MYTHOPOEIC NARNIA

Memory, Metaphor, and Metamorphoses in
THE CHRONICLES OF NARNIA

Salwa Khoddam

MYTHOPOEIC NARNIA:
MEMORY, METAPHOR AND METAMORPHOSES IN
THE CHRONICALES OF NARNIA

Copyright © 2011 Salwa Khoddam

second edition July 2013

Winged Lion Press
Hamden, CT

All rights reserved. Except in the case of quotations embodied in critical articles or reviews, no part of this book may be reproduced or transmitted in any form or by any means, electronic or mechanical, including photocopying, recording, or by any information storage or retrieval system, without written permission of the publisher. For information, contact Winged Lion Press www.WingedLionPress.com

Winged Lion Press Press titles may be purchased for business or promotional use or special sales.

10-9-8-7-6-5-4-3-2

ISBN 13   978-1-936294-11-4

To David Shelley Berkeley

in memoriam

1918 – 2011

CONTENTS

Preface — i-vi

Acknowledgments — ix-xi

Introduction — 1
   Towards a Definition of C.S. Lewis's Mythopoeic Aesthetics

Chapter 1 — 16
   The Roles of Memory, Metaphor, and Metamorphoses in Lewis's Mythopoeia

Chapter 2 — 41
   Light and Sun Iconography in Narnia

Chapter 3 — 50
   Mnemosynē in Narnia :
   Prince Caspian and *The Silver Chair*

Chapter 4 — 70
   Satanic Cities in Narnia:
   Charn, the Castle of Ice, and Underland

Chapter 5 — 104
   A Tale of Two Cities of Man:
   Tashbaan and Anvard in
   The Horse and His Boy

Chapter 6   123
> The City of God: Cair Paravel in
> *The Lion, the Witch and the Wardrobe*

Chapter 7   135
> The Gardens in Narnia

Chapter 8   159
> The Sea-Serpent, the Ship,
> and the Bifurcated Sea in
> *The Voyage of the Dawn Treader*

Chapter 9   180
> The Narnian Apocalypse in
> *The Last Battle*

Chapter 10   202
> *Ovide Moralisée* in Narnia:
> Metamorphoses and *Thèōsis*

Conclusion   218

Works Cited   225

Index   247

PREFACE

One of Lewis's major scholars told me, "Lewis takes you places" (Jerry Root, personal conversation 2001). C. S. Lewis certainly does that in *The Chronicles of Narnia*. His pages are dotted with subtle allusions to the Bible, Plato, Dante, Spenser, Shakespeare, Milton, and many other great writers. These stories are a classical, Christian, and, early modern literature scholar's dream. At least one session, sometimes more than one, in academic conferences on Lewis deals with influences on his works or parallels between his works and other authors', sometimes subtle and sometimes not.

This book is primarily an attempt, through a study of C. S. Lewis's mythopoeic aesthetics, in *The Chronicles of Narnia*, which includes the major themes and images, to secure a well-deserved place for these stories in the history of the Western Literary Imagination as a product of the confluence of the classics and Christianity. The series is no mere collection of children's stories, or to be more specific, fairy tales, though universally categorized as such by readers and publishers, and even by the author himself in his usual reference to these stories. Nor are they "violent" or "pornographic" as some readers have conceived them to be (Hooper *Past Watchful Dragons* 25-26); nor written just for entertainment, though all literature should be entertaining in Lewis's opinion; and nor simply "psychologically therapeutic" moral tales (Bettelheim 9).[1] The *Chronicles* represents the highest example of scholarship and imagination, intertwined with Christianity, so that an observant reader can relish the motifs and strands in this work that draw him/her to the Western Tradition of art and literature and find a place for it there.

Lewis's intention for writing these fairy tales is clear to those who have studied him, although not to all readers. The stories are a literary, and subtle, form of what he had reiterated in his Broadcast Talks, which were later published in *Mere Christianity* (1952), and other apologetic and literary works (assuming one can separate the two), that the purpose of life is to live in imitation of Christ, indeed, to become "a little Christ" (177), i.e., the doctrine of *thèōsis*.[2] Lewis's readings and the images that sprang into his mind from these readings which he incorporated into the Narniad, and what he believed about them, will thus be the foundational thread of this study. As Charles A. Moorman argues, "Lewis's images . . . remain deeply grounded in the traditions from which they are drawn" (66). Since his images are the vehicles of his beliefs, and grounded in traditions, they will be the center of every chapter on each chronicle in this book.

While reading the *Chronicles* the first few times, one is drawn to literary and art works, to philosophy and mythology, to the Bible. This journey into the Western Literary Imagination enriches one's enjoyment of the *Chronicles*, knowledge of Western authors, and Lewis's personal creative abilities and Christian beliefs. As Bishop Kallistos Ware has written about Lewis, "It is primarily in the imaginative writings that his theological vision can be found expressed with the greatest depth and originality" (55). They are the best tutorials in the Great Books and the imagination that created them. In this study I hope to share with readers these images, themes, and traditions that have enriched Lewis's imagination. I will describe what they are, follow their development, and answer such questions regarding how Lewis uses these traditions in his own way to support his themes.

My approach to the *Chronicles* is based on the chronological view, that they are actually one whole mythic story, paralleling the Gospel Story, from Creation to the Apocalypse, with all types of struggles in-between.[3] However, the chronicles are not discussed in the chronological order, but presented according to their core images.

The research presented in this book is vast in scope and the treatment is broad. No other methodology is adequate to unlock the key to his "scholarship of imagination," i.e., "his absorption and transmutation of details and motifs from his vast reading" (Nicholson 42). Lewis's mind was unique, packed with learning, retentive of all that he read and re-read. He was also blessed with a typological and iconographical cast of mind that helped him synthesize the different strands from his readings into coherent literary works, though this coherence may not seem obvious to all at first reading. His sources, particularly of his images, are varied and extend over a vast expanse of time: from Plato, classical mythology, Norse myth, Ovid, and the church fathers, St. Augustine most notably, to more recent authors, like Dante, Spenser, and Milton, especially Spenser, as well as modern authors like Rider Haggard.[4] Therefore, a more general question to be answered in this study is, how does Lewis achieve the fusion of all these elements with his Christianity in his art, since his wide readings must have taken him away from his Christian faith? T. S. Eliot has the answer which I believe applies to Lewis's stories: He writes that wide reading is valuable, not as "hoarding knowledge," but

> because in the process of being affected by one powerful personality after another, we cease to be dominated by anyone, or by any small number. The very different views of life, co-habiting in our minds, affect each other, and our own personality asserts itself and gives each a place in some arrangement peculiar to ourself. ("Religion and Literature" 102)

In one of his powerful passages about reading literature, Lewis writes that in reading literature, "we seek an enlargement of our being. We want to be more than ourselves. . . . We want to see with other eyes, to imagine with other imaginations, to feel with other hearts, as well as with our own. . . . [I]n reading great literature I become a thousand men and yet remain myself" (*An Experiment in Criticism* 137, 139). For Lewis to have succeeded in integrating all his sources with his own Christianity reveals his strong creative abilities as well as his deep Christian convictions. His readers are challenged to do the same. Once they go backward to his sources.

The problem with source studies is that they could degenerate into mere source-hunting, which, as another major expert on Lewis' writings states, is futile unless the differences in usage by the authors is determined, "how one thing becomes a different thing in another book" (Hooper, *Past Watchful Dragons* 108-09). I will try to avoid this trap by exploring how the images, themes, and images woven in motifs (recurring incidents in the plot) and motifemes (i.e. large units of motifs) sparked from Lewis's readings and filtered through his unique mythopoeia and shaped into these Christian fairy tales. Moreover, at every opportunity I will link his images/motifs to the traditions of the Western Literary Imagination, pagan and Christian. The plan in this book is to explore Lewis's "mythopoeic aesthetics" in the introduction, which will reveal his basic views on mythopoeia, myth, and the fairy tale. Terms like "myth," "mythopoeia," "iconic images," and "fairy tale" will be defined based on Lewis's (and others') views. In chapter 1 I will continue with further discussion on the roles of the major three elements/themes that constitute his mythopoeia: Memory, Metaphor, and Metamorphoses. Metaphors, or the uses of the images in his fiction, are at the center of this triad. They are the vehicles of Memory to bring about Metamorphosis. I will analyze the four major images in the *Chronicles* and inter-woven themes and motifs that are attached to them: light, the city, the garden, and the sea. These images work in interesting configurations and patterns of contrast and continuity in the stories. Since the image of light is pivotal in all the chronicles, I will discuss its history and significance in chapter 2. From chapter 3 on, I will proceed with analyzing and interpreting the major images and themes in each chronicle. I will show how each image and its binary opposite are at the center of the story, not only structurally, but also thematically. For example, the themes of tyranny, scientism, materialism, and progress (all marks of the Earthly City) will be contrasted with the values of its polar opposites, the garden and the City of God (Cair Paravel being the closest type of this City in Narnia) to bring into sharp relief Lewis's own themes. An individual, Narnian or human, must always make a choice: *Pax Babylonis* vs. *Pax Calestis*, Babylon vs. Zion. As much as possible, I will study how one set of motifemes accompanying each of the images in one period or mythology can shed light, in contrastive or comparable ways, on another set of events and images in another period and mythology, reaching up to Lewis's own images and mythology in the *Chronicles*. I will also focus on analogous correspondences between classical and Christian images and themes to help readers see the *Chronicles* as layered like an "onion," Tumnus's term for the Real Narnia (*The Last Battle* 225) but with layers growing larger as they are peeled away to get to the real center. Finally, in chapter 10, I will sum up Lewis's specific theme of metamorphosis in the *Chronicles*, at the foundation of his mythopoeic aesthetics, which I believe is linked in his mind to the doctrine of *thèōsis* that dominates all his work, and discuss some incidents where it is operative in the *Chronicles*. Thus the classical metamorphosis is *thèōsis*, and mythopoeia is *evangelium*. The road to Narnia is straight but covered with thickets, and like Aslan's followers, we must struggle in the undergrowth to find our path to the center.

    There are abundant scholarly works on textual influences in the *Chronicles*. These stories have received much attention from Lewis scholars in recent years, due to the movie productions of 2005 and 2008. Many recent works are textual analyses and helpful guides like

Leland Ryken and Marjorie Lamp Mead's *Through the Wardrobe: A Reader's Guide* (Downers Grove, IL: InterVarsity Press, 2005); David Downings' *Into the Wardrobe: C.S. Lewis and the Narnia Chronicles* (San Francisco: Jossey-Bass, 2005); and Peter J. Schakel's *The Way to Narnia: A Reader's Guide* (Grand Rapids, MI: Eerdmans, 2005). The influences on Lewis's chronicles have already been studied to some extent. In "C.S. Lewis's Narnia and the 'Great Design'" (*Longing for Form: Essays on the Fiction of C.S. Lewis*, ed. Peter Schakel [Grand Rapids, MI: Baker, 1977]), Charles A. Huttar has declared that the *Chronicles* deserves "serious critical consideration" (121) and that it "has been hailed as a major achievement of the mythographic imagination and some think that Lewis's place in history will owe as much to the Chronicles as to anything else he wrote" (122). Huttar discusses some significant echoes from Milton, Ovid and others in the *Chronicles*. In 1994, Doris T. Myers published her substantial work, *C.S. Lewis in Context* (Kent, OH: Kent State UP), in which she explores parallels between Lewis' *Chronicles* and Edmund Spenser's *The Fairie Queene*, in structure and use of "speaking pictures" and "allegorical cores" (123) as well as in the stages of the characters' Christian commitment (134). Marvin D. Hinten has studied, to a limited extent, the mythical, Biblical, and biographical backgrounds of Lewis's symbols in the *Chronicles* in *The Keys to The Chronicles: Unlocking the Symbols of C.S. Lewis's Narnia* (Nashville, TN: Broadman & Holman, 2005). Among the most recent studies of influences is Elizabeth Baird Hardy's notable *Milton and Spenser and* The Chronicles of Narnia (Jefferson, NC: McFarland, 2007) and Michael Ward's *Planet Narnia: The Seven Heavens in the Imagination of C.S. Lewis* (Oxford UP, 2008). However, no extensive attempt has yet been made to situate Lewis's fairy tales in the broad spectrum of the history of Western Literary Imagination.

Endnotes

1. Bruno Bettelheim has considered the fairy tale as a secular, moral children's story, reflecting the inner psychological experiences of children, thus focusing more on readers than on the intention of the author. He writes, "The juxtaposition of opposite characters is not for the purpose of stressing right behavior. . . [but] permits the child to comprehend easily the difference between the two" (9). In his view, and others like him, the fairy tale contributes to one's development emotionally, imaginatively, and intellectually—more of a therapeutic exercise to develop confidence in one's self.

2. I would like to refer the reader to two passages by Lewis where he states that the Christian meanings in his chronicles are subtle and meant to "steal past those watchful dragons [childhood inhibitions]" to catch a wider audience ("Sometimes Fairy Stories May Say Best What's to Be Said," *On Stories* 47); also in his letters he explains his idea of "supposal" that Aslan is what would Christ be if transported to Narnia (*Collected Letters* 3: 1004-05,1157-59, 1244, 1460).

3. This chronological approach takes *The Magician's Nephew* as the first story in the series. On this approach, see Peter J. Schakel, *The Way Into Narnia: A Reader's Guide* (Grand Rapids: Eerdmans, 2005) 15; see also Walter Hooper, *The Narnian Chronicles of C.S. Lewis: Past Watchful Dragons* (1971. London: Collier Macmillan, 1979) 32.

4. On Lewis's debt to St. Augustine see Sarah McLaughlin, "The City of God Revisited: C. S. Lewis's Debt to Saint Augustine," *CSL: the Bulletin of the New York C.S. Lewis Society* 23.6 (April 1992): 1-9; Thomas Ramey Watson, "Enlarging Augustinian Systems: C. S. Lewis's *The Great Divorce* and *Till We Have Faces*," *Renascence* 46.3 (Spring 1994): 1-12. EBSCOhost, 26 Aug. 2006; and Charles A. Moorman, *The Precincts of Felicity: The Augustinian City of the Oxford Christians* (Gainesville: U of Florida P, 1966). Lewis was heavily influenced by Augustine. In *The Four Loves* he rejects one of Augustine's ideas on charity, and he writes, "I do so with trembling," referring to Augustine "as a great saint and a great thinker to whom my own glad debts are incalculable" (167). On Lewis's debt to Dante see Joe R. Christopher, "Mount Purgatory Arises near Narnia," *Mythlore: A Journal of J.R.R. Tolkien, C.S. Lewis, Charles Williams, and Mythopoeic Literature* 23.2 (Spring 2001): 65-90; Marsha Ann Daigle, "Dante's *Divine Comedy* and C.S. Lewis's Narnia Chronicles," *Christianity and Literature* 34 (Fall 1984/Summer 1985): 41-55. For Rider Haggard's influence on Lewis, especially *Ayesha*, see Mervyn Nicholson, "C. S. Lewis and the Scholarship of Imagination," *Renascence* 51.1 (Fall 1988): 41-62. See also Salwa Khoddam, "From Ruined City to Edenic Garden in *The Magician's Nephew*," *Truths Breathed through Silver: the Inklings' Moral and Mythopoeic Legacy*, eds. Jonathan B. Himes, Joe R. Christopher, and Salwa Khoddam (Newcastle, UK: Cambridge Scholars Publishing, 2008) 27-50.

ACKNOWLEDGMENTS

The strength of this work is that a large community of scholars has contributed to it. Its weaknesses are my own. I would like to extend my deep thanks to the following scholars: Dr. Leland Ryken, Professor of English at Wheaton College, Illinois, who has read the whole work and made some significant suggestions which I gladly and gratefully accepted; Dr. Joe R. Christopher, Professor Emeritus of English at Tarleton University, Texas and Lewis scholar, for his immaculate job in editing parts of the document and giving numerous helpful suggestions and corrections; Dr. Jonathan Himes, Professor of English at John Brown University, Siloam Springs, Arkansas, for reading parts of the manuscript and offering advice; Dr. David Rozema, Professor of Philosophy at The University of Nebraska at Kearny, for working with me on a section on memory; Dr. Mitzi McGuire, English Professor at Oklahoma City University, for her helpful suggestions on organization; and Drs. Stephen Griffin, Mark Griffin, Randall Auxier, and John Starkey, longtime friends and former colleagues at OCU, for reading bits and pieces of the initial draft and discussing the contents with me over coffees and lunches. In fact, this book is the fruit, and, for me a celebration, of the ten years of animated discussions in "The Faith and Scholarship Forum," which we organized to promote faculty scholarship at OCU.

This book is also the fruit of ten years of presentations at the annual conferences of the C.S. Lewis and Inklings Society (CSLIS) from 1998 to the present and at The C.S. Lewis Foundation Institutes at Oxbridge 2002, 2005, and 2008. The CSLIS also started at OCU and spread nationally due to the dedicated work of Dr. Mark Hall, Professor of English at Oral Roberts University, Dr. Christopher, Dr. Martin Batts, Professor of English at LeTourneau University, Texas; later on, other professors joined our organization and became active members of the Executive Board, namely Dr. Himes and Dr. Larry Fink, Professor of English at Hardin-Simmons University, Waco, Texas. My deepest gratitude to these colleagues is fathomless and unending.

I am also grateful to the librarians at the Bodleian in Oxford, UK and the Marion E. Wade Center at Wheaton College for their generous help, notably Colin Harris of the Bodleian and Marjorie L. Meade, Laura Schmitt, and Heidi Truty of the Wade Center. My gratitude also goes to Robert E. Bryant at the Dulaney-Browne Library at OCU, who made sure I had every book or document I needed, even from abroad, and delivered it to me personally. I would like to thank Matthew Randall for typing and retyping the whole work with nary a complaint. I can seriously say that this book could not have been written without him. My thanks go to Dr. David Evans and Dr. Terry Conley, former deans of the School of Arts and Sciences at OCU, for two course-releases in 2005 and 2008, the OCU administration for granting me a sabbatical in 2001, which I spent at the Bodleian and the Marion E. Wade Center doing research on Lewis, and the Committees on Faculty Scholarships and International Education at OCU for partially funding my trips to the UK to attend and present at the C. S. Lewis Foundation Summer Institutes in 1994, 2002, 2005, and 2008 and the C. S. Lewis Summer Institute in 2001.

I would also like to thank my reader Christine Colbert for her meticulous work in editing the manuscript and uncovering hard-to-find errors. My deepest gratitude goes to Robert Trexler, my editor and publisher, who read the whole manuscript and offered unending support and insightful comments and suggestions. There are many others who supported me one way or another and I am grateful to them also. Most importantly, I would like to dedicate my work, with immense affection and respect, to Dr. David Shelley Berkeley, my dissertation advisor at Oklahoma State University and a distinguished Milton and Lewis scholar, now deceased, who was the first to show me what scholarship really is and to direct me to Lewis's works. And that has made all the difference.

Special permissions:

Extracts from C.S. Lewis's works copyright © The C.S. Lewis Pte. Ltd. Reprinted by permission.

Extracts from my articles published in *CSL: The Bulletin of The New York C.S. Lewis Society* and *Mythlore: A Journal of J.R.R. Tolkien, C.S. Lewis, Charles Williams, and Mythopoeic Literature* are reprinted by permission of the editors.

Illustrations:

Fig. 1, p. 17, "Visions of the Triple Soul in the Body" from Robert Fludd's *Utriusque Cosmi*, 1617. Reprinted by permission of Oxford University Press.

Fig. 2, p. 32, "Minotaur" by George Frederic Watts © Tate, London, 2010.

Fig. 3, p. 46, "The sun of justice" by Andreas Friedrich, from *Emblèmes Nouveaux* p. 68 (Frankfurt, 1617). Reprinted by permission of Columbia University Libraries.

Fig. 6, p. 54, "Io turned into a heifer." A sixteenth-century illustrator shows her through a window in the cow's flank. Reprinted by permission of Bibliothèque nationale de France.

Fig. 11, p. 141 from Francis Quarles' Emblemes. Reprinted by permission of The Huntington Library.

Fig. 12, p. 155, "Butterfly." Reprinted by permission of The University of London Library.

Fig. 18, p. 215, "Ezekiel's fiery wheel" from the Geneva Bible (1576). Reprinted by permission of The Huntington Library.

INTRODUCTION:

Toward a Definition of C.S. Lewis's Mythopoeic Aesthetics

> *He sees no stars who does not see them first*
> *of living silver made that sudden burst*
> *to flame like flowers beneath an ancient song,*
> *whose very echo after-music long*
> *has since pursued.*
>   J. R. R. Tolkien "Mythopoeia" (87)

Lewis does not have much to say about the term "mythopoeia" though scholars have attempted to define the term for him. Early in 1928, he wrote Owen Barfield that he needed a word for the "science of the nature of myth," and he had thought of "mythopoeia" as a possible appropriate word (*Collected Letters* 1: 765) *(CL)*. The term appears in other places in his works as well. In "Historicism" (1950) he equates "mythopoeic" with "esemplastic" (a Coleridgean term for the shaping imagination) in referring to the faculties that tend to make us perceive vague pictures of the past (105). He lists Keats's *Hyperion* and Wagner's *The Ring of the Nibelung* as mythopoeic in that they express the Myth of "Evolution" before scientists did (*Christian Reflections* 84). Colin Duriez has explicated Lewis's term "mythopoeia" as the "making of myth" (133). Another scholar, Rolland Hein, believes that "mythopoeia" is a term for "stories that are composed in time, but which suggest . . . something covert but eternally momentous . . . . that is beyond time, inexplicable but thrilling" (5-6). Harry Slochower maintains that "mythopoeia" is an individual's retelling of a myth, which can be a critique of social norms (34). For example, Dante's Catholicism in *Divine Comedy* is "mythopoeia" (110). These definitions, including Lewis's own, apply to stories in *The Chronicles of Narnia*: they are "esemplastic" works, retellings (to a limited extent) of the Christian myth, and thrilling tales suggesting something eternally momentous. Lewis's "hero," Aslan, is in constant struggle with the corrupt norms of Narnia as it falls under witches' and tyrants' rule. One can say that the author identifies with his hero, who would change Narnia. Lewis's mythopoeic aesthetics in the *Chronicles* includes four interconnected concepts: 1) the concepts of myth and myth retelling as the foundation of mythopoeia; 2) the belief in a sacramental, dynamic, transformative cosmos; 3) the recognition of the fairy tale as the most appropriate genre for mythopoeia; and 4) the acknowledgement of the important role of memory (and inspiration) as a theme and an agent of invention, since remembered ideas and images from scriptural, mythic, literary, and philosophical traditions form the staple of Lewis's chronicles; metaphor as the tool of his imagination; and metamorphosis as the intended goal of his literary work. Since the last concept is multi-faceted, I will devote chapters 1 and 10 to discussing its subdivisions fully.

I. Myth

The word "myth" is notoriously polysemous. "To define myth ... is in part to destroy it" (Kilby xiii). It appears in many of Lewis's works, but the four works that contain a clear explanation of it are, in chronological order, "Myth Become Fact" (1944), *Miracles* (1947), the introduction to *George MacDonald: An Anthology* (1947), and *An Experiment in Criticism* (1961). He states in "Myth" that "what flows into you from the myth is not truth but reality (truth is always *about* something, but reality is that *about which* truth is")" (*God in the Dock* 66). This reality is defined later on as a "gleam of the divine truth falling on human imagination" (*Miracles* 138), which indicates that myth is beginning to have a divine meaning in Lewis's mind. In *George MacDonald* Lewis makes an important and unique distinction between myth and narrative: myth is independent from narrative since as a "pattern of imagined events," it can be expressed in any medium, not necessarily in words (xxvii). Perhaps the most detailed explication of myth is in *Experiment*, where he discusses the characteristics of myth: 1) its independence from any literary narrative, therefore its lack of suspense or surprise; 2) its preternatural themes; and 3) its "grave but awe-inspiring" effects (43-44). Walter Hooper provides a passage from one of Lewis's notebooks that deserves to be quoted fully because it summarizes Lewis's views on myth:

> A *Myth* is the description of a state, an event, or a series of events, involving superhuman personages, possessing unity, not truly implying a particular time or place, and dependent for its contents not on motives developed in the course of action but on the immutable relations of the personages. (*Past Watchful Dragons* 16)

Lewis thus concludes that myth is the most powerful means to connect with the reality of God. Through myth one can express one's complex relationship to Him. He suggests in *The Weight of Glory* that poets and mythologies know all about this (12). It is common knowledge that his conversion to Christianity was achieved through the study of myth, which enchanted him deeply and led him to accept Christ as the antitype (completed type) of the pagan dying god. In *Experiment* Lewis again refers to myth as a storehouse of truth that is distinct from narrative: The great myths "rise up like elms" in our memory, i.e., the great myths of Balder, Orpheus, Ràgnarök, and others (42). The typological mind of Lewis, which viewed all myths as shadows of the Christian historical "myth," reached back into pre-Christian times for sources to create his fictive worlds.[1] Typology (the view that events from the Old Testament and pagan myths are shadows of, and thus prefigure, events from the New Testament) appears to have been central to Lewis's view of mythology, providing him with an analogical view of history like the church fathers', the center of which is Christ. Consequently, he believes that a good pagan can provide some images about reality that are not only significant but also more relevant than those of some systematic theologians. In "Religion without Dogma?" Lewis reveals this typological cast of mind when he writes,

> These stories [of pagan myths] may well be a *preparatio evangelica*, a divine hinting in poetic and ritual form at the same central truth which was later focussed and (so to speak) historicized in the Incarnation. To me who approached Christianity from a delighted interest in, and reverence for, the best pagan imagination, who loved Balder before Christ and Plato before St. Augustine, the anthropological argument against Christianity has never been formidable. (*God in the Dock* 132)

The *Chronicles* reflect Lewis's understanding of myth as the handmaiden to Christianity. Lewis's fairy tales are certainly a series of imagined events, "grave" and "awe-inspiring" about transcendent reality in the form of the numinous Aslan, the center of the monomyth from the Creation to the Apocalypse in the Narnian cosmos. One can say that the work is a modern form of re-mythologizing Christian beliefs, of linking the *eucatastrophe* (Tolkien's term for "the Consolation of the Happy Ending" and escape from Death and the familiar ["On Fairy-Stories" 68]) of the fairy tales with the *evangelium* of his apologetics. As Harry Slochower writes, "Every epoch has its own myth which provides the center of its life, gives the tone, manner and rhythm to its existence, permeates its institutions and thought, its art, science, religion, politics, its psychology and its folkways—that is, the myth organizes the values of its epoch" (16-17). Lewis's new mythology not only brings us face to face with our modern issues, but also "opens up our perception of the old story" (Fiddes 147).

II. Holy Ground

For many artists and writers, Nature in all its variants is neither merely a backdrop for plots and characters to develop and unfold, nor topographical descriptions, nor even places of destination. The seasonal cycle of Nature is woven with the supernatural. Indeed, the vast expanse of landscape is open for symbolic interpretation in the imagination of artists: gardens, rivers, mountains, deserts, and even cities—since the latter can be considered man-made landscapes—can become symbolic images of conditions within the human psyche and links to a spiritual reality. They are integral elements of quest narratives and pilgrimages, but more important, they provide a map of the human soul or the "collective voice of [a] people" (Besson 281). In fact, it is landmarks, feelings, and memories of people that make a landscape a type of a home and not merely a place (Jonathan Smith 25).

In his study of George Herbert's poetry, Stanley Stewart writes, "To the Christian the seasons' round, often represented by a contrast between spring garden and winter wilderness, is a natural figure of man's spiritual life" (105). As the modern poet Luci Shaw asserts so eloquently, "This is the benison of the sacramental view of life: our realization that all of creation rightly belongs in the house of faith" (xiv). She goes on to define "faith" as the "widening of the imagination, a leap into the transcendent, a taste of the numinous, the ability to see the extraordinary in the ordinary" (77). Another Christian writer, Flannery O'Connor, states, "The Christian novelist lives in a larger universe.

He believes that the natural world contains the supernatural" (qtd. in Ryken, *Triumphs of the Imagination: Literature in Christian Perspective* 228). "In the sacramental pattern of life, everything means something, everything may be a pointer to the holy" (Shaw 53), recalling "For of him and through him, and to him, are all things: to whom *be* glory for ever" (Rom. 11.36).[2] Simply put, "These things have meaning because God made them" (Ryken, *Triumphs* 39).

So was it for C. S. Lewis. In a sermon titled "The Grand Miracle" (1945) Lewis follows Christian tradition in interpreting winter as death and spring and summer as Christ's Resurrection (*God* 87-88), which he will again use in *The Lion, the Witch and the Wardrobe (LWW)*, in the scene of the melting snow at the approaching of Aslan. In *Surprised by Joy* Lewis writes that it was a blessing for him that his father had no car, for modern transport "annihilates space" and "deflower[s] the very idea of distance" so that one cannot experience the "infinite riches" of the landscape as early pilgrims and travelers did.[3] Nature shares divinity with man in that it was created by God, not to be devalued by the standards of modern transport as "a little room" (156-57). A narrow, materialistic world without imagination, without the light of the divine, was inadequate to him.

For him, like for the poet Gerard Manley Hopkins before him, "the world is charged with the grandeur of God" ("God's Grandeur" 1). "Lewis saw nature in strongly sacramental terms" (Ware 63). In *Letters to Malcolm: Chiefly on Prayer* (1964), Lewis writes, "[A]ll ground is holy and every bush (could we but perceive it) is a Burning Bush. . . .We may ignore, but we can nowhere evade, the presence of God. The world is crowded with Him. He walks everywhere *incognito*. And the *incognito* is not always hard to penetrate" (75). In "Horrid Red Things" (1944) Lewis writes, "But we [Christians] must insist from the beginning that we believe, as firmly as any savage or theosophist, in a spirit-world which can, and does, invade the natural or phenomenal universe" (*God* 69).

This belief is powerfully illustrated in *LWW*, as in other chronicles, in scenes which I will call, from the literary point of vew, "synchronic moments,"or "tableaux" (e.g. the still scenes where the transcendent overwhelms the concrete, linear narrative) if there is no movement in them, but "pageants" if there is. Lewis defines a "pageant" as "a procession or group of symbolical figures in symbolical costume, often in symbolical surroundings" (*Spenser's Images of Life* 3). However, there is no direct interaction between Spenser's heroes in "*The Fairie Queen*" (*FQ*) and the major pageants (29) (i.e., the pageant of the seven deadly sins in 1.5) and, in fact, they are "utterly cryptic to them" (82). In contrast, the pageants in the *Chronicles* are composed of Aslan physically interacting with his followers. Also, Lewis's pageants are not processions of allegorical figures as in *FQ* but mostly focused on Aslan as an iconic figure beyond time and space.

These pageants function as transitions from the linear level to the Christological center of the story, because Aslan is what the son of God might have been like had he been incarnated in a magical world of talking animals, trees and mythic beasts (see preface vi n2). From the philosophical point of view, these scenes of intersection with the holy will be called "eternal moments," and from the religious point of view "miracles," and examples of *thèōsis*. All these terms are very close in meaning and are parts of the general process of "metamorphoses," as will be discussed in more detail in chapter 1.

In short, every part of Lewis's fictional world in the *Chronicles* is potentially holy ground, open to what Mircea Eliade would describe as "an incursion of the sacred" in our world (*Images and Symbols* 51), i.e., a visitation from Aslan.[4] Lewis's imagination was incessantly at work in his fiction, baptizing physical places in Narnia into landscapes of the soul. This lifting of *topos* ("area," "physical place") into a *cosmos* (an ordered universe created by God) is well illustrated in the *Chronicles*. For what happens in the story's tableaux is of more significance, in my opinion, than what happens linearly (see below the section on "The Fairy Tale"). Aslan transforms the Narnian landscape, whenever he appears, with extraordinary visual effects that suspend it out of time and place and link it to him, and, by analogy, Christ in his glory bridges humanity and God in our world. These sanctified scenes of the Great Lion are "real" in a sense that renders the frame narrative primarily a fictional vehicle. No ordinary map could adequately transcribe this fictional *topos* of changing colors and light. No ordinary aesthetic is up to describing this transformative experience to characters and readers.

These moments of transcendence with Aslan present or approaching are like miracles in our world, or eternal moments, when the divine enters into the fluid-dynamic, God-centered cosmos. Through these atemporal moments, when the characters (and readers) are suspended out of time and place, art becomes mythopoeic in that it reflects these changes in characters, words, and forms, and exaggerates them. In fact for any metamorphosis to occur in one's mind, one must believe in this type of fluid universe. The mythic view depends upon seeing the divine in the familiar or the real (Barkan 18). It is the drama of God's intervention and transformation (Shaw xiii). Mythopoeic art is thus centered upon transformation, a "positive" metamorphosis of the being to a higher state, as opposed to the "negative" metamorphosis which is the reverse, and provides us with narratives of creation, of the miraculous, and of sacred mysteries. The mythopoeic narrative genre can be termed "divine fantasy," of which the fairy tale, in Lewis's and his friend and fellow Inkling J. R. R. Tolkien's opinion at least, is a subgenre.

III. The Fairy Tale as a Mythopoeic Genre: Interaction of Theme, Structure, and Purpose

How does one map a sacred place? Without the ancient sacred pole, the cosmic pillar and their replicas, church and temple, how does one know the Center of the World, the *axis mundi*, the place where the two cosmic planes, Earth and Heaven, intersect (Eliade *Images* 36-42)? And how does one write about it, having experienced it as a Christian? A special topography is needed, a topography guided by the Christian imagination. To Lewis and Tolkien, the fairy tale may provide such a topography, since as a type of fantasy literature it offers readers imaginary worlds as settings, where the benevolent, supernatural forces defeat the evil ones at the end of the story. This is the fairy tale promise.

A. Genre

Lewis and J. R. R. Tolkien were among the staunchest supporters of the "fantasy genre" in literature as the vehicle of their new mythology. When Tolkien was writing his essay "On Fairy-Stories" in 1947, he could find no definition of "fairy tale," or what he liked to call "fairy-story," in the *Oxford English Dictionary*, although he could find a somewhat vague and unsatisfactory definition in the Supplement (4);[5] but he did think that the fairy tale is as old as man himself: "To ask what is the origin of stories (however qualified) is to ask what is the origin of language and of the mind" (17). The fairy story certainly has deep roots in tradition and scholarship. It is based on a long-existing tradition built around a human faculty termed "fantasia," or sometimes in the Renaissance "fancy," early terms for the faculty of imagination. Lewis makes a distinction between bad "fantasy" (termed "fancy") in the medieval/Renaissance faculty psychology and good "fantasy" that builds the Secondary World of the fairy tale. One is Egoistic, the other Disinterested; one is castle-building, the other fiction (*Experiment* 52-53). In its dark aspects, "fancy" can lead to illusion, a failure to grasp reality, which can become demonic and allied to black magic, which Lewis calls *goeteia* (see ch. 1). In its good aspect, "fantasia" (*magia*) can be a divinely inspired faculty that leads to what Lewis and Tolkien call "sub-creative" acts, a term that Tolkien coined for natural outcomes of man's creation. Tolkien upheld "fantasy" as an "elvish craft" (49). He writes, "Fantasy remains a human right: we make in our measure and in our derivative mode, because we are made: and not only made, but made in the image and likeness of a Maker" (56). In such fantasy, a "new form is made; Fairië begins, Man becomes a sub-creator" (23). Thus, the "fantastic" is a pure and potent form, neither "suspect" nor "illegitimate." The good "fantasia" can lead to fiction, containing a substantial element of the supernatural, acts of wonder and awe which include anything outside the normal space-time continuum of everyday life. Although Tolkien was exacting in his definition of the fairy tale, one can consider it as one of several types of the "fantasy genre," the other two being space fantasy (like Lewis's Space Trilogy), and theological romance (like Lewis's *The Great Divorce*).

There are four integrated, unique features that make up the Christian fairy tale, the most important of which for this study are 1) the creation of a Secondary World, beyond time and space, yet still linked with the Primary World; 2) a pervasive quality of enchantment; 3) the clarification of good and evil for the reader as a consequence of the first two; and 4) the *eucatastrophe*, the happy ending. According to Tolkien fairy tales "open the door on Other Time, and if we pass through, though only for a moment, we stand outside our own time, outside Time itself, maybe" (32). In "On Stories" Lewis argues that this Secondary World is simply "that of the spirit" (*On Stories and Other Essays on Literature* 12). Moreover, the Secondary World must provide a credible, consistent world, founded on reason, for a reader to be able to participate in it. Tolkien states that fantasy "certainly does not destroy or even insult Reason; and it does not either blunt the appetite for, nor obscure the perception of, scientific verity. On the contrary, the keener and the clearer is the reason, the better fantasy will it make" (55). Lewis agrees. While at school, as he writes in "On Three Ways of Writing for Children," "the fantasies did not deceive me: the school stories did" (*On Stories* 37). Created with its own inner logic, the Secondary World of the fairy tale can then work its spell on a reader, enchanting him into "longing for he knows not what. It stirs and troubles him (to his life-long enrichment) with the dim sense of something beyond his reach" (38). Tolkien also admits to the enchanter's power to create worlds that readers can enter, not by "suspension of disbelief" but by a desire for enchantment, for glimpsing the Other-worlds, for Fairie. Tolkien insists that this enchantment is not escape, but a means of approaching or evaluating the Primary World. It is like a rehearsal for coming back into the Primary World, a consolation, and a recovery of freshness and vision, away from Death, from the "rawness and ugliness of modern European life" (Dawson qtd. in Tolkien 64). "We need, in any case, to clean our windows" (58), Tolkien writes, so that we could "look at green again, and be startled anew . . . by the blue and yellow and then perhaps suddenly behold, like the ancient shepherds, sheep, and dogs, and horses—and wolves" (57), recalling Edmund's comments on the intense colors on the way to the Celestial Garden in *The Last Battle (LB)*.

This consolation of the happy ending, the *eucatastrophe*, is "the true form of fairy-tale, and its highest function" 68). It "denies . . . final defeat and in so far is *evangelium,* giving a fleeting glimpse of Joy, Joy beyond the walls of the world, poignant as grief" (69). Lewis also maintains in "On Three Ways" that the reader of fairy tales "does not despise real woods because he has read of enchanted woods: the reading makes all real woods a little enchanted" (*On Stories* 38). Moreover, the wholesome effect of the fairy tale is seen in this passage also: "The whole story . . . strengthens our relish for real life. This excursion into the preposterous sends us back with renewed pleasure to the actual" (14). In *LWW,* Aslan tells the children, "This was the very reason why you were brought to Narnia, that by knowing me here for a little, you may know me better there [in the Primary World]" (270). In his study of Spenser's *FQ* Lewis puts it differently: "Evil is tired, good is full of vigour. The one says, let go, lie down, sleep, die; the other, all aboard! Kill the dragon, marry the girl, blow the pipes and beat the drum, let the dance begin" (*Spenser's Images* 95).

The tremendous significance of the fairy tale is quite obvious in that both authors consider it a "sub-creation" following God's creation. The fairy tale is thus a training for the reader to think that he/she might assist in the process of "effoliation," in this world, Tolkien's term for "the multiple enrichment of creation"(73). For Lewis these outcomes for readers are the very reason we are brought to Narnia with the children.

The fairy tale for him is expressed best by Lucy in *The Voyage of the Dawn Treader (VDT)* as a "spell 'for the refreshment of the spirit.'. . . about a cup and a sword and a tree and a green hill" which she can hardly remember, but which will always remind her of the effect the story had on her, the "refreshment of the spirit" (121). This passage reflects Lewis's focus on "atmosphere" or "tone" as one of the essential considerations for an author of fiction (see ch. 4 n5; Ward 15-18, 22, 65, 73-75, 227). In *Weight* Lewis reminds us of our need for "spells": "Remember your fairy tales. Spells are used for breaking enchantments as well as for inducing them. And you and I have need of the strongest spells that can be found to wake us from the evil enchantment of worldliness which has been laid upon us for really a hundred years" (5). The fairy tale, for both Lewis and Tolkien, is an *evangelium* (Good News), a triumph of good over evil, of salvation through Grace. Indeed, no Christian work, fairy tale or not, can stay at the level of a tragedy, for the meta narrative of the Gospel Story is always a Good News story: "Joy is the serious business of Heaven" (*Letters to Malcolm* 93).

B. Theme

The process of *eucatastrophe* for Lewis is based upon two concepts: the nature of evil and the response to evil. Lewis adhered to the Augustinian view of evil as the absence of good or spoiled good. It preys on what is good and has no independent existence, "like a hole in a shirt it is nothing without the shirt" (Markos). So without God, there can be no Satan; without Othello, no Iago; without Aslan and his followers (the Pevensie children and the Talking Animals), no Jadis, no White Witch, no Green Witch, and no Shift—all these are archetypes of evil, i.e. universal elements of human experience, or the "building blocks of literature" (Ryken, *Triumphs* 83-84).

There is a word in medieval writing that completely encompasses the meaning of such evil in Christianity. That word is *acedia*, associated with spiritual sloth, one of the seven deadly sins, which leads to, or coexists, with despair. It is the state of the broken-up, bitter soul, fragmented and fractured by a lack of hope. It forces the sinner to withdraw into the self and indulge in destructive anti-social behavior. Such is Satan (formerly Lucifer) in John Milton's *Paradise Lost*—a whiny, grumpy angel driven by a sense of "injur'd merit" (1.98), for being passed up by God in His choice of an "assistant" (Milton's theology), and fed by "immortal hate"

(1.107) of God. He wreaks havoc in God's universe and destroys His beloved children. He states his manifesto: "To do aught good never will be our task, / But ever to do ill our sole delight" (1.159-60). Dante places such sullen and violent sinners in the fifth circle of the *Inferno* immersed in the river of mud. Such is Iago in Shakespeare's *Othello*— an underling who turns against his master Othello and plans to topple him: "I follow him [Othello] to serve my turn upon him" (1.1.42). These characters, with Satan in the lead, and many others trailing behind like Edmund in *King Lear* and Richard III, are more examples of archetypes of evil; they seem too blinded by their self-centeredness and aggravated by despair to seek other options out of their dilemmas. Having lost faith in God, or the good, they rationalize their way into Hell, or destruction. In *The Magician's Nephew (MN)*, Lewis defines this sin as obeying "one's heart's desire" (191) rather than "the desire of the Faierië" (Tolkien, "On Fairy-Stories" 41) or the desire of Aslan (Christ in our world); or it is a clinging to what is desired over what is given (*Perelandra* 246; see *Letters to Malcolm* 26).

People in despair are determined to get what they want, not what God offers them. In *The Pilgrim's Regress*, Lewis, like Edmund Spenser, attributes much power to despair. Eventually all these characters get what they want; they do not always like it (*MN* 208). Jadis the Witch, the White Witch, the Green Witch, and Shift and their numerous accomplices are the major evil characters in the *Chronicles*, all driven by despair, and isolated from goodness and hope as a result of choosing to rebel against Aslan. (They will be discussed in the following chapters).

The *Chronicles*, however, in true fairy tale manner, also provides the way out of despair. In fact, another running motif in all of Lewis's life and works is the idea of Joy, *Sehnsucht*, a term that Lewis defines as "the unsatisfied desire which is itself more desirable than any other satisfaction," like "Milton's 'enormous bliss' of Eden" (*Surprised by Joy* 16-18). Lewis's experiences of this longing were first stimulated by beauty, natural and literary, before he later found its satisfaction in God: for example, his brother's miniature toy garden, Beatrix Potter's *Squirrel Nutkin*, the experience of "Northerness" in Norse mythology (*Surprised* 16-17). Eventually, he discovered that Joy is a pointer to God, rather than an end in itself. He describes one of the stages of his conversion, which can be considered a type of positive metamorphosis from despair to Joy, as the taking off of a tight corset, removing one's armor (*Surprised* 224), a movement from the dry desert into the "land of longing" (217), although he refers to himself as "the most dejected and reluctant convert in all England" (228-29). We find this experience of Joy powerfully illustrated in each chronicle as in all of his works, and always as an antidote to despair that leads to evil. Because of the established polarity between Joy and Despair in his mind, it was easy for Lewis to create good characters in his chronicles as opponents to Jadis the Witch, the White Witch, the Green Witch, and Shift the Ape—all of whom would bring about destruction in their evil reign. Lewis advises, "Look for yourself, and you will find in the long run only hatred, loneliness, despair, rage, ruin, and decay. But look for Christ and you will find Him, and with Him everything else thrown in" (*Mere Christianity* 227).

C. Structure

Fairy tales can provide the most appropriate structure for such an opposition of good and evil. Lewis writes in "Sometimes Fairy Stories May Say Best What's to Be Said" that he fell in love with this form because of "its brevity, its severe restraints on description, its flexible traditionalism, its inflexible hostility to all analysis, digression, reflection and 'gas'" (*On Stories* 46). Such a pure form would allow the author and reader to focus on the polarities of good and evil. Central to an awareness of these oppositions is a possible move to progressive mediation (Silva 86). But Lewis resolves the tension by having his characters, based on his own life experience, move from one to the other, from evil to good, despair to hope. No mediation or reflection is possible, only a final, positive metamorphosis.

As a mythopoeic art, fantasy stories like fairy tales are closely connected to metamorphoses. In fact, metamorphoses belong to the genre of fantasy stories (Ferzoco 6). Francisco Vaz da Silva goes so far as to state that to understand fairy tales one has to understand metamorphoses. Fairy tales offer a rich representation of Lewis's iconic universe and thus facilitate reading the *Chronicles* analogously to clarify our Primary World in relationship to the created Secondary World of the author. Nowhere are borders between species more clearly merged than in these fairy tales, where Primary and Secondary Worlds flow into each other in the imagination of the readers. In the *Chronicles* Lewis focuses on metamorphoses to bring about the miraculous in the actions of Aslan and his followers, leading to the *eucatastrophe* (as explained above). Aslan and his followers will transform evil into good, despair into Joy, albeit sometimes temporarily. Lewis creates his own myths using stories of metamorphoses that are analogous to stories from mostly classical and somewhat Norse mythology, and ultimately analogues to Christian conversion experiences (see ch. 1).

The fairy tale has other unique structural ingredients also. A look at Claude Saussure's two structural principles in a narrative, the diachronic (in time) and the synchronic (out of time) can be helpful to understand its structure. David Quint informs us that the "epic teleology characteristically invokes a higher vertical dimension of synchronic meaning to explain the horizontal world of diachronic action in which the romance adventurer is normally confined" (253). Saussure's terms as well as epic teleology that leaves nothing to chance (Quint 253) operate in the *Chronicles*, creating two-in-one narratives: 1) a major linear frame narrative of journeys for rescue, adventure, quest, or fulfillment of a prophecy enacted by Narnian Kings and Queens; and 2) a non-linear series of tableaux beyond space and time, composed of images that are at times iconic, marshaled by Aslan, to suggest a transcendental Reality. I will argue in this study that the scene, or tableau, is more significant than the event itself (see ch. 1).[6] Intense colors and rich variegated shapes speak to us in these scenes with interplay of light and dark in the background. The narrative is not an allegory, but the interspersed, heightened events, because of the iconic tableaux, take on more than a literal meaning. In every chronicle the reader is quickly catapulted into the transcendental world of Aslan in the Secondary World.

D. Purpose

Thus the fairy tale, for both Tolkien and Lewis, is *evangelium*. Its purpose is to rehabilitate virtues and create a change in perception in the reader, to open up his/her imagination to the Christian reality beyond the walls of familiar perception. Lewis hoped that the spell of materialism would be broken by the deeper spell of the fairy story, arousing in readers a longing for something inaccessible in the world, and thus causing them to experience Joy. Each Narnia story is built upon moments of Joy, moments that usually come at the end of the story in an event somewhat like a pageant (see ch. 1 on *Thèōsis*). Perhaps Narnia would never have come into existence had Lewis not come to finally and fully understand the meaning of Joy (Hooper, *Past Watchful* 2). In a recent article published in *The New Yorker*, Adam Gopnik writes, "As a child Lewis was overcome by an experience called 'Joy'; as an adult he created a kingdom that would contain it" (89). These metamorphic movements from despair to Joy, fear to hope, are at the foundation of each chronicle and suggest the underlying theme of Metamorphoses in the whole series.

Thus Lewis and Tolkien succeed not only in putting up a strong defense of the fairy tale as a high form of art proper for both children and adults, but also in illustrating their convictions in their accomplished works. Lewis concludes in "On Three Ways," "I am almost inclined to set it up as a canon that a children's story which is enjoyed only by children is a bad children's story" (*On Stories* 33). He confesses to enjoying fairy tales at 54 more than he did in childhood (35). Similarly, Tolkien writes, "If fairy-story as a kind is worth reading at all, it is worthy to be written for and read by adults" ("On Fairy-Stories" 45).

Endnotes

1. This section on Lewis's typological cast of mind is taken from my article, "Balder the Beautiful: Aslan's Norse Ancestor in *The Chronicles of Narnia*," *Mythlore: A Journal of J. R. R. Tolkien, C.S. Lewis, Charles Williams, and Mythopeic Literature* 23.2 (Spring 2001): 65-90.

2. All quotations from the Bible in this text are from the Authorized King James Vers.

3. Tolkien shares this belief and made his hobbits with large feet so they can travel by foot and appreciate the land (Wood 24).

4. Although there may be no clear evidence that Lewis read Eliade, the images in the *Chronicles* are universal and have traditional ties with ancient mythological thinking, so that it is fruitful to study them using Eliade's thoughts. Lewis, also, respected all myths as a means to approach God.

5. In the Supplement, "fairy-tale" is defined as a) "a tale about fairies, or generally a fairy legend"; b) an "unreal or incredible story"; and c) "a falsehood" (4).

6. For a contrary opinion see Charles A. Moorman. He writes, "[Lewis's] images never usurp the position of the main argument or narrative line, but are instead adjuncts, though very necessary adjuncts to it" (67).

CHAPTER ONE

The Roles of Memory, Metaphor, and Metamorphoses in Lewis's Mythopoeia

Memory opens up this life for us; only in memory does the past take on everlasting meaning; only in memory is the past both canceled out and preserved for all time.
            Hannah Arendt, *Essay on Understanding* (26)

Nothing can last, I do believe, for long / In the same image.
            Ovid, *Metamorphoses* (15.258-59)

PROSPERO: *Graves at my command / Have wak'd their sleepers, op'd and let'em forth / by my so potent art.*
            Shakespeare, *The Tempest* (5.1. 48-50)

Although Lewis has not devoted a specific work to an explication of the role of Memory in the creative mind and its interaction with Metaphor and Metamorphoses, all of which form the fourth concept of his mythopoeic aesthetics, his general ideas on the interaction between author, text, and reader are prevalent in *Experiment* and scattered in his other works. This chapter will explain how these faculties interact in Lewis's creative process in the *Chronicles*.

I.   Memory and Mythopoeia

The faculty of memory, along with his imagination, has a fundamental role to play in Lewis's mythopoeic aesthetics as the most powerful source of inspiration, being a storehouse of ideas and images from his readings. Some common classic beliefs regarding memory and the process of recollection can be useful in explicating Lewis's mythopoeia and some of the themes in the *Chronicles*.

Memory has a long royal history. The classic authors thought deeply and wrote extensively about memory. Indeed, the mother of the muses in Greek mythology was Memory (the classical goddess Mnemosynē)—wife of Zeus, mother of the muses, as well as a daughter-in-law (among many) of Kronos (Time). Treatises upon treatises have been, and still are, being written on this human faculty, its functions, and its parts. From Plato and Aristotle, and other less well-known philosophers, a long tradition of memory theories grew that continued to develop through the writings of St. Augustine, St. Aquinas, the Arab philosophers and into the Renaissance with Giordano Bruno and others.[1] (See fig. 1).

Like Milton's, Lewis's learning springs from his memory, which was large and strong, holding almost everything he ever read—especially the basic books he read and re-read. This faculty allowed him to draw upon his "scholarship of imagination" for rich metaphors or metaphoric thinking, for *topoi* or commonplaces gathered from a lifetime of reading.

However, this literary depth must be combined with an acknowledgement of divine inspiration in the creative act. Lewis writes, "An author should never conceive himself as bringing into existence beauty or wisdom which did not exist before, but simply and solely as trying to embody in terms of his own art some reflection of eternal Beauty and Wisdom" ("Christianity and Literature" 7). Lewis uses the example of Homer's poet Phemius in the *Odyssey* who is original, yet completely dependent on a supernatural teacher (8). Like Tolkien Lewis believes, as shown in the introduction, in the writer's role as sub-creator, created in the image of God. Mnemosynē must work not just with her daughters the muses, but also with their father Zeus to inspire works of art, and perhaps with her father-in-law, Kronos (Time) as will be discussed in chapter 3.

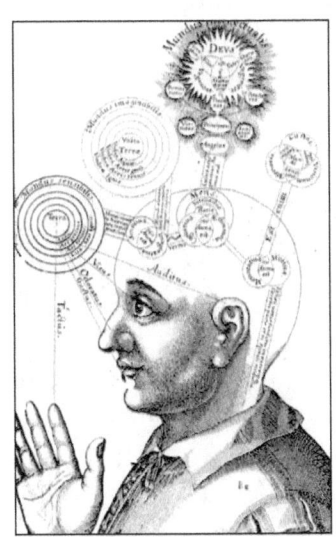

FIG. 1 THE SENSES OF THE OUTER BODY ARE LINKED TO 'SOULS' INSIDE THE BRAIN, WHICH INCLUDE 'THE IMAGINATIVE SOUL, OR FANTASY', ACCORDING TO THE NEOPLATONIST SCHEME OF ROBERT FLUDD ('VISION OF THE TRIPLE SOUL IN THE BODY' FROM *UTRIUSQUE COSMI*, 1617). (WARNER FIG. 33)

II. Metaphor and Mythopoeia

While memory *simpliciter* is a passive state of thought, the end of the comprehensive process of memory is recollection (Aristotle *De memoria et reminiscentia* 452^{a}12-13), which is an active process (Bloch 75, 88). Socrates admits this process is difficult for humans because our mortal bodies pull us downward to earthly things (*Phaedrus* 245^c-250^d). Although sometimes called "artificial memory" in more modern theories of memory, for Augustine recollection is a function of the rational soul and operates through a series of images that move one to the memory of the desired object—God. This process results in a change, a strengthening of character, and a return of lost happiness: "come to You, O lovely light" (*Confessions* 10.7). The image, as a verbal or pictorial artifact, is at the foundation of this memory tradition. Inversely, Aristotle believes that the imagination works on sense impressions to provide material for the intellectual faculty to work with, like the marks of a seal on wax. Memory is "a collection of mental pictures from sense impressions but with a time element added" (*De memoria* 450^a 30). In other words, "the [rational] soul never thinks without a mental picture" (*De anima* 432^a 17). For Renaissance writer Giordano Bruno "the function of the imagination of ordering the images in memory is an absolutely vital one in the cognitive process" (see Yates 257). Everything is better understood through images. Making the connection between the remembered image and recollection, another philosopher, Albertus Magnus, argues that mental visualization is the greatest necessity to moral wisdom (*De bono*, point 20, p. 249 qtd. in Yates 67). All of these thinkers agree that a pivotal element in this process is the remembered image.

One interesting discovery that has emerged from this particular portion of my research is the closeness of Lewis to the classical writers in his focus on the image in his creative process and admission that we cannot think without metaphors. Lewis does not miss an opportunity to tell us how significant images were to him: "Everything began with images," he writes in "Sometimes Fairy Stories," and "then came the Form" (*On Stories* 46). In the case of *LWW*, the images were of a faun holding packages and walking in the snow and a great lion jumping into the scene later. Lewis felt that it is imagery that can work with *poesis* (fiction making) to carry the story forward. The soul never creates without an image. As Luci Shaw puts it, "The artist is called upon to present pictures through words and paint to express God's creation, to bridge the human and the divine (15), for "imagination must serve truth" (49-50). For Lewis mental images play a significant role in prayers also. He writes, "I doubt if any act or thought or emotion occurs in me without them [mental images]" (*Letters to Malcolm* 86). In his scholarly work on the Middle Ages, Lewis explains the important role of memory in the imagination according to medieval faculty psychology and shows that the faculties of memory and imagination are closely related, occupying two close "dens" of the brain as two of the five wits (*The Discarded Image* 162). All experience, thoughts, and sensations are stored for future use in memory, which becomes a place for putting things away as well as discovering new things, a source for knowing God and soul/self as well as discovering ideas, all connected somehow. In this manner authors, by drawing on their memory, are linked to their Christian predecessors, which explains Lewis's "scholarship of imagination" and the symbiotic relationship of memory and his metaphors. Only through imagery can one participate in the Great Dance, Lewis's ultimate image of harmony and Joy in the unity of every human with God/Christ, or the God/Christ figure in his fiction (see the following section on *Theōsis* and ch. 10). To encourage participating in the Body of Christ, the church, or the Christian community is the goal of good literature in his opinion. Yet these images of Joy must not be mistaken for Joy itself, the experience of knowing God; otherwise they turn into idols. Nor should they be rejected if the numinous light beyond them is not perceived because in them "the thing signified is really in a certain mode present" ("Transposition" 23).

But there is something unique, something very fascinating about Lewis's images, especially in the *Chronicles*. At certain moments when they are placed with Aslan in a dramatic tableau and most energized with rays of light, they become "iconic" (see ch. 2). Lewis admits that the most powerful pictures are ikon-like in that they point to ideas beyond themselves (*Experiment* 17). Although there is at least one powerful moment of this sort in each of the chronicles, the term "iconic" does not apply to all images in the stories. Such powerful images strike "roots far below the surface of [the] mind" (*Experiment* 49). For example, one of the most "iconic" and awe-inspiring scenes in the *Chronicles* is that of Aslan standing at the center of a circle of his newly created animals, which he had selected by touching their noses with his. It was a solemn scene. "Digory's heart beat wildly" (*MN* 137). In this act of creation Aslan is analogous to the God of Genesis. The image of light surrounding him and the music elevate him to an iconic figure that points out to characters and readers the presence of divinity. Another example of an iconic scene is the appearance of Aslan in the midst of the dancing trees, shining white in the moonlight in *Prince Caspian* (*PC*). (See ch. 10 for a full discussion of this and other scenes/pageants from the *Chronicles*.) Vigen Guroian describes Aslan's appearance in the moonlit forest as "an objective correlative of the Transfiguration of Jesus" (59).

To examine how mythopoeia works in Lewis's fairy tales, one must explicate the symbolic landscape already described in the introduction as numinous and having points of contact with a long literary intellectual tradition. Metaphors are bridges between the world of reality and imagination, making the world numinous and the landscape dynamic and symbolic. Every object or image has a story, and every story is a metaphor of passions, love, and personal desires. Not only particular objects, but also the whole cosmos comes alive: "The sacred place embodies divinity as physical objects embody spirit" (Barkan 89). Lewis's own cosmic images are the ruling metaphors in the *Chronicles*. They create the geography of Narnia, and also "motifs"—units of meaning in the form of objects, characters, and events that are loaded with rich associations from Western thought. They are variants used in universal "motifemes" (types of plots, for example Slaying the Dragon) that give shape to the whole story (Dundes 99-101). These rich images not only create the geography of Narnia, but also become metaphoric in the way Lewis uses them as integral tools in his mythopoeic aesthetics. Lewis's images are the pivots that move his plots in order to create "synchronic" moments out of time and place, pointing to the transcendent. He constructs these images as "speaking pictures" by drawing from classical authors, theologians, and other poets and fiction writers, to build his theme of Metamorphoses.

I have based my classification of Lewis's images in Narnia not on his own narrow classification of images in *Spenser's Images*. Instead of using his categories of the false and the true forms of life as a framework for his interpretation, I am using more open categories that embrace the vast vista of these metamorphic journeys in Narnia: the natural and man-made forms (images) in the landscape. I will focus on four specific images, one man-made and three natural, all of which have been widely used by writers to narrate the Christian Story: the light, the city, the garden, and the sea.[2] As Diane Jacobson states in her analysis of biblical imagery, "For though the biblical journey begins in the garden, it moves quickly to the city and remains there, moving back and forth from city to city, until finally one rests in the heavenly garden transformed into a city" (395-96). St. Augustine's spiritual journey started with an exodus from Targaste to the unholy loves of Carthage, to the sophisters of Rome, and finally to a garden in Milan (Dougherty 37). We can say of the British children in Narnia, in a general sense, their journey began in a pre-Narnian fallen city (Charn in *MN*), moved to the Created Garden (*MN*), to other sinful cities (Castle of Ice in *LWW*), to the ideal city Cair Paravel (in *LWW*), across the seas to the Garden of Restoration (*VDT*), into the City of the Underworld (*The Silver Chair*) (SC), and finally up to the Celestial Garden (*LB*), with intermittent returns to their own Primary World. However, there is also the sea voyage image that has enchanted the human imagination from the *Odyssey* until the present, and the light images of the sun and moon that illuminate everything.

A. Lewis's Metaphoric World (1): The City [3]

Babylon and Jerusalem. Two of the richest binary oppositions of the city in the human imagination, used by writers and artists to explore human foibles, as well as achievements and successes, in humans' relationship to God. Jerusalem has lived in the imagination as the city that reaches its fulfillment in the vision at the end of the Bible, "a synonym for the universe . . . for happiness, peace, and redemption" (Georgi 167). On the other hand, Babylon (and many other biblical cities like Babel, Damascus, Sodom and Gomorrah) has become an archetype for wickedness and sinfulness, pride, and uncontrollable pleasure seeking.

The human imagination has always been engaged in shaping and interpreting the city. Here one may consider man-made buildings such as castles and homes as metonymies of cities. Furthermore, modern psychology's interpretation of the house as symbolic of the subconscious part of the human mind needs also to be noted. As James Dougherty argues, "Man cannot regard neutrally his manifold artifact, the city" (53). Peter Hawkins agrees: "The city [is] the place to tell one's time" (82). This interest in the city is due partly to the complexity of its structures and partly to the fact that as a work of man, it reflects the human psyche. What better place to study man's moral and religious imagination, ordinary everyday behavior, psychology, and culture than in the city? Indeed, as T. C. Stewart suggests, the city, in general, is a symbol of man's psychic structure (3). It is "man writ large" (Huard 42).

Mircea Eliade believes that the city is the product of man's creation, his development of chaos into cosmos (*Myth of the Eternal Return* 18).

For centuries earthly cities have borne the blame for wickedness in the world, receiving the curses of outraged biblical prophets and even God Himself. As Diane Jacobson states, "The Bible is anti-city" (395). Notably, the first city was built by a murderer, Cain, who in rebellion toward God gave it the name of his son Enoch (Gen. 4.17). The tyrant Nimrod created the Tower of Babel in rebellion against God (Gen. 11.1-9). The biblical book of Chronicles continues to condemn cities as dens of iniquity and wickedness. God's anger against nearly all the ancient cities of the Near East is recorded in Amos 1. As Jacques Ellul writes, "The consciousness is there [in biblical teaching] of the city as a world for which man was not made" (42). He continues, "God has cursed, condemned the city instead of giving us a law for it" (47). It was considered good for Israel to destroy a city (Num. 21.2). [4] While one may conclude that gardens and mountains function as settings for restorative metamorphoses, it is the wilderness, the wastelands, as well as cities that form the background for the themes of decay and degeneration, or destructive transformation. The city is also a place of wild living, chaos, disintegration, distortions, a *monde reversé*: "reversal of everything ordained for mankind by the Almighty" (Palmer 27). The medieval conception of Hell as a "state where the divinely ordained laws of nature have disintegrated into chaos" (27) applies to all these settings. In the spoiled garden various forms of doubt, rebellion, restlessness, failure, and fear exist (McGrath 24 and *passim*). In *Mere Christianity*, Lewis attributes the spoiling of our world to a state of rebellion against God: "Enemy-occupied territory—that is what the world is" (46). One of the deepest effects of rebellion is the vortex of despair, the antithesis of hope, which crushes a being's reason and distorts the imagination (see introduction). At some point in the modern literary imagination the city and the wilderness blended, as in William Blake's and T.S. Eliot's early poetry. Eliot elaborated on this view in the forties, writing that cities were necessary, not evil, but that "without the life of the soul from which to draw its strength, the urban culture must lose its source of strength and rejuvenescence" (qtd. in Crawford 228).

The image of the city is an important element of the Narnian landscape. It is a framing device, as Charles A. Moorman argues, since the plots in the *Chronicles* involve journeys from and back to cities, but, more importantly, it is an objective correlative of all the urban issues that concerned Lewis: isolation, fear, violence, egoism, slavery, tyranny, and materialism.

B. Lewis's Metaphoric World (2): The Garden [5]

At the other end of the spectrum from the city is the garden. To be able to interpret the major gardens in Lewis's *Chronicles*, one must study the motifs of the various types of gardens in classical, biblical, and secular literature upon which Lewis fashioned his own. A. Bartlett Giamatti's *The Earthly Paradise and the Renaissance Epic* is of great help in exploring these traditional garden motifs. Giamatti defines a garden, before it was linked to any specific place like the Garden of Eden, as "a place of perfect repose and harmony" (11). As the earthly paradise, the garden was thought by many Western church writers to be a terrestrial place "in some normally inaccessible part of the earth, which might become the goal of man's search and, in a literal as well as metaphorical way, the object of his dreams" (Ladner qtd. in Giamatti 15). The blessed regions of Elysium (*Odyssey* 4.561-68), the garden of Alkinoös (*Odyssey* 7) with its "trees, fruit, water, Zephyr, and perpetual springtime" (Giamatti 35), Virgil's *Eclogues* and *Georgics*, Claudian's *Epithalamium de Nuptius Honorii Augusti*, and Hesiod's description of the Golden Age (*Works and Days* 109-20) are the classical foundations of later depictions of blessed places (16). It is impossible to understand the English garden without referring to Horace or Virgil (Thomas 265). J. T. Rhodes and Clifford Davidson also affirm, "The beginning and end were marked by the garden" (95).

The biblical Garden of Eden shares these motifs (as will be discussed in chs. 6 and 7). The Song of Solomon is also of notable interest as another source for Lewis because it contains a garden with some of these traditional motifs allegorized by biblical exegetes. The book is a dialogue between the male and female principals with at least one chorus, the daughters of Jerusalem.[6] While a literal reading of the Song of Sol. interprets it as an epithalamium of romantic wedded love, an allegorical reading renders the male beloved as the Bride-groom, Christ, or (for Jews) Yahweh, and the Shulamite as the church, the soul, or (again, for Jews) Israel.

Another version of the garden in medieval and Renaissance art and literature that may have provided motifs for Lewis is the enclosed garden (*hortus conclusus*) which was also a common trope, so common that, as Stanley Stewart states, "Scarcely an event from the life of Christ exists for which some artist at some time or other has not provided a backdrop of an unfinished enclosure" (47). He goes on to add, "The touchstone of the enclosed garden [was] an emblem (*hortus mentis*) of man's inner being. This is how the figure was used by St. Teresa and St. John, and how it was used by Herbert, Vaughan, and Marvell" (169). (Of course, the figure also may be parodied, as with the quasi-Edenic enclosed barnyard of Chaucer's "The Nun's Priest's Tale.") The generic motifs of this garden in its ideal form are trees, fruits, sweet odors, a well, fountain, or rivers, and a form of enclosure so that direct access is impossible. It is also situated on a mountain, "a befitting spot of worship" (Porteous 45) set in the East (Ramos 98). "Paradise is the highest land on earth; it is so high it touches the sphere of the moon" (Ramos 78). Also, as Stanley Stewart writes, "Night cannot fall in the enclosed garden because the sun, who is the Son, has eternally risen" (110).

Other biblical passages are at the basis of Lewis's depiction of gardens in the *Chronicles*. Building on Genesis 2.8-10 as well as the image of the vineyard in Isaiah 5, John 15, and 1 Corinthians 3.9, biblical exegetes saw vineyards as "lands enclosed from the open wilderness by the art of man's husbandry" (Stewart 53). To Isaiah the vineyard is Jerusalem, the Lord's garden built on a fruitful hill and surrounded by a fence (5. 1-2), the City of God. Early medieval and Christian commentators went on to view the vineyard as a metaphor of the church, a divine enclosure with God/Christ as gardeners, set off from the rest of the world through God's mercy. On the individual level, the garden is the soul; the wilderness is the corrupted flesh. Man acting in cooperation with God/Christ will attain a place in the Celestial Garden, or Heaven. Thus the "wild is separated from the regenerate" (54). Stewart states that these traditional gardens—with their green vistas, water, shade, fragrant, gentle winds, and in some account their locations on a mountain top where trees touch the sky—appeared later in apocalyptic and rabbinical commentaries and "anticipate gardens and paradises of medieval literature which culminated in the earthly paradise of *Divine Comedy*" (50).

Before writing the *Chronicles*, Lewis had explored in depth this long tradition of garden poetry in *The Allegory of Love* (1936). In his discussion of *Roman de la Rose*, the most famous and influential of all garden poems of the Middle Ages, he contrasts Claudian's garden of the Hesperides, "the land of longing, the Earthly Paradise, the garden east of the sun and west of the moon" (75-76), to the Good Shepherd's pasture which is the true garden, the celestial paradise. Giamatti describes the latter "as a green meadow with the Lamb leading the flock amid the joys of eternal springtime and daylight in a glistening, flowery landscape" (64). Lewis writes, "When we have seen the true garden we look back and realize that the garden of courtly love [of Guillaume de Lorris] is an impostor" (151). Scholars have also noted the motif of the enclosed garden in Lewis's Space Trilogy (Downing *Planets in Peril* 80; Pitts 3, 5). These motifs will appear in the description of the gardens in the *Chronicles*.

C. Lewis's Metaphoric World (3): The Sea

To classical and Hebrew writers the sea was a supreme mystery, evoking nothing less than terror. It was chaos, a deep abyss, and to Hebrews, the unfinished part of creation or a "remnant of the Flood" (Corbin 6). In Genesis 1.2 darkness is associated with "the deep"; in Psalm 36.6 God's unfathomable judgment is likened to "a great deep." Also, in the vision of a new heaven and earth in the Book of Revelation there is no sea. "When Christ returns, the sea will have disappeared" (Corbin 6). For Plato, everything that comes from the sea corrupts, is unhealthy, "motley" (*Laws*, 746). The City of Laws must be built inland far from the shore (Charbit 18). In *FQ*, Edmund Spenser, who felt most horror of the sea, calls the sea a "wild wildernesse," a "waste wildernesse," (7.8) or a "watrie wildernesse" (2.12.29.9). He compares the dragon to the raging seas (*FQ* 1.11.21.1-9).[7]

In describing Satan's voyage to earth in *Paradise Lost*, John Milton includes a vivid description of the sea as part of a horrifying chaos:

> Before their [Satan's and Sin's] eyes in sudden view appear
> The secrets of the hoary deep, a dark
> Illimitable Ocean without bound
> Without dimension, where length, breadth and height
> And time and place are lost; where eldest *Night*
> And *Chaos*, Ancestors of Nature, hold
> Eternal Anarchy. (2. 890-96)

According to Alain Corbin, who based his ideas on an early work by Thomas Burnet (1681), "This quivering vast expanse, which symbolized, and actually was, the unknowable, was frightful in itself. There is no sea in the Garden of Eden. There is no place within the enclosed landscape of Paradise for the watery horizon whose surface extends as far as the eye can see" (2). Islands and caves are also byproducts of the Flood, "random and anarchic" in their distribution (4), and the ocean, nothing but "an abyss full of debris" (4). Chaos (or the dragon) would return if moral order is violated. Corbin concludes, "A creature fashioned in the image of God would never make his abode outside the garden or the city" (2). Thus the sea remained alien, untouched by human culture, and repulsive to human beings until the Romantics, who looked at the sea as a symbol of infinity and liberation from society.

However, though demonic, ominous, and untouched by human culture, the sea, like the city and the garden, is a part of an individual's or a nation's psychic and spiritual landscape. Like them, the sea is a screen on which to project man's deepest fears and desires, such that it, and all the elements associated with it, can be a metaphor of cultural experience (Klein 2, 7). The sea's fluctuation and instability not only terrified people but also represented the fluctuations of fortune, and, for Christians, the sins of the first humans (Corbin 2). The metaphor of the sea as fortune is a common trope in early British literature, most powerfully expressed by Shakespeare. In *H IV* (*I*), Prince Henry replies to Falstaff's comment about the moon governing the sea: "Thou sayest well, and it holds well too; for the fortune of us that are the moon's men doth ebb and flow like the sea, being governed, as the sea is, by the moon" (1.2.30-33). Also, Brutus, talking to Cassius, links fortune to the sea.[8] The concepts of "time" and "tide," the latter associated with the sea, are transposed to express human affairs, specifically the success of ventures. The unpredictability of the sea was a specter that courageous men had to face down every time they set sail. Some of the masterpieces of art and literature depict these voyages.

Voyaging provides many metaphors for the human condition. The sea voyage, with its constituents—the ship, the tempest, and the sea monsters—is at the foundation of any maritime narrative. There is no doubt that navigation was commonly considered physically dangerous in itself and a cause of many ailments and infections (Corbin 5). For classical authors, man's ability to navigate was comparable to the invention of fire, but more evil. To attempt to fathom the mysteries of the sea is a challenge to supernatural forces. Classical writers saw navigation also as an infraction of the rule of "keeping within limits." There was a traditional criticism of post-Golden-Age man for wanting to travel, captured in an image of trees turned into boats (Barkan 28). Jason's sea voyage on the Argo was considered to be the first in classical mythology. He was "the first violator of the deep" (Curtius 470), and, as a result, cursed. "The cursing of the invention of navigation [was] a favorite commonplace in poetry" (476). Both Ovid in *Heroides V, XII*, and Jean de Meun in *Roman de la Rose* view the Argo's voyage negatively (Curtius 483, 485). Odysseus and his sea voyage into the Atlantic were also viewed with some aspersion. As Corbin states, "Nowhere does Homer say that Ulysses [Odysseus] really loves the sea" (12). In fact, in some versions of the Ulysses myth, notably in Dante's *Inferno* canto 21, it is Ulysses' sailing through the Pillars of Hercules, the limits of the known world at that time, into the Atlantic Ocean that cost him his life and gained him a place in Dante's circle of fraudulent counselors. Aeneas's sorrows were caused by his storm-tossed sea voyage in the *Aeneid*. Horace also condemned navigation as unsociable and a challenge to the gods (Corbin 11). According to David Quint, Milton conceives of Satan's voyage over chaos in terms of a sea voyage, evil because of Satan's motives of destruction and imperialism and his reliance on chance: "Milton demonstrates that the evil will gives itself to the play of chance, that its activities are ultimately random and fortuitous: there is only one coherent plan of action in the universe, and it belongs to God" (256). Sea voyages were the works of the devil. According to W. H. Auden, "A [sea] voyage, therefore, is a necessary evil, a crossing of that which separates or estranges . . . The ship . . . is only used as a metaphor for society in danger from within or without. When society is normal the image is the city or the garden" (8).

Sea voyages were condemned also for their commercial purposes even up to the eighteenth century at the zenith of the age of exploration. These voyages of "enterprise," a Baconian term used for such purposes, included searching for treasures, slave trading, piracy, and colonialism. Traders were put down by Homer in the *Odyssey* and set against the heroic ideal (Quint 260). Jason was referred to disparagingly not only as "the first violator of the deep" (Curtius 470) but also as "merchant Jason" (Quint 259). A disparaging picture of maritime slave traders is found in *FQ* 6.11.9 where Pastorell is lying in prison, pretending to be sick in order to avoid the captain's advances. [9] These slave merchants are described as thieves, abusers of bodies. Piracy was also a criminal offense as well as colonizing, the latter being perceived as taking away the rights of natives to self-determination and prosperity. According to Arnold Schmidt, piracy and colonialism are intimately related, both using brute force for possessions (95). Milton's subtext of Satan's journey in *Paradise Lost* as a colonial enterprise is the journey of Vasco da Gama around the Cape of Good Hope to India as told in *Os Lusiadas* by Camões (*PL* 2.615,

638-39, 4.159-165; 10.440, 468), which, ironically, is the national epic of Portugal. The concept of the sea as a means of commerce, enterprise, and mercantile ambitions flourished in the novels of exploration in the early eighteenth century, as in *Robinson Crusoe*, the first English novel.

Other important motifs in the traditions of the sea voyage that enhance the feelings of horror, instability, and disorder associated with the sea are the tempest and the tempest-tossed ship, a tableau which symbolized life exposed to fortune whether at court or in a love relationship. Just as the city, the garden, and the sea in general function as symbolic landscapes of the human soul, so do the sea storm and the ship, which are subjects of a long list of explorers' and authors' works and the toil involved in these hard adventures. As Katherine Williams explains, "The sea may be that of fortune or of human passion, on which the mortal ship is tossed and in danger of destruction, yet the wise man can choose the right pilot and keep steady his course" (137). Various writers have explained the tempest metaphor. St. Paul's encounter with a tempest and his agonizing experience are described in Acts 27. In Old English poetry there is *Beowulf* and the exquisite "The Wanderer" and "The Seafarer," both narrating the pain of exile at sea and the dangerous fascination with it, respectively. In the alliterative medieval *Troy-Book* the storm is described in detail as full of "clater and clowdes" (31.12501). The *Pearl* poet's "Cleanness," about the destruction of Sodom and Gomorrah, describes the swaying masts and the spinning ship due to the winds, and "Patience," a retelling of the story of Jonah, includes some sea passages (see Treneer 70-74). Drawing on his own experiences on a voyage to the Azores with Essex and Raleigh in 1597, John Donne depicts the sea in "The Storm" neither as a thing of beauty nor as a mirror of God, but a place of anguish and exasperation: "Compared to these storms, death is but a qualm" (line 65). The storm has no grandeur for him. Nietzsche explains the metaphor of the shipwreck: "Not only is life a sea voyage, but we are always wrecked" (qtd. in Habermann 105).

However, the view of the sea as a receptacle of all evil forces is only one side of the bifurcated view of the sea. The other side is the view of a calm, harmonious sea, the sea of baptism, or at the least, of spiritual healing. Pious thinkers attempted to reconcile the image of the sea as evil, Satanic, and horrific with its image of inherent goodness as part of God's creation. For many poets, "the sea hides the secret of God, and is interesting only as showing the mind of God" (Treneer 236). As John Peck states, "The association of the sea can never entirely be negative, for the sea is a sphere of adventure, and the source of new things and renewal" (15). The sea is, after all, "father of all things" (Boccaccio qtd. in Williams 137). Natalis Comes, the Renaissance mythographer, emblematizes Neptune, the Roman god of the sea, as a divine figure protecting waters from corruption and working under Divine Providence (*Mythologie* 534 qtd. in Williams 136). In *FQ* the sea brings justice to Amidas and Bracidas in the *Book of Justice*. What the sea had once possessed, "He may dispose by his imperiall might" (5.4.19). Similarly, Shakespeare has the ocean deliver wife and daughter to Pericles. Moreover, the beauty of the marine world was not ignored by some. The sea was perceived as well-ordered and fecund, rich with the beauty of its creatures. Its submarine creatures were full of magnificence, more luminous and colorful than the land ones. To those versed in natural theology, the sea's creatures were not monsters and some were replicas of God's created animals on earth, only more perfect. In *FQ* Edmund Spenser portrays the sea as ambivalent, a source of terror and confusion (3.8.24) as well as fertile (4.12.1-2). All these motifs and motifemes of the sea from Lewis's vast reading percolated in his imagination as he composed *VDT.*

III. Metamorphoses/*Thèōsis* and Mythopoeia

At the beginning of *Metamorphoses*, Ovid sings of a universe of change where nothing dies: "Of bodies changed to other forms I tell; / You Gods, who have yourselves wrought every change, / Inspire my enterprise and lead my lay" (1.1-3). At the foundation of any definition of metamorphoses is the concept that we live in a world in flux, that reality is fluid (Barkan 3) and that change, whether or not prompted by Eros, one of the primordial entities of the cosmos, is a vital principle of Nature.[10] As Sister M. Bernetta Quinn argues, "Metamorphosis begins and ends the history of man, from baptism to resurrection, affecting the world within him and the world without" (1). Metamorphoses, in a general sense, can be defined as transformation in appearance, character, psychological state, or circumstance. As stated in the introduction, there are two types of metamorphoses, one positive, the other destructive (one to a higher state of being, the other to a lower state of being). Any discussion of metamorphoses entails an explanation of some closely related terms like "wonder," "illusion," the "miraculous," and, of course, "magic," and, I believe, the Christian doctrine of *thèōsis*.

A. Types of Metamorphoses

Of the many types of metamorphoses, natural, or organic change, is the most basic. No day is the same, no season is like the one before it, and creatures and humans grow, develop, and then decay. This natural change surrounds us as "leaf subsides to leaf" and "dawn goes down to day" (Frost "Nothing Gold Can Stay" 5, 7), as chickens hatch from eggs and butterflies from cocoons and "innumerable forms [are regenerated] out of an amorous and metamorphic impulse" (Barkan 228). In the *Two Cantos of Mutabilitie*, which Lewis praised as a work where "all the powers of the poet are more happily united than ever before; the sublime and the miraculous, the rarified beauties of august mythology and the homely glimpses of daily life in the procession of months, combine to give us an unsurpassed impression of the harmonious complexity of the world" (*Allegory of Love* 357), Edmund Spenser, one of Lewis's major influences, gives us a taste of a metamorphic incident of organic growth, in the following lines:

> But th' Earth for herself, of her owne motion,
> Out of her fruitfull bosome made to growe
> Most dainty trees, that, shooting up anon,
> Did seeme to bow their blossoming heads full lowe,
> For homage unto her [Nature], and like a throne did shew.
> (7.8. 5-9)

Some of these natural changing processes we fail to understand rationally and so we call them "wonders" because they usually point to a meaning beyond themselves flooding with awe. At the root of this glorious type of metamorphoses are the psalmist's words: "This is the Lord's doing; it is marvelous in our eyes" (Ps. 118. 23), which one encounters continually woven into the *Chronicles*.

Change also occurs on a bigger time scale. Evolution attests to this process of change as some may think, an "escape from bestial bondage" (Asker 53). "Evolution means species getting less and less like one another," says Professor Dimble, a character in Lewis's *That Hideous Strength* (646). Changes are also produced when man enters the picture and creates materials to build cities and attempts to imitate the laws of Nature, rearranging cells and molecules, and like, Icarus and Faustus,[11] sometimes overreaching and stepping out of natural order, in creating artificial intelligence. The protean powers of the artist and magician seem also to change Nature in a variety of ways, but both can work only with already created objects, God being the only true creator since He created the world out of nothing (as Aslan does in *MN*). The poet and magician build castles in the air, in our imagination, and we become recipients of the poet's Truth through his mythopoeic art or victims of *tompe l'oeil* through the magician's art. As Christine Rees asks, "What is poetry but a metamorphosing power, turning fantasy to shapes and giving what is mortal a kind of immortality" (268)? At the heart of all art and magic, as well as religion, is the belief that the natural world can be intersected by the supernatural reality in many forms (see introduction), one of the fundamental beliefs of mythopoeic aesthetics. Without the view of the universe as sacramental, there can be no mythopeia, no metaphor, and no metamorphosis. The doctrine of correspondence is an essential element of the fluid yet somehow ordered universe—a classical belief that has pervaded literature in the Middle Ages and the Renaissance, based upon analogical links between the microcosm (man himself), the macrocosm (society), and the cosmos. In other words, what happens on one level of existence can have an impact on the others. For example, Claudius's murder of his brother the king in *Hamlet* not only corrupts him, as an individual, but also the kingdom of Denmark on the social level and the whole Nature (moral order), thus requiring retributive justice.

The art of the theater, itself based upon a conflation between illusion and reality, art and nature, also challenges our notions of perception. The ancient Greek art of *ekphrasis* (the verbal representation of visual representation" (Heffernan 3) transforms visual into verbal art (and back again in the reader's perception), thus reminding us of a higher dynamic universe. In mythology, we have obvious challenges to our perceptions: partial zoomorphizing of humans like centaurs, minotaurs, sphinxes, mermaids, and other such hybrids; and sometimes there is full degradation of humans transformed into dragons, wolves, serpents, and the like, some keeping their human self, some not. As boundaries between species thus collapse and inner and outer entities merge, questions arise about identity: Do humans retain their identities in these destructive metamorphoses? The question also applies to reverse metamorphoses, exemplified in the Talking Animals in Narnia, which can be considered a way of translating human qualities into the natural world, the essence of the literary device personification, a form which I call positive metamorphoses.

Indeed, there was much anxiety among theologians, as there is now, over species crossing and body hopping, as in Ovid's *Metamorphoses*, for these processes went against traditional beliefs such as "like generates like," the body and soul are one," and "individual identities are unique" (Bynum 98, 110; Warner 2). Add to these the traditional, rigid beliefs in hierarchies of beings and polarity of good and evil (Ferzoco 4). According to Warner, "In medieval eschatology, metamorphosis by almost any process belongs to the devil's party; devils, and their servants, witches are monstrously hybrid themselves in form, and control magic processes of mutation. Within the Judaeo-Christian tradition, metamorphosis has marked out heterodoxy, instability, perversity, unseemliness, monstrosity" (35-36). (See fig.2). In Lewis's chronicles, one can generally observe that the mixed creatures are evil if they have human bodies but animal heads, and good if it's the other way round, suggesting the Renaissance concept of reason as the highest faculty (Hinten 17). But such collapses of boundaries also open up the way for thinking about the "miraculous"—since miracles are types of positive metamorphoses, created by divine power alone, not by Proteus or Loki, artist or poet alone (Warner 41).

Because of these questions that challenged the notions of unique individual integrity of identity in Judeo-Christian tradition, Ovid's *Metamorphoses* was probed by medieval thinkers for hidden, moral, or Christian meanings and composed in the early fourteenth century as *Ovide Moralisée* (*The Moralized Ovid*).

FIG. 2. THE MINOTAUR BY GEORGE FREDERICK WATTS.

1. Magic

The word "magic," a type of metamorphoses, is a slippery word and demands precise definition. As Manuel Ramos reminds us, "It is easy to confuse the action inspired by divinity with acts of sorcery, deceit, enchantment, and poisoning" (196) and that the line between the two may indeed seem blurred. According to Stuart Clark, a review of the natural philosophy in the Middle Ages shows a positive view of magic as descended from the *magia* of the ancient Persians, signifying it was thought to be a genuine science or universal wisdom (215). The scientist was seen as a magus. Thus it was understood by Renaissance thinkers like Cornelius Agrippa and Pico della Mirandola. Magic even paralleled religion in its attempt to link earth and heaven. It was not until the birth of the new science in the Renaissance that attempts were made to distinguish natural philosophy (science) from the occult. Consequently, magic was condemned as demonic (Clark 246) and became, I might add, *goeteia*, while to Lewis and others it is that same "new science" which can be equated with *goeteia* (see *Abolition of Man*). In *Hideous* Professor Dimble distinguishes between these types of magic in terms of the individual's use of Nature. He says that the people of Belbury (headquarters of N.I.C.E.), who represent the evils of scientism "thought the old *magia* of Merlin, which worked in with the spiritual qualities of Nature, loving and reverencing them and knowing them from within, could be combined with the new *goeteia* – the brutal surgery from without. No. In a sense Merlin represents what we've got to get back to in some different way" (648). This new *goeteia*, Dimble says, is based on the modern view of Nature as "something to be worked, and taken to bits if it won't work the way he [modern man] pleases" (648). The old *magia* of Merlin is what Tolkien considers the essential fact of Fairie ("On Fairy-Stories" 26).[12] In a letter to Dom Bede Griffiths in March 25, 1946, Lewis defined magic (presumably white magic, or *magia*) as "the artificial and local recovery of what Adam enjoyed normally"; like prayer, it is based on trust and work for the betterment of humans, although magic, in general, usually works automatically (*CL* 2: 841-42). In *English Literature in the Sixteenth Century* Lewis attempts to distinguish between the two types of magic: *magia* is Merlin's or Prospero's magic in *The Tempest* which would arouse no practical or quasi-scientific interest in the readers' minds, while *goeteia* is the dark magic of a Faustus or the hags in *Macbeth*. Lewis makes much of the Witch's magical abilities, defined as "making things look like what they aren't" (*LWW* 152). These two categories of magic are represented in the *Chronicles* by Aslan (*magia*) vs. the Witches (*goeteia*). For instance, when

Aslan is singing Narnia into creation, Jadis the Witch "felt that this whole world was filled with a magic different from hers and stronger" (*MN* 118). It is *magia* rather than *goeteia*, the Deeper Magic that will conquer her Deep Magic, although the Deep Magic here is not diabolic magic, but can be interpreted as pre-Christian morals and religious laws that limit human behavior and forces humans to adhere to them (*Mere* 24-25). Christians believe that God is associated only with positive types of metamorphoses that bring regeneration to his believers, i.e. miracles. Jesus's miracle of turning water to wine is, according to Lewis, not a break in the law of Nature, but of "feeding new events into [the] pattern"(*Miracles* 64), since God has been making wine in Nature all along through the process of natural, organic change. The Bible labels witchcraft as sin and condemns witches and soothsayers (Ex. 22.18; 1 Sam. 15.23; Micah 5.12; and Nahum 3.4).

2. *Thèōsis*

As mentioned in the introduction, Tolkien proffers *eucatastrophe* as the purpose of the fairy tale, which means an escape from Death or the familiar, and links it with *evangelium*, the Good News and the good ending (Wood 8). Lewis does that also in his fairy tales. The "enlargement of our being" which he discusses in *Experiment* as the end of literature (137) is a secular statement of the Christian metamorphosis that is his purpose to offer his readers, however subtlely, in the *Chronicles*. The powers the readers get from Lewis's work have to do with the understanding of the transcendent Aslan which translates to the understanding of the divine nature of Christ in our world. This Christian transformation in the hearts of the readers is a gift from Lewis, a gift of power, light, and energy that facilitate their unification with Christ. i.e. *thèōsis*. I would like to suggest that this transformation has a striking affinity with the doctrine of *thèōsis*, which is a translation of the Greek word, "deification" (being made God) and has much the same meaning as "apotheosis" (Rakestraw 260). It is a state of glorified human nature, "transformed above its own limits" (260). This doctrine is confusing in lay terms, especially since it has not been adequately explained by the early Church Fathers, controversial (Finlan 5-7), and too complex to discuss in detail here. For some theologians, it is effected by the Holy Spirit when man observes the commandments of God, acquires the evangelical virtues and shares in the sufferings of

Christ" (Archbishop Basil Krivocheine qtd. in Rakestraw 261). For others, it is fully realized after resurrection, but one has to participate in it in this life (Lossky qtd. in Rakeshaw 262). For still others, it is the transformation into a mystical union with God (Jensen 1) and the participation in the energies of God, but not His essence (Finlan 19). For St. Irenaeus, the Greek Church Father, *thèōsis* means restoring the divine image (God) and likeness (man) (Finch 87). This doctrine was grounded mainly on Pauline themes such as "the participation of man in the life of God." (2 Peter 1.4; 2 Cor. 5.17) It was given its fundamental form first by St. Irenaeus, with his acclamation of "our Lord Jesus Christ, who died through His transcendent love, became what we are, that He might bring us even what He is Himself" (*Adversus Haeresis* 5 qtd. in Finch 86). Later, St. Athanasius, also a Greek Church Father, in his *De Incarnatione*, to which Lewis wrote an introduction, reiterated this same concept: "He, indeed, assumed humanity that we might become God" (93). In the Western Church, St. Augustine uses the language of "participation in God" in Sermo 192.1, where he states, "To make gods those who were men, He was made man who is God" (qtd. in Puchniak 122).[13]

Several scholars have found echoes of this orthodox doctrine, or what may be a strand of it, in Lewis's writings.[14] Chris Jensen stresses the importance in Lewis's thought of the themes of joy, myth, and sacramental life, which are related to *thèōsis*. The work that contains statements of this doctrine, albeit without the use of the term, is *Mere Christianity*. Lewis writes that God shows Himself not only to individuals who are good, but also to those who are united in the community of the church, "for that is what God meant humanity to be like; like players in one hand, or organs in one body" (*Mere* 165). In "Membership" (1945) Lewis writes that "the Christian is called, not to individualism but to membership in the mystical body" (*Weight* 33). Yet one "will not be himself until he is there [union with Christ]" (41). The creature will then be a child of God. This union is an ongoing process of learning to become humble, aware of original sin, but also to be charitable. Lewis writes, "The whole purpose for which we exist is to be thus taken into the life of God" (*Mere* 161) and "Every Christian is to become a little Christ. The whole purpose of becoming a Christian is simply nothing else" (177). And who can forget the following lines from his sermon in 1941: "There are no ordinary people. You have never talked to a mere mortal" (*Weight* 15)? As Chris Jensen puts it so eloquently, *thèōsis*, "is the capstone to his [Lewis's] theory of Joy insofar as it explains the means of which the "old ache" of longing [*Sehnsucht*] finally will be satisfied" (5).

One of the ways where *thèōsis* appears in the *Chronicles* is in Lewis's use of memory not just as a mental faculty for invention, as discussed above, or for grasping "the presence of eternity in the coherence of time" (Plass 357), but as a middle term between eternity and temporal existence (352), between God and man (to be discussed in ch. 3). Lewis relies on a medieval theory that, in practice, led to an elaborate exposition of mnemonics in rhetoric and, later in the Middle Ages, to the art of ethical living. Indeed, in the Middle Ages, the art of memory was concerned ultimately with remembering heaven and hell, the virtues and vices, as illustrated in the treatises of Albertus Magnus and Thomas Aquinas (Yates 57), who may have founded their moralistic interpretation of memory on Boncompagno de Sigma's *Rhetorica nouissima* (A.D. 1235). Boncompagno writes, "We must assiduously remember the invisible joys of Paradise and the eternal torments of hell" (278 qtd. in Yates 59, 60).

However, *thèōsis* is not only tied to memory in Lewis's Narnia stories, but also to several other aspects of his mythopoeic aesthetics. I have already discussed in the introduction Lewis's belief in divine immanence, which renders Narnia a land of enchantment and magic, a holy ground. This belief is bound up with a focus on myth and specific imagery that reflects Lewis's "language of participation" with the divine that no other type of language can (see chapter 2). *Thèōsis* is expressed best through poetic language. Other essential elements of *thèōsis* like baptism and Holy Communion are also major themes in the *Chronicles*. Furthermore, there are the metamorphoses of characters effected by the "dynamic pulsating activity" of Aslan/God/Christ, which Fiddes links with *thèōsis* (295). By observing this process actually happening to characters in the stories, readers can reflect on their own Christian transformation, an interesting dialectic of Myth become Fact (Fiddes 146). This motifeme, the story of suffering heroes, being tested, following their god's commandments, sharing with his struggles, metamorphosing into fellowship and being in-folded in their god, and finally receiving salvation, is everywhere in the *Chronicles*. Because of the importance of this motifeme of metamorphoses, and its Christianized form (*thèōsis*), I have devoted chapter 10 for further discussion and specific illustrations of it in the stories themselves, although I will point out some instances of metamorphosis throughout this study.

The significance of this universal theme of Metamorphoses in literature and life experiences, and especially its links with the Christian doctrine of *thèōsis* in the mythopoeic mind of Lewis, sparks the need for a fresh approach to the reading of the images in the *Chronicles*. Among the many approaches to these stories, not the least fruitful is an examination of the Metamorphoses theme and its interaction with Memory and Metaphor, as heuristic strategy, focusing on metaphor as the liason between the two. It is clear that the tool of metamorphoses is metaphor (Barkan 269) which can be defined as "a way of translating personal qualities into the physical world" (Barkan 37). To Sister M. Bernetta Quinn, metaphor is metamorphosis, "the creation of resemblance by the imagination" (65). Metaphoric thinking is based on a vision that the universe "is under the metaphor of things. Metamorphosis becomes the quintessential corporal metaphor based on the belief that the nature of a thing can be read into shape" (Barkan 88). These three subdivisions of the last element of Lewis's mythopoeic aesthetics—Memory, Metaphor, and Metamorphoses—actually work together as one, each being an integral part of the whole work. All three are present simultaneously in the act of Lewis's creative imagination in the *Chronicles*. The archetypal metaphors form the fabric of Lewis's chronicles, culled from his memory, to construct his plots, in order to achieve his purpose in this work: metamorphosis/*thèōsis*. I hope that the focus on the core images (with associated, motifs, tableaux, pageants, and themes) in the Narnian chronicles in the following chapters will elucidate this link.

Endnotes

1. I am indebted for most of my information on memory to Frances A. Yates, *The Art of Memory* (Chicago UP, 1966) and Mary Carruthers and Jan M. Ziolkowsky, eds, *The Medieval Craft of Memory: An Anthology of Texts and Pictures* (U of Penn P, 2002), who present a historical review and discussion of memory theories and their authors. For this paper, I have selected a few but important remarks from these theories as well as from St. Augustine as they apply to Lewis's fairy tales.

2. I will devote chapter 2 to a discussion of light imagery in Narnia since it is prevalent in all the chronicles.

3. See my chapter, "From Ruined City to Edenic Garden in *The Magician's Nephew*," *Truths Breathed through Silver: The Inkling' Moral and Mythopoeic Legacy*, eds. Jonathan Himes, Joe R. Christopher, and Salwa Khoddam (Newcastle, UK: Cambridge Scholars Publishing, 2008) 26-50.

4. A contradictory opinion regarding anti-city biblical bias is offered by Robert R. Wilson, who does not believe that this anti-urban bias is found in the Old Testament text (5). According to him, it is the wilderness [in the Bible] that is described as a hostile place, which resembles nothing so much as the underworld, the realm of the dead, the very antithesis of life. Like the underworld, it is a land of dangerous traps for the unwary, a land of drought and supernatural darkness where no light penetrates, a land of no return, where no one lives (5). He presents Jer. 2.5-7, which refers to the wilderness as a land of drought and deep darkness, a hostile place, a land that none passes through, where no one dwells "as evidence of discrediting life in the desert as opposed to life in the cities" (5). The wilderness is the realm of the dead, the very antitheses of life (5).

5. Some parts of this section have been published elsewhere. See Salwa Khoddam, "The Enclosed Garden in C.S. Lewis's *Chronicles of Narnia*," *CSL: The Bulletin of the New York C.S. Lewis Society* 37.1 (Jan/Feb 2006): 1-10.

6. The figure of the garden appears in other contexts in the poem. In her invitation for the beloved to possess her, the soul extends the figure of the garden (Ryken, *The Bible as Literature* 227). When refreshed, the soul becomes also a garden for the beloved: "A garden enclosed is my sister, my bride" (4.12); "I am come to my garden, my sister, my bride" (5.1).

7. All quotations from Edmund Spenser's *The Fairie Queene* are from *The Works of Edmund Spenser.* Ed. Henry John Todd. London: Edward Moxon, 1856.

> He [the dragon] cryde, as raging seas are wont to rore,
> When wintry storme his wrathfull wreck does threat;
> The rolling billowes beate the ragged shore,
> As they the earth would shoulder from her seat;
> And greedy gulfe does gape, as he would eat
> His neighbour element in his revenge:

8. There is a tide in the affairs of men
    Which, taken at the flood, leads on to fortune
    Omitted, all the voyage of their life
    Is bound in shallows and in miseries.
    On such a full sea are we now afloat
    And we must take the current when it serves
    Or lose our ventures.   (*JC* 4.3.217-22)

9. During which space that she thus sicke did lie,
    It chaunst a sort of Merchants, which were wount
    To skim those coastes, for bondmen there to buy,
    And by such trafficke after gaines to hunt,
    Arriued in this isle, though bare and blunt,
    T'inquire for slaves; where being readie met
    By some of these same Theeues at th' instant brunt,
    Were brought unto their Captaine, who was set
    In his faire patients side with sorrowfull regret.

10. For the discussion on metamorphoses I am indebted to Leonard Barkan, *The God Made Flesh: Metamorphoses and the Pursuit of Paganism* (New Haven: MA, Yale UP, 1986). All quotations from Ovid's *Metamorphoses* are from a translation by A.D. Melville (Oxford UP, 1986).

11. In Greek mythology Icarus is the son of Daedalus, who equipped him with wings of feather attached to his body with wax, in order to fly back to Greece. Icarus did not heed his father's advice not to come too close to the sun while flying for fear the wax on his wings would melt and he would fall. He became in literature the symbol of overreaching and over confidence. Faustus is the protagonist in Christopher Marlowe's play whose ambition drove him to turn to *goetia* and in the end he was destroyed.

12. Later in "On Fairy-Stories" Tolkien states that "magic" is only a "technique," not art; "its desire is power in this world, domination of things and wills" (53).

13. Lewis might not have fully accepted this doctrine, but the dynamic universe in the *Chronicles* does contain echoes of it which he skillfully ties with the classical concept of metamorphosis.

14. As attested to by several scholars, Lewis was well acquainted with Eastern Orthodox Church doctrines and some of his work was seen to include them. One Greek bishop from Constantinople referred to him as an "anonymous Orthodox" (Andrew Walker 64). Close to him in Oxford there was a Russian Orthodox community, a member of which by the name of Nicholas Zernov became his friend. Zernov founded the Fellowship of St. Alban and St. Sergius for discussions between the Eastern and Western Christians. Lewis gave a paper on "Membership" to the Fellowship and another one on icons (never published) at a meeting at St. Gregory's House in Oxford. He attended a Greek Orthodox mass and liked it because it has no "prescribed behaviour" (*Letters to Malcolm* 12). He knew the theology of St. Athanasius,

having written on him an essay and an introduction to a translation by his friend Sister Penelope. He also wrote an introduction to Charles Williams's "The Figure of Arthur" in which Williams reviewed the history of the doctrine of the Holy Eucharist by the Church Fathers. He would have agreed with Charles Williams on this theological doctrine which Williams spelled out in *The Descent of the Dove: A Short History of the Holy Spirit in the Church* (Grand Rapids, MI: Eerdmans, 1972). In his early poem "Dungeon Grates" Lewis, though yet not a Christian, describes a vision of Beauty in a "language of participation" with the divine, peculiar to believers in the doctrine of *thèōsis*:

> But only the strange power
> Of unsought Beauty in some casual hour
> Can build a bridge of light or sound or form
> To lead you out of all this strife and storm;
> . . . .
> O! but we shall keep
> Our vision still. One moment was enough,
> We know we are not made of moral stuff.
> . . . .
> For we have seen the Glory—we have seen. (17-20, 36-38, 42)

According to Andrew Walker, Lewis used "the ransom theory" of the early Greek Fathers in *LWW* (64). Greek Orthodox Archbishop Kallistos Ware has noted some other parallels between Lewis's fiction and theology and Eastern Theology, namely, God's hiddenness, the Trinity, creation, personhood, and the church (69). See chapter 2 for further discussion on Lewis's iconic imagery that also connects him to the Eastern Orthodox church. For a study of Lewis's mysticism see David C. Downing, *Into the Region of Awe: Mysticism in C.S. Lewis* (Downers Grove, IL: InterVarsity Press, 2005).

CHAPTER TWO

THE LIGHT AND SUN ICONOGRAPHY IN NARNIA

In one form or another light is naturally the most appropriate of all emblems of truth.
           Samuel Chew *The Virtues Reconciled* (34)

I. Icons, Images, Tableaux

In its original meaning, an "icon" is an image (Gr. *eikon*) which refers to a sacred image of the Orthodox Eastern Church, guiding and instructing in the spiritual life.[1] It is Platonic in origin, a holy archetype for the purpose of pointing to a reality beyond the earthly one. The sense in which I use the term "icon" in this study approaches St. John of Damascus's fourth type of image: the object and creature that suggest the Divine by analogy (Barasch 232). The icon is not an idol. The colors and lines of its composition, including shapes like circles and crosses, aid viewers in pointing to the Divine. Under such a general classification, however, the entire universe to the Christian imagination is imbued, like Lewis's, with holiness because it participates in God's incarnation in the creation (see introduction). The spirit permeates the flesh. As John Doebler points out, icons are at the point where all worlds meet in a single moment of action (16). These single moments in the *Chronicles* are, as I indicated earlier, the intersection of the synchronic (out of time) and the diachronic (in time) levels of the story, the eternal and the present, producing tableaux and pageants that are linked to the transcendent and are metamorphic in experience for characters and readers. In Lewis's chronicles some of the imagery is "God-intoxicated imagery" (Houston Smith 163) or, rather, "Aslan-intoxicated imagery," which intersects with the linear narrative to create, in the minds of characters and readers, a bridge between earth and heaven or, in Narnian terms, between Narnia and Aslan's Country. These tableaux and pageants gloss the main line of action to "narrate" for the readers the story of the Christian soul's regeneration from the powers of evil, indeed, the Gospel Story. As the Narnian Kings and Queens accompanied by Talking Animals (friendly fauns, birds, beavers, lions, dragons, wolves, and satyrs) navigate the Narnian landscape, Aslan appears (mostly late in the plot) in haunting and evocative tableaux out of time and space to create first and then regenerate the world of Narnia, protect his followers, draw them to him, as well as to fulfill primeval prophecies—whatever the *eucatastrophe* requires. It is in these situations that Lewis's "images of life" become iconic, pointing to Aslan in Narnia and by analogy to Christ in our world, as his main protagonists rise above any mediation between good and evil. These "speaking pictures," are "divine compositions" exhibiting increasing intricacy in Lewis's usage of imagery as he narrates his metamorphic journeys, one after another, across cities, gardens, and the sea—the topography of the human soul in Narnia.

In his study of icons, Leonard Stanton defines the icon as God's "penetrating energies" into created time and space (16). Stanton goes on to state that the icon is presented in "a complex spatial, perspectival, epistemological relationship to what lies beyond its palpable, sensible portion" (20). Creatures and objects thus are distorted, space and perspective inverted in order to pull the readers (or, in the case of visual arts, the viewers) into its center. The icon portrays reality not as it appears to our senses. "It is not the viewer who judges the icon, but the icon who judges the viewer" (Pitkin 16). The icon is like a prayer in that it draws one to God. Léonide Ouspensky explains, "What we see in the icon is so unlike what we see in ordinary life. The Divine Light permeates all things, so there is no source of light . . . . All is bathed in light, and in their technical language iconographers call 'light' the background of the icon" (40). However, in literary texts, "icon" has a verbal shape, a fictional image created by words that engage the writer's and reader's imagination. The meaning of the icon exists at the halfway point in the dialogic imagination of icon painter/writer and icon viewer/reader and always within liturgical events such as the Creation, Communion, Transfiguration, Resurrection, and with liturgical figures (angels, saints, and Fathers of the Church). Though Lewis's characters are neither angels, nor saints, nor Fathers of the Church, they do participate in events which may be considered liturgical or iconic.

The Creation in *MN*, the Resurrection of Aslan in *LWW*, the fulfilling of the prophecy at Cair Paravel in *LWW*, the pilgrimage in *VDT*, the regeneration of the Narnians in *PC*, and the apocalypse in *LB* can be considered liturgical-like pageants with a series of tableaux in the narrative—all bathed in iconic light. In the *Chronicles*, these iconic scenes point to the mystery of Aslan's (Christ's) presence. They allow Aslan/Christ to be manifest (temporarily) in the iconic image or become an iconic image himself. At the heart of the Narnia stories is the "inverse perspective" of the icon mentioned by Stanton, which breaks the laws of time, space, and reason to produce seeming paradoxes and riddles that engage readers. For example, the Narnia stories are set in an ambiguous Narnian time, with Talking Animals and Trees, and children who travel to Narnia by magic rings, through a painting, a wardrobe door, or some such magical way to become Kings and Queens of Narnia. Most important, the hero of these stories is the Golden Lion who inspires *mysterium tremendium*, forever treading in a halo of light in the darkest of nights—the greatest Talking Animal of all. And he always has a good story to tell. Iconic light imagery accompanies the daily situations of the characters on their journeys to find and assist Aslan in his metamorphic powers over nature and souls. Aslan is not visible in all scenes, only when he is about to bring regeneration into the Narnian universe. When he is present, the tableaux and pageants with their metamorphic powers become iconic. We find space and time transcended in the *Chronicles* in Aslan's presence in tableaux, composed with him at the center, always surrounded by light in gardens or woods and with his followers. At the end of each story, the imagery is usually unified in a ritualistic tableau (the final pageant). These scenes act like doors that bring characters in Narnia and readers to Aslan, as icons bring people to Christ in our world.

Admittedly, all conventional features of icons are not found in the *Chronicles*, nor do Lewis's images adhere to conventions of Renaissance iconology, but there are some scenes where the imagery seems to have some features of the icons and can be called "holy images," scenes of intense brightness that point to eternal, transcendent reality. In exploring Lewis's views on Eastern Church doctrines, Chris Jensen has shown that Lewis also used various images common to the Eastern Church like "face," "dance," "fountain," "winged horse," and others (Jensen 2) Lewis's sensitivity to beauty and *Sehnsucht*, his longing for Joy, may have led him to appreciate the beauty of the icon as a "sacred image."

II. Lewis's Views on Iconography

Lewis himself had a few things to say about iconography that corroborate the approach the present writer takes to the study of some of Lewis's particular verbal images. He writes that iconography is at the basis of Neo-Platonic art since the artist models his work after an image in his mind, created from prolonged reflection on sacred iconography (*English Literature* 319). Lewis defines iconography as traditional images filled with ancient wisdom and used in "divine compositions" (*Spenser's Images* 11). In this manner iconography is an accompaniment of life, rather than a criticism of it (*Spenser's Images* 11). He also refers to iconography as scenes and characters in a story that provide its readers with explanations of their experience (*Experiment* 3). He believes that the function of the icon is "not to fix attention upon itself, but to stimulate and liberate certain activities in the child or worshipper" (17). For example, a crucifix diverts the worshipper's thoughts and feelings to the Passion (17).

In a letter to Alastair Fowler on November 22, 1960, Lewis cautions him about "refining" the story or allegory "to the neglect of the general, iconographical, emblematic, or philosophical elements" (*CL* 3: 1212). More pertinently, Lewis believes that iconography is the language of images. He defines images in this context as "the 'moods' or 'spirits' themselves—the powerful expositions of terror, gloom, jocundity, cruelty, lust, innocence, purity—in them each man can clothe [or incarnate] his own belief" (*Four Loves* 36). Clearly, Lewis puts a higher value on imagery than on plain theological beliefs (see introduction and ch. 1). The image is essential to the belief for the latter to be "incarnated" (37). He continues with this most powerful statement about iconography: "I do not see how the 'fear' of God could have ever meant to me anything but the lowest prudential efforts to be safe, if I had never seen certain ominous ravines and unapproachable crags" (37). Although nature did not teach him any theological doctrines, she gave him the meaning of the word *glory* (37). And, most importantly, "If nature [with its iconic images] had never awakened certain longings in me, huge areas of what I can now mean by the 'love' of God would never, so far as I can see, have existed" (37). Yet he does caution us against carrying the love of nature into a "nature religion" (38). We need to go back to our studies, parishes, and churches for answers to our theological questions and to complete our journey to God. Love of nature and its images is a valuable initiation in this journey—but not the end. Fowler is convinced that had Lewis lived longer, he would have written more in the iconographical tradition (Hannay 161).

III. Light and Sun Iconography

Lewis follows a long tradition that views light as a symbol of the spirit (Cirlot 187-88) and, in the case of Christianity, an image of Christ or God. This tradition stems from pre-Christian primitive and classical mythologies that view light not only as a symbol of the spirit, but also as cosmic energy, and creative force (Cirlot 187-88). Some of Lewis's sources in his use of light are the Bible, Plato, Dante, Spenser, and Milton. Lewis's own writings reflect the significance that he attaches to light as a component of his own Christian iconography. In *Studies in Medieval and Renaissance Literature* (1966), he states that light is a natural symbol for God, for "God is, or is like, light . . . for every devotional, philosophical, and theological purpose imaginable within a Christian, or indeed, a monotheistic frame of reference" (71). In *Miracles* (1947), he describes God as light that illuminates Nature from beyond (124). In *The Four Loves* (1960), he compares light to the ultimate reality that remains a mystery while giving meaning to everything else: "We cannot see light, though by light we can see things" (175). As for Christ, Lewis describes Him as "always . . . streaming forth from the Father, like light from a lamp or heat from a fire, or thoughts from a mind" (*Mere* 151). In *The Great Divorce*, the regenerate spirits who choose to stay in Heaven are the "bright spirits" (119) and in the landscape of Narnia Aslan is the brightest of spirits.

In ancient cultures, the sun represented generally the source of life and light (Cirlot 319). Later on this tradition, as well as heliocentric theories, was adopted by the Neoplatonist Christians who focused on the analogy between the Diety and the Sun. "The orderly movement of the 'great lords of the upper sky' symbolizes the law of God, and the king must imitate the order of Heaven in wise laws to govern the movements and relationships of his subjects" (Myers 136). Not only the Diety, like Jove, was represented by the sun, but also the monarch on earth as a representative of Jove, and therefore, of justice. According to Jane Aptekar, in her study of iconography and thematic imagery in book 5 of Spenser's *FQ*, "The sun and Jove themes are related . . . There is an early seventeenth-century emblem which perfectly illustrates the generally accepted connection between monarchy and justice, the god which they serve and mirror, and the sun" (73). (See fig. 3). To Plato, the sun is the symbol of the ultimate good to which all creatures must turn (*Rep.* 5. 507-08). Christian typology links solar imagery in the New Testament to Christ: "[His] countenance *was* as the sun shineth in [H]is strength" (Rev. 1.16), and "I saw an angel standing in the sun" (Rev. 19.17). A passage from Malachi (4.1-2) also identifies Christ as 'the Sun of Righteousness." Spenser bases his character Una (the True Church) in *FQ* on Revelation 12.1: "And there appeared a great wonder in heaven: a woman clothed with the sun." He describes in book 1

> Her angels face
> As the great eye of heauen shyned bright,
> And made a sunshine in the shadie place;
> Did never mortall eye beheld such heavenly grace. (1.3.4.6-9)

In *Spenser and the Numbers of Time* Alastair Fowler writes that "in Pythagorean and Orphic thought Sol was associated with the monad because both were key images of deity" (77).

FIG. 3 THE SUN OF JUSTICE, BY ANDREAS FRIEDRICH FROM *EMBLEMES NOUVEAUX*, P. 68 (FRANKFURT, 1617). (APTEKAR FIG. 14).

As for the iconic image of the sun, Lewis also draws on ancient classical mythology and Christian traditions to establish its role as a companion of Aslan in these "divine compositions." In *Arthurian Torso* (1938), a collaboration of Lewis and Charles Williams, Williams quotes the following passage by Honorius of Autun (d.1130) in his historical review of the act of communion, which links Christ and the sun:

> [A]s the sun is the same in its heat and in its brightness, and yet produces different results in these two aspects, namely, burning the earth by its heat and giving light by its brightness, so the flesh of Christ remaining the same produces different results in different persons, incorporating the righteous with himself, separating the unrighteous from his life. (201)

In *The Allegory of Love* Lewis remarks that the image of God for Spenser was the sun (342). In *The Problem of Pain* (1962), Lewis defines a "blessed spirit" as "a body ever more completely uncovered to the meridian blaze of the spiritual sun" (151). He also declares, "I believe in Christianity as I believe the sun has risen, not only because I see it, but because by it I see every thing else" ("Is Theology Poetry" 92), alluding to the above mentioned Platonic concept of light. One of the famous representations of this image in the visual arts is an engraving by Albrecht Dürer, whom Lewis highly esteemed,[2] entitled *Sol iustitiae*, inspired by the above passage from Malachi. This engraving links the

FIG. 4 *SOL IUSTITIAE*, ENGRAVING BY ALBRECHT DÜRER (1499).

triad: Christ, sun, and lion (Panofsky 262). (See fig.4) A medieval tradition also underlies Lewis's linking of Aslan to the sun: the lion was a sun deity, his mane shone like the sun, and the astrological sign of the sun was Leo (Houston Smith 68). Based on these early pagan, classical, and medieval traditions, Aslan is a sun god, a Christ figure, shedding light on the benighted world of Narnia. In Luci Shaw's powerful words, "God and his truth and beauty are like a sun that fills the sky. Huge verities flare off from its center like the flaming tongues of a corona, utterly overwheliming us in our insignificance" (124).

A chronological reading of the *Chronicles* shows that Lewis handles light imagery as an iconic device that creates artistic unity in the series and renders them "divine compositions." As actual light passes through the various layers of glazes in an icon, transfiguring its earthly material, wood and paint (Proud n.p), so do the moon, the sun, and the stars transform the landscapes in the *Chronicles*. Lewis's mythopoeic Christian imagination uses the ancient primitive contest of light (as good) vs. darkness (as evil) not only as a tool for drama and suspense, but also for endowing the landscape of Narnia with holiness and mystery. Like a spotlight on the stage, the moon or the sun follow the moving good forces, isolating them for the reader to imagine and reflect upon. Light is always present in the iconic tableaux of Aslan, his world, and his good forces, which represent divine order, moral virtues, as well as beauty. It is a framing device that holds the varied plots together with Aslan as a numinous figure. He is everywhere, for his followers to see; Madeleine L'Engle writes, "To be truly Christian means to see Christ everywhere, to know him as all in all" (32). However, as reality, especially Christian reality, becomes more complex in the *Chronicles* series, light and dark become more tightly interlaced as good and evil often are. While in the earlier *MN* and *LWW,* the White Witch and her followers are juxtaposed against Aslan and his followers, the plots and characters of the later chronicles are more complex as Aslan's role becomes more subtle and protean. He appears in various feline shapes in *The Horse and His Boy (HHB)*, in more ambiguous dream-like visions to Lucy in *PC,* and in seemingly different forms in *VDT.* Aslan scratches Aravis's back as punishment for her treatment of her slave in *HHB*, and many characters in *LB* emphasize that he is "not a tame lion." Like an icon painter who allows light to pass through various layers of glazes, Lewis uses light to reveal as much as he can of the multi-layers of his Christian reality. As a result, his *Chronicles* are enhanced with an iconic quality, which, as L'Engle reminds us, is the quality of all true art (29).

Endnotes

1. Some parts of this chapter have been published in an article titled " 'Where Sky and Water Meet': Christian Iconography in C.S. Lewis's *The Voyage of the Dawn Treader*.'" *Mythlore: A Journal of J. R. R. Tolkien, C.S. Lewis, Charles Williams, and Mythopoeic Literature* 23.2 (Spring 2001): 36-52.

2. In a letter to Arthur Greeves on May 20, 1917 Lewis wrote, "Yesterday I came across some postcard reproductions of his [Dürer's] pictures . . . I like them greatly." "I do wish Dürer had illustrated 'The Fairie Queene,'" he wrote in another letter to Greeves on February 16, 1919. Lewis believed Dürer was the "founder of the fantastic and illustrative school now represented by Rackham and Heath Robinson" (Hooper *CL* 1: 207, 434). See illustrations of Dürer's art on pages 47 and 128 and of Rackham's art on page 79.

CHAPTER THREE

Mnemosynē in Narnia: Memory in Prince Caspian and The Silver Chair

And in my memory too I meet myself—I recall myself, what I have done, when and where and in what state of mind I was when I did it.
St. Augustine *Confessions* (10.8)

Great is this power of memory, exceedingly great, O my God, a spreading limitless room within me.
St. Augustine *Confessions* (10.8)

Aside from functioning as a storehouse of images and ideas for the creative writer as discussed in chapter 2, memory is also a major theme in the Narnia chronicles. Memory, according to St. Augustine, is a means of discovering God, and therefore one's self identity, through journeys in time, journeys from *Kronos* (chronological time) to *Kairos* (eternal time). While this is the basic journey of discovering the self in *Prince Caspian*, the journey in *The Silver Chair* includes the added concept of language as an aid to memory.

Of all seven of the *Chronicles*, *PC* is the one that speaks most to memory, followed by *SC*. Its plot is composed of an interweaving of journeys of memory that makes its chronological place in the series quite singular. Its Narnian plot, a sequel to *LWW*, has been interrupted by the story of *HHB*, about strange non-Narnian characters travelling through non-Narnian territory, Calormenes on their way to Archenland through the exotic city of Tashbaan. Although many Narnian years have elapsed since they were Kings and Queens of Narnia in *LWW*, the same Pevensie children in *PC*—Lucy, Peter, Edmund, and Susan—have deep buried memories about their experiences in *LWW*, which slowly come to consciousness through recollection as the plot unfolds. However, the plot of *PC* is different from that of *LWW* in that no White Witch or archetype of universal evil like her is present. The struggle in *Prince Caspian* is less archetypal and more moral and political since the evil character to rally against is a mere wayward Telmarine king, a tyrant and a usurper. On the diachronic narrative level, the main purpose of the plot is to crush the usurper King Miraz and restore the rightful heir, Prince Caspian, to the throne. But the plot is complex, tri-partite, and temporally disjunctive, at first glance. When one completes the reading of the story, one finds that the "synchronic moment" or the "eternal present" that initiates metamorphosis is facilitated through memory. The three structural components of the plot are: 1) the travel back in time in the children's memory to the past glorious state of Cair Paravel, stimulated by the children's encounter with Cair Paravel's ruins;[1] 2) the dwarf Trumpkin's long flashback narrative of remembered events, i.e., King Miraz's tyrannical rule and his conspiracy to murder the fleeing Prince Caspian and his supporters, who are to battle Miraz at Aslan's How (the setting of Aslan's martyrdom in *LWW* and the *eucatastrophe* of the story); and 3) the children's voyage to Aslan's How in the present to join forces with Caspian and defeat Miraz. The journey is filled with the children's memories of the old Narnia and tableaux of Aslan, who makes a rather late appearance, as in most of the chronicles. This tripartite plot, held by strings of memory, allows Lewis to draw on his scholarship in classical, medieval, and Renaissance theories on memory and recollection, specifically from St. Augustine's concept of time in *Confessions*, to present in a creative and subtle way his favorite theme of metamorphosis on many levels: spiritual, moral, and political.

This classical and Christian link of memory to the eternal through the image (as discussed in chapter 1) concerns Lewis the most in *PC*, for the eternal to him is Aslan, who must be remembered by the children and all the inhabitants of Old Narnia before any regeneration is to occur in the land, as Christ must be remembered on earth. The ruins of Cair Paravel in the first scene in *PC* act as mnemonic objects, giving emotional impetus to the children's memory to recall something else, something or someone half-forgotten—the city of Cair Paravel in the Golden Age of Narnia and the one who offered it to them, Aslan. The details from the children's memory, Trumpkin's flashback narrative, and the children's travel through Narnia coalesce to represent the sacral quality of Cair Paravel. (See fig.5).

FIG. 5 *MNEMOSYNE* (AKA *LAMP OF MEMORY* OR *RICORDANZA*), OIL PAINTING BY DANTE GABRIEL ROSSETTI (C.1876-1881). (THE NATIONAL GALLERY)

I. Memory and Time

In *Confessions*, which records Augustine's personal struggles in understanding memory and which is one of Lewis's favorite books, and which affected him the most as he wrote to Don Bede Griffiths (Hooper *Letters* 2 1044), [2] Augustine states that eternal being is "present all at once" (11.6.3) when past, present, and future are linked in believers' understanding of the Gospel Story. In other words, past and future can be linked to the timeless typologically, where one past event reminds us of another, for example, Jonah in the whale and Christ in the tomb—a system of typological representation important to Lewis as well (see introduction). As Thomas Ramey Watson explains, this experience of time as a merging of present past (in memory), present, and present future (in expectations) is something akin to Incarnation:

> Those who participate in the Incarnational task of expressing the Word in the world have the God-like duty of seeking to move hearers from the mutable and partial perspective of earthly time, chronos, to the immutable and complete perspective of eternity, kairos . . . in which time and eternity, earth and heavens, partiality and fullness meet forever. (6)

Watson further states that this process happens because of the "interior teacher, identified variously with Christ, the interior presence of God, the indwelling Word, in some sort of combination of the human mind" (5). Alister McGrath puts it eloquently: "The journey of faith [for Christians] is sustained by *memory* on the one hand and *anticipation* on the other" (25). Remembering the act of redemption through the martyrdom of Christ in the past will inspire us to live in anticipation of a future union with God and entry into the New Jerusalem. Past and future are merged in the present, when we recall what God has done for us. This is the "eternal moment," or "synchronic moment," in time yet out of it (see introduction), when the narrative is intersected by an out-of-time experience, the diachronic with the synchronic, at the moment of transformation, effected by Aslan's presence. This is *Kairos* as opposed to *Kronos*. Lewis has something similar to say about time and memory in *Divorce* through his guide in the novel, George MacDonald, who tells the narrator that time confers freedom on humanity, "the gift whereby ye must remember your maker and are yourselves part of eternal reality" (141). To remember their creator the ghosts must go with the bright spirits to the distant mountains.

Paradoxically, the Narnian stories contribute to the history of a world pivoted on Creation, Fall, Redemption, and Judgement. As a practicing Christian for about twenty years before any of the chronicles were written, Lewis understood history through his deep Christian beliefs. In "Historicism" (1950) he states that actual human history "is indeed the divine revelation *par excellence*, the revelation which includes all other revelations" (*Christian Reflections* 103). The most important sense of history for him is

> the real or primary history which meets each of us moment by moment in his experience. It is very limited, but it is the pure, unedited, unexpurgated text, straight from the Author's hand. . . . God is every moment 'revealed in history,' that is what [George] MacDonald called 'the holy present.' Where except in the present can the Eternal be met? (113)

This view explains, for Lewis, the Christian view of history which links through memory the first and second chapters, Creation and the Fall, and its last chapter which is the Judgment and Salvation.

II. Memory and Self-Discovery

Augustine's theory that verbal signs embody spiritual truths for believers parallels the classic mnemonic sign theory of memory. While both are based on linking the present to the past, Augustine's theory extends this link to include the future. Consequently, memory not only stores images and sensations, but is also an instrument of self-discovery: "And in my memory too I meet myself—I recall myself, what I have done, when and where and in what state of mind I was when I did it" (*Confessions* 10.8). As Robert Louis Wilken has written, "He [Augustine] recognized that memory has to do not only with recalling what one has experienced, but also with discovering what was already there buried deep within the recesses of the mind" (n. page). For Plato, remembrance of our true nature is of immense significance in our life (*Rep.* 621^c). At the same time, as a cognitive instrument of one's personal history, remembering one's identity is untouched by any change of outside form that occurs with the process of metamorphosis (Perutelli 23). The act of recognition occurs *within* transformation (25, italics mine). For example, in classical mythology, Cadmus, Harmonia, and Io, were transformed into serpents, and cow, respectively, but retained their intellectual capacity and remembered their human forms, sometimes with sorrow, like Io (26). (See fig. 5). In *VDT* Eustace retains his human self though he is changed into a dragon. This discovery, however, is a metaphor for the act of remembering God as our Father in this world. Aside from being an instrument of remembering God and self-knowledge, memory, in its variant forms, also releases the four passions of the mind: desire, joy, fear, and sorrow. In his explication of the happy life that all humans seek, Augustine uses a triadic figure to show how happy life (sought by the will), joy (accessed by memory), and truth (discovered by the understanding), all linked together (Puckett 865). For Christians, true nature is being God's children. One can make an interesting observation here: Memory and Time – Mnemosynē and her father-in-law Kronos – work together in Metamorphosis.

FIG. 6 IO TURNED INTO A HEIFER. A SIXTEENTH-CENTURY ILLUSTRATOR SHOWS HER THROUGH A WINDOW IN THE COW'S FLANK. (WARNER FIG. 9)

III. Memory, Recollection, and the Image

The image, however, must have a locus in the imagination for it to be remembered, and must be an image of a physical place or object to which meanings are attached, a starting point (Aristotle *De memoria* 452^a 12). These mnemonic loci, whether natural like branches of a tree or man-made like architectural objects (a house, an inner space, a theater, an arch, and the like), can be used as memory signs (Yates

6). Recollection requires one to work deliberately and with effort to interpret these images/signs, which function as starting points of the full memory process. Furthermore, it is essential that the memory images be arranged in an orderly manner to facilitate recollection. The cognitive processes involved in reconstructing the object of memory are based upon the principles of association and differentiation, through attention to likeness and opposition between present and absent things, and a logical determination to assemble these images in a meaningful way. These processes make recollection a means of investigation of a truth, rhetorical or ethical (Yates 34; Carruthers 150). In his *Commentary on Aristotle*, Albertus Magnus provides a summary of the recollection process, setting down tenets of earlier Aristotle interpreters: 1) "the representation of an image as an image"; 2) the filling of its shape with what it ought to be; and 3) the discernment process of assembling all steps and attaching characteristics of the object by likeness, opposition, place, time, and so forth (*On Recollection* ch. 1 qtd. in Carruthers 137). Memory thus works as part of transformation in accelerating recognition and self-knowledge, and storing as well as accessing images which express thoughts. As Alessandro Perutelli states, recognition is the confirmation of remembrance and occurs within transformation (25). Memory may arouse nostalgia for the past and so spur on action, and in this manner the past, present, and future are unified. These functions of memory and the art of recollection through mnemonics seem to be drawn by Lewis in *PC* from his classical sources to explain the children's process of discovering their relationship to Aslan.

IV. Cair Paravel Recollected Through the Art of Memory

After many Narnian years, we find in *PC* that the castle of Cair Paravel is in desolate ruins. If the Old and New Jerusalem in our world is what Cair Paravel is supposed to be in Narnia, then one may consider the catastrophes that struck the earthly Jerusalem in AD 70 and again in the fourth century, though in different manners, as analogous to the destruction of Cair Paravel in Narnia (see ch. 6). The Telmarines under the usurper King Miraz have reduced the castle to ruins and the city to an island and abandoned them, cut down trees, and forced the Talking Animals, the oldest citizens of Narnia, into hiding. What is left of the castle are some walls of the courtyard and hall and the hidden chamber where the armor and other gifts of Father Christmas in *LWW* are hidden.

The present Cair Paravel mirrors the corruption of King Miraz, the usurper. Lewis is applying here the Renaissance microcosm/macrocosm correspondence theory that views the corruption/health of the state as a mirror of the corruption/health of its leader. At the beginning of *PC* the scene of the ruined castle of Cair Paravel is powerful, another one of Lewis's tableaux in the *Chronicles* that convey strong themes as well as that special quality of tone and atmosphere that Lewis so much admired in Rider H. Haggard's novels (see ch. 4, n5). The scene communicates utter desolation and death mixed with suspense. Narnia at present is representative of a totalitarian regime bent on suppressing its citizens. The process of regeneration for Narnia and the children will be long and arduous, punctuated with moments of recollection of the glorious past. The mnemonic objects that will lead them to remember Cair Paravel are strewn in their path as if by providence.

From England the Pevensie children first land in Narnia on a sandy beach at the edge of a wood, which they soon realize is an island. A stream leads them to a woody place, the outgrown orchard of Cair Paravel, which they do not recognize at first. The iconic image of light surrounding the castle when they were coronated earlier in *LWW* has vanished. The place is covered up with weeds, thorns, wild roses, and dead branches that tear the children's clothes (*PC* 15). After struggling through the wild bushes and brambles, they spot apple trees—from the same tree that was planted in *LWW*, whose fruit, like the silver apples in *MN*, was and will prove to be an agent of healing and regeneration. Later on, after the children discover that the ruins are those of Cair Paravel, they remember they had planted apple orchards outside the north gate in the Golden Age and that "the greatest of all wood-people, Pomona herself, came to put good spells on it" (19), Pomoma being a Roman goddess invented by Ovid and associated with fruit trees and agriculture (Barkan 81). The moment they see the apple trees is significant. Lewis writes, "They were beginning to get very tired of it when they noticed a delicious smell, and then a flash of bright color high above them at the top of the right bark. 'I say!' exclaimed Lucy, 'I do believe that's an apple tree'" (*PC* 10). The yellowish-golden apples not only ward off starvation, but also serve as the starting point of the memory process leading towards finally recollecting Cair Paravel. Very slowly, as their imagination is working with their memory and powers of observation, the children begin to recognize pieces of Cair Paravel in the ruins. Ruins, according to Françoise Besson, represent temporary chaos, a shattered community, but they also "are the image of man's questions . . . of a quest for a lost harmony with nature . . . man's own self within the circle of the cosmos . . . [an] image of the quest of his inner city" (281-82).

One after another memory signs are discovered in their path. First there is a wall, an old, broken stone wall, covered with moss and flowers, discovered by Peter. Then as they come close to it they find a great arch, where they enter into an open place surrounded by grey walls: "It was a bright, secret, quiet place and rather sad" (12). The children, and we as readers of *LWW*, are soon driven by the process of recollection. Susan is the first to conclude, from what seems to be the process of association, that "this [place] wasn't a garden . . . . It was a castle and this must have been the courtyard" (13). Peter agrees, noticing some more memory signs: a tower, a flight of steps going up to the top of the walls and another to a doorway of the "great hall" (13). Edmund's observation leads him to conclude that the castle was functioning "ages ago" (13). Peter's deliberate effort to remember prompts him to declare, "I wish we could find out who the people were that lived in this castle; and how long ago" (14). Lucy and Peter begin to experience a queer feeling they have regarding the place. When they go through the doorway, they are in the great hall. They notice it is shorter and narrower than the first hall they first entered, and the walls are higher. The children (and readers of *LWW*) are logically engaged in retrieving the absent place through the process of seeing likeness and opposition between the present and the absent objects. The terrace at the far end of the hall is interpreted by Peter through the process of association as the dais where the High Table was: "Anyone would think you had forgotten that we ourselves were once Kings and Queens and sat on a dais just like that, in our great hall" (14), he tells Susan. She picks up on this memory sign and continues Peter's recollective strain though the process of discerning likeness, giving more specific details of the setting: "In our castle of Cair Paravel. . . at the mouth of the great river of Narnia. How could I forget?" (15). Lucy's associative thinking pushes her to utter, "This hall must have been very like the great hall we feasted in" (15). After exploring the area and building a fire, the children continue to assemble pieces of information about Cair Paravel from memory signs. Later, they discover a well half-way surrounded by the remains of a stone pavement. The clincher comes when Susan finds a little gold chess-knight with "eyes in the horse's head [like] two tiny little rubies—or rather one was, for the other had been knocked out" (17). "Why!" said Lucy, "it's exactly like one of the golden chessmen we used to play with when we were Kings and Queens at Cair Paravel." She remembers "playing chess with fauns and good giants, and the mer-people singing in the sea, and my beautiful horse-and-and-" (17-18).

It is Peter who finally suggests they must use their logic, the last step in the art of memory, to assemble all the meaning from the memory signs. The apples with their delicious smell, the wall, tower, courtyard, dais, well, and now the golden chess-knight are discerned and assembled in their imagination to recreate the glorious castle of Cair Paravel from memory. "We are in the ruins of Cair Paravel itself," declares Peter finally (*PC* 18). True to a scholastic in the classical memory tradition, Peter applies logic in the process of assembling evidence for the absent object. He takes the points one by one, rebutting every argument against it. Peter brilliantly proves, using logic and the process of argument by likeness or opposition, that the objects they have seen, which stand for memory signs, all lead to their initial conclusion that the ruins are those of Cair Paravel.

First, the hall is the same in size and shape as the hall in Cair Paravel. Peter challenges their imagination: "Just picture a roof on this, and a colored pavement, instead of grass, and tapestries on the walls, and you get our royal banqueting hall" (19). Second, he observes that "the castle well is exactly where our well was, a little to the south of the great hall; and it is exactly the same size and shape" (19). Third, the chessman that Susan found is exactly like the chessmen they used to play with. Fourth, this very apple orchard was planted by the moles outside the north gate of Cair Paravel and the wood spirit Pomona put a good spell on it and funny old Lily used to say, " 'Believe me, your majesty, you'll be glad of these fruits one day' " (19).

To Edmund's first objection—"We didn't plant the orchard slap up against the gate" (20)—Peter answers that Cair Paravel was not an island during their time (20); to his second objection—that they have been gone away for too short a time, only one year, for all those changes to happen—Peter has logical responses. Lucy challenges all by suggesting that if this is Cair Paravel, there ought to be a door at the end of the dais, leading down to the treasure chamber which houses Father Christmas's gifts given to each of them in *LWW*. And so it was. The little diamond bottle with the magical cordial for Lucy, the bow and arrows for Susan, and the shield and royal sword for Peter are all retrieved. All have special meanings regarding their roles as Aslan's followers and champions.

Faced with these mnemonics of the past, the children bring to life the absent castle. They put the broken fragments together and recreate from their memory, with imagination as well as observation and discernment, the place in the Narnian cosmos to which they belong—Cair Paravel— much like pilgrims or tourists who recreate through their imagination the living city they are seeking from bare walls, or readers who recreate a story from a text, or for that matter, the author recreating stories from his memory.[3] Reading the ruins of Cair Paravel resurrects it in their minds and, most importantly, helps the children recover their identities as Kings and Queens and citizens of Narnia. Through the providential ruins and objects of memory retrieved from the treasure house of Cair Paravel, the children reclaim their identity: "And that one small noise [the twang of Susan's bow] brought back the old days to the children's mind more than anything that had happened yet. All the battles and hunts and feasts came rushing into their heads together" (28).

This memory process of self-recovery for the children echoes Augustine's concept of memory as a distended present, linked to both past and future, allowing one to conceive of the Gospel Story. But more important to our purpose in this chapter is that these images are used like hieroglyphs and emblems to give an impetus to the process of memory in the children so that they can recollect their distant past in Narnia and see what is ahead of them. The process of memory is an integral part of their growth in self-awareness. By recollecting their own city of Cair Paravel, the city over which they presided as Kings and Queens of Narnia, the children will also awaken to the moral seriousness of their calling to Narnia, although that specific purpose will not become totally clear until the dwarf Trumpkin appears. The recollection process leads to a metamorphosis, transforming them and moving forward the plot narrative as they recover their glorious city in their imagination. They realize that all Narnia is now enemy territory and that it is incumbent upon them to redress this situation. By affirming their identities as citizens of Cair Paravel and Aslan's followers, they are fired up to proceed on their quest. As Augustine writes, memory releases passion.

In *PC* Lewis demonstrates once again his "scholarship of imagination" as he fuses classical, medieval, and Renaissance theories of memory with his own metaphors to achieve his purpose, the metamorphosis of Narnians and the children (and us the readers) by empowering them against evil. As was discussed above, the purpose of memory is the return of lost happiness and self-discovery by recollecting past experiences through present images. Augustine writes that memory is so important that "without [it] the gaze of our thought has no object to return to and without love it has no reason to return to it" (*De trinitate* 15.21.45 qtd. in Teske 156). One cannot relive past happiness or blessedness without memory. Nor can one understand the Gospel Story without understanding events in history, present experiences, and revelation of the future. Moreover, one cannot remember unless one cares to remember, unless one thinks deeply about the past experience (Aristotle *De memoria* 451^{b}10). It is this Augustinian journey of memory that continues to guide the Pevensie children in *PC* until their object of desire (Aslan) and their purpose of desire, the regeneration of Narnia, are restored. Memory of the past, the present, and the future coalesce in the timeless present and gives meaning and identity to the children and Narnia. As Hannah Arendt writes about Augustine's concept of memory, "The not-yet and the no-more" gather into the present, the "mental images of absent objects," the "objects stored by the memory that are no more," and anticipations by the will of what is "not yet" (*The Life of the Mind* 1:76).

This study has shown that aside from being a story whose major diachronic plot is the return to the throne of the rightful heir, *PC* is actually about memory and its role in one's understanding of the eternal (Aslan in the Secondary World of Narnia and Christ in our Primary World). Reading the ruins of Cair Paravel as mnemonic signs is reminiscent of the classical art of memory. It is similar to Augustine's process of reading verbal signs that embody spiritual truths for the believer. Having participated in this "Incarnational task," the children's mission, especially Lucy's, is to move other Aslan followers from the perspective of Narnian time to the perspective of Aslan's time, i.e., eternity—from *Kronos* to *Kairos*. This process takes up the first part of the story, expands in the other two parts to involve the inhabitants of Old Narnia, the Talking Animals and Trees, and terminates with the defeat of tyranny and the metamorphosis of Narnia.

Lewis unites memory, purpose, and desire as the three elements of salvation to provide a view of the Gospel Story and humans' role in it. Phoenix-like, Cair Paravel springs back to life in the imagination of the children and readers, followed by the awakened forest and Talking Animals—indeed, Narnia as a whole reclaims itself through the act of remembering and achieves its previous, joyous state (see ch. 10). In explicating Augustine's ideas about *memoria dei,* Richard Ambrosini writes, "The state of confusion in which man lives when he is lost in the world is, in a way, a condition of forgetfulness of the presence of his own soul" which proceeds from the word of God within us (102).

V. Memory and God

To most interpreters of Plato (those known as Platonists), memory has "almost divine" connotations (Yates 20). In *Meno,* Socrates suggests to Meno that what is recollected is knowledge of intelligible, unchanging forms, knowledge that is inherent in the immortal soul. Something similar appears in Cicero. In *De inventione,* Cicero places *memoria* as part of the virtue of *prudentia* (wisdom), along with *intelligentia* and *providentia* (foresight) (II.3.160 see Yates 20). So does Augustine who, as a Christian thinker, goes further by conceiving of memory, in rational souls like humans and angels, as an instrument of spiritual wisdom. As Ambrosini explains, "The soul's knowledge of God can be called memory of Him" (98). Paul Plass adds that to Augustine, memory is an instrument for remembering God and, like Plato before him, Augustine links it to providential patterns (347-48). Augustine himself writes, "God is everywhere present so that creation lives and moves in him (*Acts* 17.28), and remembers him" (*De trin.* 14.15.21 qtd. in Plass 352).

Augustine's "*The City of God* [is] a remembering of the plot of history as a whole" (Plass 358). To him, God "validates the memory of human discourse" (Bergvall 26). Our memory stores the *sermo sapientiae* (*De doctrina christiana* 12.4.23) to ruminate upon it by recollection. In this manner, our words and thoughts (*verba*) become representations not only of things (*res*) but also of the mental concept, which in turn affect our patterns of thought and life. Words and thoughts become representations of the Word for God. Paul Ford maintains, "Lewis stresses the importance of remembering as a spiritual discipline" (308). As Lewis has written in *Letters to Malcolm* (75), to penetrate into the presence of God, "the real labour is to remember, to attend. In fact, to come awake. Still more, to remain awake," reminding us of Christ's words: "Thou shalt love God with all thy heart, and with all thy soul, and with all thy mind" (Matt. 22.37-39). These relationships between memory, God, and language will appear in *The Silver Chair,* where the children and Puddleglum must remember Aslan's signs in order to succeed in their quest of rescuing Prince Rilian from the spell of the Green Witch.

IV. Memory and Aslan's Four Signs in *The Silver Chair*

The journey in *The Silver Chair* is epical as Eustace and Jill, with Puddleglum, rough it from Cair Paravel through a horrible winter season, over a wasteland of icy mountains and valleys in the north of Ettinsmoor, the foreboding and sinister land of the giants, to Harfang, the Castle of the Giants, where they find out they are on the menu for the giants' Autumn Feast. They escape from the Castle of Harfang through the Ruined City of the giants down into Underland, City of the Green Witch—a maze of caves in different sizes nestled into each other, sloping down to the city of Earthmen (gnomes)—all the time carrying (or attempting to carry) Aslan's signs in their memory. The story is packed full of traditional motifs and motifemes of good and evil, and a huge metamorphic scene from one species to another. The last scene, which involves the temptation by the Green Witch of the travelers and Prince Rilian, whom they are trying to rescue, and her negative metamorphosis, is at the center of the plot. In it the Witch, by robbing them of their memory through enchantment, robs them of their identities.

The powerful, but horrific, motifeme of her negative metamorphosis is a travesty of the stone statues' de-petrifaction and Aslan's resurrection scenes in *LWW*, Eustace's "un-dragonization", and the Lamb's transformation into Aslan in *VDT*—all motifemes of Enchantment/Disenchantment. However, what is unusual about this chronicle is that Aslan's followers do not have a clearly defined archetypal evil figure to fight against like Jadis in *MN* who, in all her drama, always appears as herself, a beautiful sorceress; or the White Witch, who parades in her white furs in all her scenes in *LWW*; or like the vicious Radabash and King Miraz in *HHB* and *PC*, respectively; or the formidable sea serpent which attacks the Narnians' ship in *VDT*, providing the Dragon Slaying motifeme and making of Prince Rilian the Dragon Slayer mythic hero. What they have in *PC* is a Witch, a shape shifter, who vacillates between human and serpentine forms (like Dante's thieves in *Inferno* 7), between a pleasing Victorian lady-like appearance and a ferocious, writhing serpent, forked tongue and all. The oldest dwarf is right in his perception of her inner nature: "Those Northern Witches always mean the same thing, but in every age they have a different plan for getting it" (*SC* 240).

However, Aslan is equally ready with his own strong plan for the campaign against the sorceress in *SC*. On the diachronic level, the frame narrative, the travelers' quest, is to find and rescue Prince Rilian, which will be successful when the negative transformation (of enchantress Witch into beast) will be effected by the positive transformation (of enchanted Prince into disenchanted), ending with the ascent of Aslan's followers from the dark Underland to sunny Overland. As in *PC* the role of memory is strong in bringing about all these resolutions, this time more focused on remembrance as a discipline. The journey across Narnia and down to Underland, as well as the return to Overland, cannot be achieved without following Aslan's signs of remembrance. The children, Puddleglum, and Prince Rilian will discover their identities and succeed in their mission to the degree that they remember Aslan and follow his signs. In this sense, the lessons of Aslan's signs and memory of them trump any destructive metamorphosis in this story and help the process, at the core of the plot, from negative enchantment of Prince Rilian and his rescuers to their ultimate disenchantment, i.e. the *eucatastrophe*.

Aslan makes an unusually early appearance in this story, in comparison to other chronicles, to instruct Jill himself on how to go about the quest to find the missing Prince Rilian. She and Eustace must follow these four signs: 1) Eustace must greet an old friend as soon as he sets foot in Narnia; 2) the children must journey to the Ruined City of the ancient giants; 3) they must read and do what the writing on a stone in the Ruined City tells them; and 4) they must aid the first person in their travels who will ask for help in Aslan's name (*SC* 24). Remembering and following these signs are the only ways to succeed in their quest. "The first step is to remember" (24), Aslan emphasizes. Before he blows Jill with his breath from his high mountain to Cair Paravel, he again says, "But first, remember, remember the signs" (25). He cautions her that the signs in Narnia will not look as she expects them to look so "that is why it is important to know them by heart and pay no attention to appearances. Remember the signs and believe the signs. *Nothing else matters*" (26, italics mine). By remembering these signs, the children and Puddleglum will save Prince Rilian and escape the destructive power of the Green Witch.

A review of Lewis's thoughts on language can help in interpreting Aslan's signs. Lewis delighted in studying the etymology of words, probably considering himself the last philologist (as well as the last dinosaur!). He admired the early modern writers' use of concrete language (*CL* 2: 37) and believed that "all speech about super-sensibles is, and must be, metaphorical in the highest degree" (*Miracles* 77). However, his ideas about ordinary language stem from a traditional (post-seventeenth-century) view that the role of language is to communicate thoughts and express truth. The relationship between the signifier (word) and the signified (referent) is arbitrary, based on linguistic conventions. There is no corresponding relationship or similitude between words and things, and usually no epistemic properties of words.[3] Like his contemporary George Orwell, he believed that language can be corrupted by jargon, scientism, and technology, as shown in *That Hideous Strength*, and degenerate into complete dysphasia, confusion of tongues (Filmer 73). More importantly, a corrupt language can falsify things about the world. An example is the "green book" by Alec King and Martin Kelley, *The Control of Language*, which is attacked by Lewis in the *Abolition of Man* for discounting the teaching of values in the use of language and focusing instead on subjective feelings.

However, Aslan's signs are not ordinary words, but riddles—they are not vague because of vague thoughts. The semantics is context-dependent, and without apparent logical or temporal connections, the sentences need to be followed on faith to unravel their meaning. What gives them significance is that they come out of the mouth of Aslan, and, therefore, are not ordinary. The only option for the children to make sense of them is to remember them and act accordingly at the right time and place. As to when these conditions might be, Aslan is silent. They must learn to trust him. *Credo ut intelligam.* I believe so that I may understand. One recalls the many cases of positive metamorphoses in the Gospels, of people cured by their faith in Jesus. One also recalls the abundance of signs in the Scriptures, some equally ambiguous, that believers are asked, like the children in *SC*, to hold in memory. Moses exhorts his people to keep the Ten Commandments in their hearts: "And Moses called all Israel, and said unto them, Hear, O Israel, the statutes and judgments which I speak in your ears this day, that ye may learn them, and keep, and do them" (Deut. 5.1). He continues,

> And thou shalt teach them diligently unto thy children, and shalt talk of them when thou sittest in thine house, and when thou walkest by the way, and when thou liest down, and when thou risest up.
>
> And thou shalt bind them for a sign upon thine hand, and they shall be as frontlets between thine eyes.
>
> And thou shalt write them upon the posts of the house, and

on thy gates. (6.7-9)

Peter J. Schakel states, "The signs become for Jill what the words of the law were for Israel: a source of direction and guidance, and she must keep them before her all the time" (*The Way Into Narnia* 73). In the Gospels also believers are asked to not only hold God in all their being (heart, soul, and mind) (Matt. 22, Luke 10.27) but also to remember Him through the holy Scriptures and sacraments, especially communion: "And he took bread, and gave thanks, and brake *it*, and gave unto them saying, This is my body which is given for you: this do in remembrance of me" (Luke 22:19). Lewis writes that believers must also hold Christian doctrines in their hearts and minds (*Mere Christianity* 141). For Jesus says, "The words that I speak unto you, *they* are spirit, and *they* are life" (John 6.63). Remembering Jesus is also remembering God, and the faculty of memory leads individuals to self-knowledge and identity, recognition of their true nature as "Sons of God" (*Mere Christianity* 156). Memory of God leads to *thèōsis*.

It is important to note also that Aslan's signs are not written down, abstract thoughts or objectified rules that follow in a logical pattern. They are spoken words, *verba*, that enable the travelers to reach their destination and be transformed in the meantime through their mnemonic capacities to remember Aslan. Advocating the power of the spoken word over the written in terms of reaching the truth, Plato writes in *Phaedrus*,

> [Writing] will induce forgetfulness in the souls of those who learn it: they will not practice using their memory . . . . You have not discovered a potion for remembering but for reminding; you provide your students with the appearance of wisdom, not with reality. Your invention will enable them to hear many things without being properly taught, and they will imagine that they have come to know much while for the most part they will know nothing. And they will be difficult to get along with, since they will merely appear to be wise instead of really being so. (275 [a-b])

True knowledge (for a Christian through remembering the words of Christ) should be alive in hearts and minds rather than on the printed page. Living according to the signs is the very point of the Christian Story. In this respect, Aslan's four signs are not examples of ordinary language. Therefore, they work according to the Augustinian theory of linguistics, which is tied to his theology, that verbal signs (*verba*) represent not just things (*res*) but mental concepts of the thing. It follows that words can represent God, the transcendental reality as discussed above: "At the center of both stands the transcendental Sign that gives validity to all conventional signs": Christ and the Holy Scripture (Bergvall 26, 29).

Stuart Clark explains the Catholic understanding of miraculous situations, when language becomes extraordinary, this way:

> God's arbitrary dispensations concerning words were . . . nothing less than these miraculous efficacies that accompanied their pronouncement by privileged persons on sacramental occasions. In these ritual contexts, words did have a uniform, automatic, but, of course, supernatural power to bring about physical changes as well as sanctification of souls; they were, we might say, performative utterances of a particularly pure kind. But these were only apparent exceptions to the rule since sacramental efficacy, above all, could not rest on the power of the words themselves, only . . . on an instrumentality that they acquired from heaven. (291)

I think Lewis believes in these infractions of the rules of language when words proceed from the "powerful operation of the spirit" (Stewart Clark 291). Aslan's signs are "performative utterances" to engage his followers through trust, memory, and action in order to effect the reverse metamorphosis of a witch. All of the main characters in *SC* achieve self-knowledge and success in their quest when they remember Aslan's signs in their minds and hearts and act accordingly, but they run into trouble when they fail to do them or when they are tempted by material comforts or pride.

A chronological reading of the *Chronicles* shows how the children's memory of Old Narnia and Prince Caspian's remembrance of Cornelius's words led to the defeat of King Miraz and his followers in *PC*; how Lucy's memory of the forgotten story that she read in the Magician's House has become a standard by which to measure all stories in *VDT*; and we will see how in this story the children, Puddleglum, and Prince Rilian will defeat the Green Witch through memory of Aslan and his signs, which allow them to remember who they are and what their mission is.

Jill can recite all the signs as she is blown into the air by Aslan's breath, although she does so with some anxiety. When she lands in Narnia and tells Eustace about the first sign (to meet an old friend, the aged King Caspian the Tenth whom Eustace had met in *VDT*), he fails to remember because he is distracted by the hullabaloo as the king is sailing away to the eastern islands, hopefully to meet with Aslan to get information about his missing son, Prince Rilian. Had Eustace met with King Caspian, the children might have had help in their quest.

They would not have had to struggle with their later temptation for food and comfort, for instance, since the Green Witch might not have dared to approach them. Also, their hunger and need for comfort would have been satisfied by King Caspian's followers.

However, after a warm bath and change of clothes at Cair Paravel, Jill forgot all about the signs (43). Distracted later by the anticipated warmth, food, and comforts of Castle Harfang, the Castle of the Giants, the children forget the signs. Puddleglum again asks Jill, "Are you still sure of those signs, Pole? What's the one we ought to be after now?" (103). She replies abruptly and erroneously, "Oh, come on! Bother the signs . . . Something about someone mentioning Aslan's name, I think. But I'm jolly well not going to give a recitation here" (103). As the narrator explains, "She had given up saying the signs over every night" (103), and she did not know the "Lion's lesson" as well as she should (104). Consequently, they are trapped in Harfang for a day and would have been on the giants' menu in the Autumn Feast, had they not escaped. Aslan intervenes at this crucial moment. At night, he appears to Jill in a dream in a series of metamorphoses (reminding us of the series of shapes he appeared in to Lucy in the Dark Island in *VDT*), first as a toy horse and then as a toy lion, and finally as himself. "And a smell of all sweet-smelling things there are filled the room" (119-20). He tells her to repeat the signs, which she had forgotten, and takes her to look out of the window at the sky on which is written UNDER ME, which is the third sign. The next day, rather belatedly, they could see from the window of the Castle the ruins of a gigantic city, which they had missed the night before in the rush to get to Harfang and the comforts associated with it. The letters UNDER ME are carved across the pavement of the city:

> Down below them, spread out like a map, lay the flat hill-top which they had struggled over yesterday afternoon. . . . It had been flat . . . because it was still, on the whole, paved, though in places the pavement was broken. The criss-cross banks were what was left of the walls of huge buildings which might once have been giants' palaces and temples. One bit of wall, about five hundred feet high, was still standing. . . . The things that looked like factory chimneys were enormous pillars, broken off at unequal heights; their fragments lay at the bases like felled trees of monstrous stone. The ledges . . . were the remaining steps of giant stairs. (121)

Recognition of these two signs allows them to succeed in escaping from death at the castle of Harfang. Their escape, which takes a great deal of wit and bravery, makes it possible for them to descend to Underland and follow the last sign, which is to assist anyone who asks for help using Aslan's name.

In Underland, the Green Witch has robbed Rilian of his true knowledge of himself and tempted him with a false one. Yet ironically, he and the two children and Puddleglum regain their identities as Aslan's followers by remembering Aslan's words. In contrast, Eve in *Paradise Lost* was too engulfed by Satan's rhetoric to remember the words of God. This scene reveals the strength and constancy of faith of the children in Aslan, an experience paralleling the experience of *thèōsis* in our world. Although capable of being tempted by evil, they reveal themselves to be true followers of Aslan, "little Christs" in our world. Aslan does not intervene directly as he did in the White Witch's Castle. The travelers remember Aslan's last sign (to "help the one who utters his name") and liberate the victims of the Green Witch. They must all get out of the shadowy realm to sunlit Narnia. It is the power of Aslan that saves them through following his signs.

The grief and horror experienced in Underland is overcome by courage and rationality, but mostly by grace represented by Aslan's signs—analogous to our belief in God's saving words, the Christian Gospel in our world. Although Aslan does not interfere physically to aid his followers as he did in *PC* and *LWW*, he works through the children's memory to create a physical victory over the Green Witch and a spiritual victory through their acts of remembrance and faith in him, analogous to remembering the Lord and our own true nature as His children in this world. Again, memory is an aid to *thèōsis* as it is in Lewis's mythopoeic creative process.

Endnotes

1. Unfortunately, this important section of the story is much shortened and trivialized in the movie *Prince Caspian* (2008). This effort on the part of the children may be an illustration of Lewis's concept of creative reading, which he defines in *Experiment* as a process of reading for facts and interpreting them through memory and imagination. This theory parallels his own concept of invention (see ch. 1).

2. See also *CL* 1: 190, 225, 529, and 3: 1263.

3. Other references are provided under "language" in Janine Goffar's *The C.S. Lewis Index: A Comprehensive Guide to Lewis's Writing and Ideas*, 1995 (Wheaton, IL: Crossway Books, 1998); see also George Orwell's essay, "Politics and the English Language," *Language Awareness: Reading for College Writers*, eds. Paul Eschholz et al. 9th ed. (Boston: Bedford / St. Marin's, 2005) 138-49.

CHAPTER FOUR

Satanic Cities in Narnia:
Charn, the Castle of Ice, and Underland

Through me, the way into the suffering city.
         Dante *Inferno* (3.1)

Unreal City,
Under the brown fog of a winter dawn.
A crowd flowed over London Bridge, so many,
I had not thought death had undone so many.
         (T.S. Eliot, *The Wasteland* 59-62)

I behold Babylon in the opening Streets of London. I behold
Jerusalem in ruins wandering about from house to house,
         (Blake, *Jerusalem* 74.16-17)

Whether one debunks the city or the wilderness in the Bible as places of degeneration, there is another more significant binary opposition of the two types of cities, the sacred and the profane—the City of God (*civitas dei*) and the City of Man (*civitas terrena/perversa*)—at the heart of the Western Literary Imagination. Taking his cue from the Scriptures, St. Augustine builds his own dichotomous system of cities: the City of God and the City of Man, the first a divine gift and, therefore, pure in its heavenly form; the latter man-made and, therefore, corrupt in different degrees. Saint Augustine elaborates on the two lines of human descent that were formed as a consequence of the primal act of murder, the first from Cain and the second from Seth, another son of Adam. The first line of descendants went on to form the City of Man, consisting of those who choose to live by the standard of the flesh, and the second line went on to form the City of God, consisting of those who choose to live by the standard of the spirit (*The City of God* 15.1), as exemplified by Ishmael and Isaac who represent, respectively, man's state of nature and man in the state of grace. The City of Man is founded on self love (*amor sui*) and lust for power (*libido dominandi*), while the Heavenly city (or the City of God) is founded on love of God (*amor Dei*) (14.28). In these passages St. Augustine focuses on free will that renders humans, and angels, responsible for their actions, whether to be citizens of the City of Satan/Man or of the City of God. Augustine writes, "The right will is well-directed love, and the wrong will is ill-directed love" (14.7), thus rejecting, at least in this passage, a Manichean dualism. In his remarkable study of the image of the city, Charles A. Moorman states that there is a lack of sympathy and of exchange of burdens and troubles in the Civitas Terrena and more isolation (62). (See fig. 7).

FIG. 7 *THE CITY*, A WOODCUT BY FRANS MASEREEL (1889-1972)) (NY: DOVER).

However, this binary analysis does not distinguish between various degrees of evil that might plague the Earthly City (or the City of Man) and its inhabitants—like secularism, on one end of the spectrum, and demonic worship and blood sacrifices, on the other. Augustine's image of the city, comments James Dougherty, is an "uneasy" one with too many powerful associations that Augustine could not control (24). In fact, Augustine used "man" and "devil" interchangeably. Hawkins is of the opinion that Augustine "confuses the earthly city with the *civitas diaboli* (the City of Satan) so that the two often seem to be synonymous with one another," although in the eternal realms they are distinct (74). To his credit, Augustine later added that the two cities, "the earthly and heavenly, [are] mingled together from the beginning to the end of their history" (18.54). Indeed, Satanic self-love can dominate the earthly city.

SATANIC CITIES IN NARNIA

According to Thomas R. Watson, who uses the compound term "City of Satan/Man" in an attempt to resolve the issue, Satan introduced the dichotomy that continues and multiplies through Cain, who "fully brought to earth the City of Satan, now properly called the City of Man" (2).[1] For many, therefore, only in a natural, fertile setting can one see the face of God—or in a city that is a gift of God. As Richard Lehan has pointed out, life close to nature is good; life close to society is bad (61). W. H. Auden remarks, "The once fertile city has become, through the malevolence of others or its own sin, the wasteland" (26). Lewis's Romantic leanings and his love of nature make one conclude that he would have agreed with these notions.

In its most extreme and dangerous form, when ruled by a demonic figure, the City of Man is inseparable from the City of the Antichrist "who opposeth and exalteth himself above all that is called God, or that is worshipped; so that he as God sitteth in the temple of God, showing himself that he is God" (2 Thess. 2.4). (The temple of God here is a reference to the Jewish temple in Jerusalem, metonymically the City of God, possessed by the Antichrist.) In this context the term "city" refers to earthly cities, rather than the holy city of Jerusalem praised in Psalms 122 and 137, whose location, for the most part, is in heaven. This city is a type of hell, a *monde reversé*, as discussed in chapter 1, a city of chaos and despair—a City of Satan. In the *Inferno*, Dante especially excels in describing the City of Dis (Satan), which holds those guilty of malice and fraud in circles seven to nine and includes more specific motifs of the City of Satan than Augustine.

Charles A. Moorman believes that the image of the city elucidates Dante's poem (43). Dante alludes to this City of Satan, the "Suffering City," early on in an inscription above the Gate of Hell: "THROUGH ME THE WAY TO THE SUFFERING CITY/ . . . . ABANDON EVERY HOPE, WHO ENTER HERE (3.1.9). Ranked according to Aristotlean and Augustinian degrees of perversion of the good, or "ill-directed love" (*amor sui*, and *libido dominandi*) (*City* 14.7), these egregious sins consist of heresy, violence, flattery, alchemy (another term for black magic in the Middle Ages), false prophecy, usury, and the like as enumerated in Gal. 5.20 and discussed in detail in the *City*. All guilty of the sins put their private profit, feelings, house, or party, over the City (Moorman 43). In Dante's *Inferno*, canto 33, Satan, the father of evil, to whom these sinners ceded their will, lies frozen at the bottom of the pit, the location of murderers of kin and guests, and of traitors to their political parties and leaders.

In Lewis's chronicles, the hard core evil Cities of Satan include the Ruined City of Jadis in *MN*, the White Witch's Castle in *LWW*, the Castle of Harfang and Underland in *SC*, and Shift's Stable in *LB*, before it is transformed by Aslan into a gateway to the real Narnia. These cities are ideological and demonic parodies of Cair Paravel, the City of God (Aslan in Narnia), and its attributes of harmony and *agapé*, which will be discussed in chapter 6. They are ruled by shape-shifters, non-human, unnatural magicians, or a beast set on destroying or enslaving all the Narnians instead of "promoting the common good" (Hambnet 152). The rulers and inhabitants of the City of Man in the *Chronicles*, i.e., of Tashbaan in *HHB* and the Island of Gumpas in *VDT*, but not Anvard in *HHB*, are mostly evil—but none is as over-reaching in the lust for power as rulers of the City of Satan, who are all incarnations of the powers of evil, competing with Aslan himself as if he were their equal.

Jadis had destroyed her own city by uttering the Deplorable Word and tries to tempt Digory to eat the apple in the garden, against Aslan's will; the White Witch tempts Edmund by Turkish Delight; the Green Witch kidnaps Prince Rilian to her Underland Kingdom by seduction and keeps him there by enchantment; and the Ape Shift creates a feeble optical illusion by dressing a donkey in a lion skin to look like Aslan. Their sins are augmented by their awareness of their own evil and their tendency to blame others. Because of their treachery toward Aslan and others, they are physically isolated and spiritually banished from the rest of the beings in Narnia, surrounded only by their demonic followers. Each of the damned creates his/her own hell. Quoting Von Hugel, Lewis writes, "The characteristic of lost souls is 'their rejection of everything that is not simply themselves'" (*Problem of Pain* 123). Along the same line he writes in *The Great Divorce*, "There are only two kinds of people in the end: those who say to God, 'Thy will be done,' and those to whom God says, in the end,' *Thy* will be done'" (75). Or, as Charles Williams writes, "When all's said and done there's only Zion or Gomorrah" (*Descent to Hell* 174-75). These sinners are not offered a second chance or forgiveness by Aslan, although their followers are. "A man who admits no guilt can accept no forgiveness," writes Lewis (*Problem* 122). Their dwellings are located not in familiar social settings, but remote in a period of the past, across fields of snow, or deserts, or in the belly of the earth. Like Homer's, Virgil's, and Dante's hells, these cities are entered through a wasteland or a desert.

All these traditions, biblical, classical, and literary, have reinforced in Lewis's "scholarship of imagination" and in his memory the two-city archetypes, with their particular motifs, the sacred and the profane, the City of God and the City of Man (in its worst form, the City of Satan). I believe Lewis shares these views since in Narnia he constructs cities that are sacred or profane and makes the choice to be or not to be a citizen of a particular city a determining factor in an individual's salvation. With the exception of Cair Paravel, the ideal city in Narnia, towers (in a metronymic sense) in *PC* and *LB* and the Archenlandian city of Anvard, which are splinters of Cair Paravel, Lewis's other cities and their rulers are representations of these classical cities of tyranny: Charn, the Castle of Ice, Underland. In the *Chronicles* Lewis adheres to this traditional concept of the city, in general, as inseparable from the city of death (Lehan 181), although in its highest form it can replicate the City of God. In its worst form, the city is "a troubling territory, a place of loss, alienation, and corruption of the soul, a place of dangerous distancing from the natural world, the home of all beginnings" (21).

A. Charn and its Queen in *The Magician's Nephew*

In *MN* the two opposing binary structures in the landscape in Narnia are the Ruined City (the starting point of evil) and the Garden (the final destination of hope and triumph). They provide a moral dichotomy that lies at the foundation of this story. This dichotomy, however, is resolved at the end through a movement in the plot from city to garden which reflects a spiritual movement, or metamorphosis, in the main character, Digory, with significant thematic implications. From the Ruined City of Charn, an ancient non-Narnian city, the Witch Queen Jadis emerges to invade the newly Created Garden in Narnia and tempt Digory's soul, but, in aspiring to do so, suffers defeat by Digory and Aslan. The inter-relationship of the two main structural elements of *MN*'s landscape, the Ruined City and Garden, and their biblical, classical, and literary associations, reveal Lewis's "scholarship of imagination" at its height and his talent in interweaving motifs and motifemes to suggest his themes about sin and redemption in Christian history. These motifs of corruption, chaos, waste, and death, spanning centuries of tradition, abound in the depiction of the city of Charn and define it, as I will argue, as a type of an evil City of Man, much like the old Jerusalem, Babylon, and Rome. However, the fact that it is dominated by Jadis the witch, a devil figure, who is consumed with the lust for power not just over Narnians, but over Aslan himself, defines it more as a motifeme of Satanic City like the Dantean City of Satan, out of Narnian time but not eternal like Dante's. Thus in *MN*'s simple plot Jadis the Witch is posited against Aslan—the evil city vs. the good garden, the city of Charn vs. the Created Narnian Garden, as a place suggesting Christian Grace.

Charn, in its former corrupt state under the rule of Jadis and in its present utter ruin, is a composite of scriptural, Augustinian, and Dantean motifs. Charn is first presented to us through the eyes of Polly and Digory and, later, through the comments of Aslan. When Polly and Digory use their magic rings in the Wood Between the Worlds, they are transported to Charn. They first notice the darkness of this ruined city, the great crumbling pillared arches around a desolate courtyard, and the "dead, cold, empty silence" (*MN* 48). The vast rooms of the ruined palace open out of one another "till you were dizzy with the mere size of the place" (50). There is also a strange winged stone monster perched over a dry fountain. Inside the Hall of Images, the only inhabitants of Charn that come to the children's view are the stone figures, all seated, as the following tableau shows:

> All the figures were wearing magnificent clothes. . . . .And the blaze of their colors made this room look, not exactly cheerful, but at any rate rich and majestic . . . . The figures were all robed and had crowns on their heads. Their robes were of crimson and silvery gray and deep purple and vivid green; and there were patterns, and pictures of flowers and strange beasts, in needlework all over them. Precious stones of astonishing size and brightness stared from their crowns and hung in chains round their necks and popped out from all the places where anything was fastened. (52-53)

Polly is dazzled by their clothes and finery. However, the extravagant ornamentation is suspect since it is associated traditionally with "artifice" or "art," Renaissance terms that are linked in some instances to evil, which I think Lewis is drawing upon here (*Allegory of Love* 326).[2] The tableau is also a parody of the apostles, the elect in the Last Judgment (Rev. 3.4-5), or of a group of prophets and Sybils usually found in iconic paintings. The luxurious robes of the stone figures mock the simple white robes of the apostles and conjure up heathen cultures. The dead figures' faces range from "nice" to "very solemn" to "cruel," as well as to the most despairing (*MN* 54), suggesting to Paul Ford the theory of devolution which is later made more obvious in the view of the destroyed city (138-39). Jadis the Witch is presented last in the line, as the fiercest, yet most beautiful, of all the still figures in this desolate room of the palace of Charn.

What happens in the enchanted Hall of Images in *MN* is pivotal to the metamorphic journey of Digory and quite a contrast to the events in the garden later on. On a square pillar there is a golden arch with a little golden bell hanging from it and a little golden hammer beside it. The pillar also bears an inscription with these words:

> Make your choice, adventurous Stranger;
> Strike the bell and bide the danger,
> Or wonder, till it drives you mad,
> What would have followed if you had. (*MN* 56)

This scene with all its props is clearly a temptation to obey curiosity, the first step on the ladder of pride (Janson 201), and Digory is unable to resist. The ringing of the bell brings Jadis back to life, who will, after some other adventures, introduce evil to Narnia. Digory's succumbing to temptation here will be compensated for later by his heroic resistance to another temptation, this time by Jadis herself in the newly Created Garden. For his action in Charn, Digory is like a fallen Adam to Aslan, who states, "You see, friends . . . that before the new, clean world I gave you is seven hours old, a force of evil has already entered it; waked and brought hither by this son of Adam" (161). Lewis has reversed the biblical sequence of Creation and Fall for his own world by placing Digory's moral failing in a pre-Narnian city and his subsequent triumph over temptation in a Narnian garden. Lewis thus reverses not only the sequence, but also the locus, since the initial Fall takes place in a city, the traditional site of moral decay. The origin of evil for Narnia is thus a city that had fallen into complete moral corruption before Narnia's own history had begun. The origin of such metamorphic destruction through black magic is non-Narnian, although it will be repeated by the White Witch and the Green Witch.

When Jadis is brought back to life through the ringing of the bell, she leads Digory and Polly out of the Hall of Images to a panoramic view of the Ruined City of Charn, which she had earlier destroyed by her magic in a rivalry for power with her sister:

> Low down and near the horizon hung a great red sun, far bigger than our sun. Digory felt at once that it was also older than ours: a sun near the end of its life, weary of looking

down upon that world. To the left of the sun, and higher up, there was a single star, big and bright. Those were the only two things to be seen in the dark sky; they made a dismal group. And on the earth, in every direction, as far as the eye could reach, there spread a vast city in which there was no living thing to be seen. And all the temples, towers, palaces, pyramids, and bridges cast long, disastrous-looking shadows in the light of that withered sun. Once a great river had flowed through the city, but the water had long since vanished, and it was now only a wide ditch of gray dust. . . . "Such was Charn, that great city, the city of the King of Kings, the wonder of the world, perhaps of all worlds" [says Queen Jadis]. (68)

Mysteriously created, outside of Narnia, outside of Aslan's purview, Charn is certainly not the "wonder of the world" in its present state. It may be viewed as a type of the City of Satan in the biblical/Augustinian tradition, destroyed by its evil ruler. The imagery in this passage conveys these notions. It is vast, with courtyard opening into courtyard, like a ruined medieval castle. Its fountains, as mentioned earlier, are ornamented with strange monsters. They are dried up. The sun in Charn is withered and old, and "all the temples, towers, palaces, pyramids, and bridges cast long, disastrous-looking shadows" in this elderly light. In *MN* as in the later chronicles, light appears to possess a variety of shades projected on the landscape in different degrees. The sickly-looking light in The Wood between the Worlds where Polly and Digory first land is "a soft green light" (31); the light of the Ruined City, Charn, is a ghoulish "dull, rather red light, not at all cheerful" (46). This dismal scene is a stark contrast to the most intense bright light that always hovers around Aslan. As Hugh Crago states, "The dim light of Charn immediately places it in the same class as Underworld cities, even though it is not subterranean" (42). What comes to mind immediately is the Green Witch's Underland in *SC*. Both are infernal cities controlled by a witch, one already in ruins, and the other to be destroyed at the end of the story.

Etymological considerations of the word "charn" confirm the physical and spiritual decay of the city and its former inhabitants. "Charn" comes from the Latin root *carnale* which means "flesh," as opposed to the spirit. The word "charnel," or "burial place" with its imagery of cold, dead, crumbling, ruined masonry, holding remnants of the body/flesh also applies here to this ruined city; "Charn," moreover, recalls the word "charred" (Craik qtd. in Paul Ford 139; Crago 42). In *Alain Quatermain*, an 1855 novel by H. Rider Haggard, one of Lewis's favorite authors and a possible modern influence, there is a ruined city called Charra (Lehan 93).

Before its devastation, Charn had once been a city of cruelty and hate, a tyrannous city in Plato's terms (see ch. 5), filled with dungeons, slaves, sacrifices, noises of drums (*MN* 69)—all motifs that link it also to devastated biblical cities like Sodom and Gomorrah, rather than to a glorious past civilization, which it might have had in the unknown distant past. Jadis's account is all that there is. As one finds out from Jadis's description of events in Charn before its devastation: "The cracking of whips and the groaning of slaves, the thunder of chariots, and the sacrificial drums beating in the temples. . . . and the river of Charn [ran] red" (*MN* 69). She brags to the children about how her own great-grandfather slaughtered seven hundred guests whom he had invited to a feast (66), like the betrayers of guests in circle nine of Dante's *Inferno*. Another event links this city to the City of Satan. In a fight with her sister for the throne, Jadis had used the magical Deplorable Word (analogous to nuclear weapons in our time) and "[A] moment later," she says, "I was the only living thing beneath the sun" (71).

This murder is analogous to the Cain/Abel and Romulus/Remus fratricidal murders, condemned by Augustine as the most horrible of sins (*City* 15.5), though in this case, the rival sisters were both evil rulers (*MN* 69). Following Augustine, Dante places such murderers of kin in circle nine of the *Inferno*, the lowest circle of the City of Satan. It is a sepulchral city, metaphorically like T. S. Eliot's dreadful London. The destructive power of Jadis's words that annihilates civilization is a stark contrast to Aslan's music, which will create Narnia, and later his words in *SC* will guide the children and Puddleglum in their mission (see ch. 3). Ever afterward, there was no life in Charn at all, not even insects—only empty silence. These images of death are in direct contrast to the images of life and healing in Aslan's gardens, which will be discussed in chapter 7.

Aside from being a type of the City of Satan, Charn is also a city of a remote past. "Jadis" means "once" or "in former times" in French (Crago 42); thus her name indicates a past civilization which is irrelevant in Aslan's Narnia and which contrasts, as death to birth, with Narnia. Lewis's ambivalent fascination with the past has early roots in his life. In an early unpublished fragment titled "The Quest of Bleheris," written when he was only seventeen, he describes a young lad named Wan Jadis, who is on a pilgrimage to a romantic Land of Yesterday, where "a man can hide away from the care and moil of the world" (qtd. in Downing 48).³ Wan Jadis is eventually drowned in the Gray Marsh, showing his futile, sentimental aspirations to return to the past. Also, in the same manuscript, there are striking images of a temple in the Land of Yesterday that anticipate those used for Charn: "Flight of steps, of fluted columns, of lowering domes high above sculptured terraces of galleries, among the which stood sad and solemn monuments, and monstrous images: and because of the mist it was all shadowy as a dream, and empty as some city of the dead" (25).⁴ The "flight of steps," the "sad and solemn monuments," "monstrous images," "empty as some city of the dead"— all create a desolate atmosphere like that of Charn, revealing Lewis's wariness, even in adolescence, of inordinate reverie or of idolizing the past, whether its greatness is real or imagined. ⁵

FIG. 8 ARTHUR RACKHAM'S ROMANTIC IMAGE OF BRÜNHILDE FROM *DER RING DES NIBELUNGEN*, 1909.

Jadis the Witch is the first of the demoniacal female witches known for their supernatural power over men—an archetype of the Valkyrie from Norse mythology, of much attraction to Lewis.⁶ (See fig.8). Like Uncle Andrew, but on a much larger and bolder scale, Jadis asserts, "We must be freed from all rules. Ours [magicians'] is a high and lonely destiny" (*MN* 71), a rationalization of evil actions. Also like Uncle Andrew, she uses people for her ends.

The narrator says, "I expect most witches are like that. They are not interested in things or people unless they can use them; they are terribly practical" (*MN* 85-86). Young Digory has several brilliant insights into the Witch's character, too brilliant for a boy of his age (but then he became the wise Professor Kirke in *LWW* and owner of the house the children are staying in). When Jadis does not say anything to the children about her sickly state in the Wood Between the Worlds, the narrator remarks, "I think (and Digory thinks too) that her mind was of a sort which cannot remember that quiet place at all, and however often you took her there and however long you left her there, she would still know nothing about it" (85). Magicians, though some may claim "royal blood" or "fairy" blood in them, as the Witch and Uncle Andrew do, respectively, are blind to present realities. Moreover, the Witch has "giantish" blood in her family, and we will see her at the end of the story defeated by Digory, skulking to the north of Narnia, a direction that is associated with the evil giants in the Christian tradition. Also, magicians like the Witch and Uncle Andrew are ignorant of the extent of the power of Aslan's Deeper Magic, which manifests itself at the end of each of the Narnia chronicles. When the Witch first hears Aslan's song of creation, she understands that his Magic is stronger than hers and wants to leave this "terrible world" (120), but not before hitting him with the iron bar.

To learn more about Jadis, one needs to examine other tableaux of her. One powerful tableau describes her, earlier on in London, on the roof of a hansom, "[h]er teeth were bared, her eyes shone like fire, and her long hair streamed out behind her like a comet's tail. She was flogging the horse without mercy" (101). The fire imagery suggests a demonic quality about her which matches her obvious cruelty. This tableau foreshadows the tableau of the White Witch (who is also Jadis at a later time) as she comes into view for Edmund in *LWW*. While fiery hell torments the Witch in *MN*, icy hell will distort the heart and soul of the White Witch in *LWW*. They both create and reflect the hell they live in.

This section on the Ruined City in *MN* introduces a unique theme related to Lewis's views on time. In *MN* past civilizations do not divert the reader temporarily with grand visions of antiquity and the magnificence of a heathen past—rather with only its remoteness, irrelevance, and evil. According to Paul Ford, the degeneration of the kings and queens of Charn, ending with Jadis, supports the view that ancient empires founded upon tyranny and ungodliness, whether historical or fictional, eventually succumb to devolution, in spite of their earthly successes and grandeur (139). G. K. Chesterton states in *The Everlasting Man* (1914) that despotism is very often "the end of societies that have been highly democratic" (50). Lewis hints at the idea of devolution in our world [7] as Aslan warns Polly and Digory, saying,

> It is not certain that some wicked one of your race will not find out a secret as evil as the Deplorable Word and use it to destroy all living things. And soon, very soon, before you are an old man and an old woman, great nations in your world will be ruled by tyrants who care no more for joy and justice and mercy than Empress Jadis. (*MN* 212)

This prophecy certainly came true for Narnia and its neighbors. Democracies can change into empires and finally die out.

For Lewis, Charn, under Jadis's rule and in its ruined state, represents the absence of all good (in whatever form good—or God—took in Narnia), and so it must, and did, end. Similarly, Augustine believes that the *civitas terrena* in the end will be folded like a scroll (*Confessions* 13.15). Such empires are also ephemeral for Lewis, as they were for Plato, and not a major concern in *MN*. However, the power of such mythopoeic places to enthrall readers, particularly those who share Lewis's temperament and taste, with glimpses into realms of eldritch knowledge and beauty is not to be denied. Also, "A Nature which is 'running down' cannot be the whole story," he affirms in *Miracles* (156). We, as readers of the *Chronicles*, must wait for the apocalypse in *The Last Battle* to complete the story.

Thus, the ruined Charn is important, not just as an enigmatic setting that arouses peculiar dread, but as a past civilization that produced Jadis, the antagonist of Aslan, and as a setting for Digory's first temptation. As hinted in Lewis's early "Bleheris," and in the description of Charn, Lewis considered the value of romantic accounts of the remote past not to be simply their imaginative appeal, but their potential for spiritual instruction —if any metamorphosis in a person is to occur in "the holy present." The human soul, in a personal or general sense, must journey through its struggles from the ruins of a desolate city to the hope of a newly created garden in order to learn about and triumph over evil.

MN involves a series of metamorphoses through Aslan's grace. Two such moments in *MN* are Digory's triumph over Jadis in the garden and the healing of Digory's mother through eating the apple. These moments of the Eternal present radiate into the future lives of Digory and his mother. Here Lewis is viewing time as a unity, unfragmented, much like Augustine for whom, if one can see the past, present, and future as one process (the Gospel Story), then one can experience the Eternal moment in the present. The present includes the past, the present, and the future. It is, what I term in this study, the "synchronic moment" or *Kairos* (eternal time). Lewis explains such revelatory, metamorphic moments as miracles, the clues to the meaning of the human story, "precisely those chapters in the great story on which the plot turns. Death and Resurrection are what the story is about" (*Miracles* 102). This concept of time has already been discussed in chapter 3.

Aslan's new covenant must be instituted in a number of ways, echoing his typological cast of mind: The Ruined City is structurally and thematically replaced in *MN* by Aslan's Created Garden; the magic of the Deplorable Word, by the Greater Magic of Aslan (as later happens in *LWW* where the Deep Magic of Jadis is vanquished by the Deeper Magic of Aslan); and Jadis herself, who has the ambition to regain her former position as Queen, by the newly crowned King and Queen in *MN*. Likewise, Digory and Polly leave Charn (and earlier our world) for Narnia, and the cabby and his wife (selected by Aslan) leave our world to be given thrones in Cair Paravel. A person's and a civilization's ancient stories are not the focus in *MN*; they are only the complication that moves the plot towards glorious metamorphosis in the Created Garden.

In *MN* Lewis's "scholarship of imagination" blends classical/biblical, Dantean, and secular motifs to construct the two major structural images of his landscape, the newly Created Garden and the Ruined City of Charn, as settings for the children's pilgrimage—which suggests the journey of the Christian soul, its struggle, and restoration through grace. Charn is one of the most evil cities of Narnia because its ruler is self-deceived and, consequently, attempts to deceive others by manipulating the truth in favor of illusion as was evident in the garden. Jadis and her followers in *LWW*, as will be shown in the following section, represent corrupt humanity without a spiritual center, residents of a city isolated from each other and from God. On the other hand, the enclosed garden with its silver fruit, heavenly scent, and golden gates, perched on top of a hill or mountain, is the garden of triumph over temptation in the human soul, a place of healing. The theme of metamorphoses is revealed through Digory's journey in *MN*, a journey from the sinful city of Charn to Aslan's garden of love and healing.

B. The Castle of Ice and the White Witch in *The Lion, the Witch, and the Wardrobe*

The gloomy cold wood of the White Witch and her followers is first presented to the reader through the eyes of Edmund, who has just gone through the wardrobe after Lucy and for whom the snowy wood seems different. The frozen wood is a creation of the White Witch, but also a reflection of Edmund's evil nature, since Lucy does not see exactly what he sees: for Edmund, the sky is pale, the sun just rising, but dry, crisp snow is everywhere under his feet and on the branches of the trees. Edmund is entering into a cold and quiet place similar to Dante's circle of ice in the *Inferno*. Lewis writes, "Everything was perfectly still, as if he were the only living creature in that country. There was not even a robin or a squirrel among the trees" (*LWW* 31). This desolate, deadly landscape is the background for the first half of the narrative: frozen rivers, dams, and vegetation—as well as utter silence.

The White Witch's life-denying power is nearly absolute for now. Except for the humans, her spy Mr. Tumnus (the faun), the Beavers who are the last remnants of their species, and a few other animals, the Witch has literally petrified vitually all of the woodland creatures. In this respect, she resembles two figures from classical mythology: the Gorgon, who petrifies men, and indirectly Circe, who changes men into swine. Her forced metamorphosis of living things into stone is the inverse of the incarnation in our world: she destroys life while Christ gives it. One is reminded of Christ's words here: "The thief cometh not, but for to steal, and to kill, and to destroy: I am come that they might have life" (John 10.10). Also, this cold wasteland and the Gothic-looking icy castle she operates from are similar to Charn in *MN*, where life is extinguished by Jadis, the White Witch under a different name. Both wastelands are types of Hell or locations for Cities of Satan and can be compared to Gomorrah, according to Glen GoodKnight. In Charles Williams' *Descent*, Stanhope, a Christ figure, asks, "Do you know how quiet the streets of Gomorrah are?" (174). Like Charn in *MN*, the White Witch's Castle is solemn, silent, and sterile, its classic representations being Homer's Hades, Virgil's Hell and Dante's City of Ice in Circle 9 of *Inferno*. Lewis paints an eerie tableau of the Witch's

Castle in the moonlight, with its long, pointed spires that are like huge "dunce's caps or Sorcerer's caps" (100), suggesting it is a product of the Witch's Art (black magic, *goeteia*) which substitutes for Nature, unlike its antitype, Cair Paravel, which blends Nature and Art, and is therefore sacred in landscape and edifice. The Witch's *goeteia* is a favorite topic of Lewis which he associates with the violations of natural law and the sacredness of life through scientism (tantamount to black magic for him) and with the false belief that technology is a solution to the problems of humanity (Eustace's dreams in chs. 8 and 10).

Inside the walls of the Witch's Castle, Edmund later encounters a horrible scene of devastation. The whole courtyard is like a graveyard filled with petrified creatures: a dwarf, a centaur, a winged horse, a dragon, and faun—all motionless like Lucifer and the other frozen inhabitants of the deepest pit of Dante's *Inferno*. And "just inside the gate, with the moon shining on it, stood an enormous lion crouched as if it was ready to spring" (101). But the lion is not Aslan. These creatures are not there because of their own will, and, unlike Dante's sinners, they are not denied salvation. They are victims of the White Witch's magic wand, the main instrument of her *goeteia*. On the other hand, Edmund later is tempted by Turkish Delight but is allowed to live as an informant.

As Edmund is contemplating the snowy wasteland, the eerie silence of the frozen Narnian wood is suddenly broken by the sound of ringing bells as if announcing the entrance of a royal figure. The White Witch emerges from her evil-looking Gothic type castle on the frozen landscape only to destroy good, thus adding a motif of horror to this fairy tale and establishing the motifeme of Defeating a Witch in the Edenic Garden later on. Her purpose, according to the diachronic frame, is to thwart Aslan's plan to institute humans on the throne of Cair Paravel, thus preventing the fulfillment of three prophecies: 1) that when Aslan comes, spring will return to Narnia (*LWW* 85); 2) that "when Adam's flesh and Adam's bone / Sits at Cair Paravel in throne, / the evil will be over and done" (87); and 3) that "when two Sons of Adam and two Daughters of Eve sit in those four thrones [at Cair Paravel], then it will be the end, not only of the White Witch's reign but her life" (89).

The tableau describing her entrance and her ridiculous entourage is a travesty of a queen's or a goddess's entrance, a point that goes unnoticed by the enchanted Edmund. The Witch is regally poised on a *sledge* and accompanied by a strange *fat dwarf* in *bear's fur* wearing a Christmassy *red hood* with a long tassel. The sledge is pulled by *horse-like* reindeer with *gilded horns*—a congloramous, ridiculous tableau. The dwarf is a mischievous travesty of the dwarf in Spenser's *FQ*, Una and the Red Cross Knight's faithful companion. The gilded horns of the reindeer present another jarring detail that makes these unnatural looking animals a mockery of the sacred sacrificial bulls in ancient Greece and also, on a more mundane level, of the typical Christmas reindeer. The White Witch has a beautiful face, albeit proud, stern, cold, and white, like "paper or icing-sugar," notes Edmund (34)—appropriate images of death. Such perverseness and an obvious lack of charity in her behavior are also suggested by her title, "white" being the color of snow, cold, and even death. In Revelation 6.8, "the pale horse" can be interpreted as a symbol of Death and Hell who "kill with sword, and with hunger and with death and with the beasts of the earth." The Witch will later kill Aslan with her Stone Knife and the help of her monstrous beasts. "White" is also the color of disease, nausea, and the future sickness of Edmund (Filmer 109). In *FQ*, foul Meleager's face is "as pale and wan as ashes" (2.11.22.1). The phrase "covered with white fur up to her throat" suggests lupine characteristics. Instead of a scepter there is a golden wand in her hand, which we later find out turns living creatures into stone.

The Witch is no Daughter of Eve, although she masquerades as one to get the throne of Cair Paravel in her attempt to put an end to the prophecy (mentioned above). In one of his letters to W. L. Kinter, dated July 30, 1954 (*CL* 3: 497), Lewis places her in the tradition of the Witch archetype, performing black magic like the sorceress from Greek mythology Circe (Alcina being her Latinized name). He had already addressed this archetypal figure in a poem about a witch called "Lilith," where he mourns over the destruction caused by her seductions of the hero by offering him a cup of wine (*Pilgrim's Regress* 189). GoodKnight suggests that in creating the White Witch, Lewis may have been influenced by George MacDonald's novel *Lilith*, but that in *LWW* Lewis emphasized her hatred of humanity and her child stealing more than her attractiveness (18).

In *LWW* Mr. Beaver explains that the White Witch goes back far in time to such demonic ancestors as Jinns (Arabic term for demons who take human or animal shapes), Efreets (Arabic term for evil spirits), and giants. According to some Christian traditions, Satan has often been seen as a giant (Cirlot 118) from whom descended the evil giants of the Old Testament who slept with women and brought evil into the antediluvian world (Gen. 6.4; Num. 13.33). Northern Narnia is the habitat of the murderous giants and the White Witch; the North is also associated in the Christian tradition with Satan. In *Paradise Lost*, Lucifer leads the rebellious angels towards the north of heaven. In *MN*, Jadis, the earlier appearance of the White Witch, skulks to the North after being routed by Digory (Professor Kirke now in *LWW*); and in *SC* the Green Witch appears on the "north" side of the pool, and her city is in the North of Narnia. Lilith, on the maternal side of the White Witch, was the first wife of Adam but made from a different lump of clay. According to some traditions, she left him in disobedience but was forever jealous of Eve and her children: "Lilith's rebellion against God is a much more severe and intense act than Adam's fall" (GoodKnight 18). Lilith was always accompanied by wolves. In Semitic mythology, "She is known as a demon of the night, of the wind, and a stealer of the light" (GoodKnight 15).

In predicting the downfall of Edom, the prophet Isaiah says, "And the wild-cats shall meet with the jackals, and the satyr shall cry to his fellow; yea, the night-monster shall repose there, and shall find her a place of rest" (34.14, The Jewish Publication Society of America Translation qtd. in GoodKnight 15). Glen GoodKnight explains that the translation of the Hebrew word "night monster" is "Lilith," the mother of demons (15). All the above mentioned characteristics of Lilith are associated with the White Witch of Narnia: she has kept the land in a Christmasless freezing winter for a hundred years, is hunting human children, is wolf-like herself, and appears with her major accomplice, the grey wolf, mostly during the night. Perhaps another source for the White Witch is explained in the following passage from a January 26, 1951 letter from Lewis to Sarah Neylan: "A missionary told me that he had seen a little ruined Kraal where the natives told him a white witch used to live who was called She-who-must-be-obeyed" (*CL* 3: 89). In the letter to Kinter mentioned above, Lewis humorously remarks, "No good asking where an individual author got that. We are born knowing the Witch, aren't we?"

Lewis makes much of the Witch's magical abilities, defined as making things look like what they aren't" (*LWW* 152). She operates under the Old Law put forth by the Emperor-Over-The-Sea which allows her, under its principle of justice, to turn traitors into stone with her golden wand or enslave all human sinners that she succeeds in luring.

A would-be traitor, Edmund was lured with the addictive magical candy, Turkish Delight, for the purpose of spying on his siblings. She develops in him a habit of intemperance and incontinence, much like Archimago in *FQ* who tempts the Red Cross Knight through sexual dreams, and Satan, who tempts Eve through her fancy and senses. As A. Bartlett Giamatti observes, sense and sexuality can corrupt the will (327), the central faculty of the human being. GoodKnight makes an interesting observation that during the nineteenth century, Turkish Delight often had the ingredient hashish added to it (17), a fact that would have been available to Lewis.

Like Jadis in *MN*, the White Witch's evil nature is reflected in her terrifying appearance, notwithstanding her "beautiful" face. When she appears at the Stone Table, shudders run down the children's backs. The animals start growling (154). "Every sinner is mine," she brags (170). But her temporary power will soon be routed by Aslan and the gifts of Father Christmas to the children: sword and shield, horn and bow and arrow, and cordial. These, especially the cordial, will effect incidents of positive metamorphosis in Narnia through its ability to heal creatures. The White Witch's despair, as in all evil creatures, feeds her greed, as explained in one of Lewis's early poems entitled "Deadly Sins," in which the speaker mourns over the destruction caused by greed's seduction:

> Greed into herself would turn
> All that's sweet: but let her follow
> Still the path and greed will learn
> How the whole world is hers to swallow. (*Poems* 5-8)

In short, the Witch, in Mrs. Beaver's opinion, is "bad all through" (*LWW* 88).

After a series of brilliant pageants—the Resurrection of Aslan, the Liberation of the Statues in the Castle of Ice, the battle of Beruna and the defeat of the Witch, the children are crowned at Cair Paravel. Some of these pageants will be discussed in chapter 10 as powerful illustrations of metamorphosis/*theōsis*.

C. The City of Underland and the Green Witch/Serpent in *The Silver Chair*

During the parliament of owls to which Jill and Eustace are taken after they arrive at Cair Paravel from Aslan's Country in *SC*, the oldest owl Glimfeather narrates the story of Prince Rilian's disappearance in a "northern" wood, a direction of potential evil as has been discussed earlier. The story-within-story is a vivid vignette, which functions as a prelude to what will happen in Underland, the central motifemic scene of metamorphosis. In that wood, Glimfeather says, there is a seemingly idyllic place where Prince Rilian and his mother the queen (Ramandu's daughter in *VDT*) would go riding. In one of the rides, they came upon "a pleasant glade where a fountain flowed freshly out of the earth" (57). This place contains motifs of earthly gardens which turn out to be false. Prince Rilian and his mother dismounted and drank. While the queen was sleeping, a great green serpent came out and stung her, causing her death. Lewis refers to the serpent as the "worm," thus linking it quite clearly with the biblical dragon and the dragon of Norse mythology. He describes it: "It was great, shining, and as green as poison, so that he [Rilian] could see it well; but it glided into the bushes and he could not come at it" (57). (In *Paradise Lost*, John Milton describes the Serpent/Satan skulking into the bushes after its temptation of Eve). In that location, while looking for "that venomous worm," he would later disappear, fallen to the temptation of the Green Witch, a serpent in the form of a beautiful woman. What seemed to be an idyllic place becomes a type of a garden of loss, of actualized temptation as opposed to the the Edenic Garden in *MN* and the beautiful Garden of Restoration in Aslan's Country in *VDT*. This mysterious incident of the queen's death and the equally mysterious later seduction/abduction of Prince Rilian deserve close analysis in order to expose the evil nature of the Green Witch/Serpent and her devastating effect on those she comes in contact with, primarily Rilian's mother, Rilian himself, and later the British children and Puddleglum.

We know that Prince Rilian's mother is the daughter of the prophet/priest and retired star Ramandu in *VDT*. Descended from such noble blood, she must have some extraordinary graces bestowed upon her. There are similar intriguing characteristics between her and the Green Witch, which may have made it easier for Rilian to be seduced by her. As described in *VDT*, Ramandu's daughter was stunningly beautiful, as beautiful, one might add, as the Green Witch: "When they [the voyagers] looked at her they thought they had never known what beauty meant" (215). In *SC* she is described as "a great lady, wise and gracious . . . And men said that the blood of the stars flowed in her veins" (58). Also like the Green Witch, she is involved with enchantment, albeit in an indirect way. She was the prize for Prince Caspian after the three sleeping Narnian lords were disenchanted in *VDT*. Yet, despite her supernatural gifts, she is surprised by a green worm and falls victim to its poisonous bite. The poison was too strong for her, coming from the Green Witch/Serpent who is considered in folklore an agent of death, belonging to the Diabolic category. She is like the serpent Typhon in classical mythology, a serpent who is the offspring of Hera, symbolizing the principles of irrationality and disorder as used in Apuleius's novel *The Golden Ass* (Asker 115) (which Lewis will draw upon later in 1956 for his novel *Till We Have Faces*). The Green Witch/Serpent shares these attributes.

Despite his noble ancestry, Rilian falls prey to the Green Witch as his mother had, but in a different manner. The Green Witch's intense beauty (mixed with evil to which Rilian is blind) is the primary factor in his mysterious seduction by her. Glimfeather continues with his story: "But about a month after the Queen's death, some said they could see a change in him. There was a look in his eyes as of a man who has seen visions, and though he would be out all day, his horse did not bear signs of hard riding" (*SC* 58). The Prince is having a mysterious relationship with this diabolic creature, which is effecting a change in him. Finally, he confesses to Drinian, a Narnian knight who had traveled with Prince Caspian in *VDT*, "I have seen there the most beautiful thing that was ever made" (59). Glimfeather and Jill both realize that the serpent and that woman are the same person. Glimfeather, in fact, associates the beautiful woman with the White Witch of *LWW*: "This may be some of the same crew" (61). When Drinian sees her, he too can accurately fathom her at first sight:

> At noon Drinian looked up and saw the most beautiful lady he had ever seen and she stood on the north side of the fountain and said no word but beckoned to the Prince with her hand as if she bade him come to her. And she was tall and great, shining, and wrapped in a thin garment as green as poison. And the Prince stared at her like a man out of his wits. . . . It struck in Drinian's mind that this shining green woman was evil. (*SC* 59-60)

This woman will lure Rilian to Underland and put him under a spell. Rilian's relationship with the Green Witch has gone on for ten years before the plot of the story begins, long enough for readers to speculate about its nature. Lewis is markedly silent about this matter, although it will be made clear later, through Rilian's words when he is under the Green Witch's spell, that he has a dark, possibly perverse, mother/child relationship with her. But the relationship certainly did not start out this way. What we know are the following facts: she is tall, beautiful, shining, but her garment is as green as poison. She appears to Drinian at the north side of the fountain, and at noon, both foreboding evil. We have already established the sinister association of the "north" as the home of the evil giants. Also, noon is the time when the "noonday" devil is supposed to roam (Ps. 91.6).[8] She appears next to the travelers as "a lady on a white horse. . . . [wearing a] long, fluttering dress of dazzling green." She speaks to them in a musical voice (*SC* 89).

To further understand the strange relationship of Rilian and the Green Witch, we must turn to folklore and literary tradition. The Green Witch in folklore has been associated with Ophidian motifs, a version of the Woman/Dragon. She is also the "serpent-as-poison-damzel" (Ramos 178) or the Witch/Bride/Enticing Woman, a variation on the Loathly Lady/Bride/Dragon in biblical tradition and folklore (Silva 31, 100-01; Rev. 12.3-4). (She is the opposite of the loathly lady figure in folklore as in Chaucer's "The Wife of Bath's Tale," who is a lovely princess on the inside but a hag on the outside). The color of green in medieval fairy tales symbolizes death as in *Sir Gawain and the Green Knight*. In the above passage from *SC* we also see a sketch, albeit faint, of the *femme fatale* figure of folklore: a combination of beauty and evil. Patrick Quinn defines the *femme fatale* as an archetypal figure or a literary construct of a masculine creation (200). He cites the following passage from Max Nordeau's *Degeneration* to sum up her motifs and significance to a man:

> He [man] feels he cannot resist the exciting influences proceeding from the woman, that he is her helpless slave, and would commit any folly, any madness, any crime, at her beck and call. He necessarily, therefore, sees in woman an uncanny, overpowering force of nature, bestowing supreme delights or dealing destruction, and he trembles before this power, to which he is defenselessly exposed. If, then, besides this, the almost never-failing aberrations set in, if he, in fact, commits things for woman which he must condemn and despise in himself; or if woman, without its coming to actual deeds, awakens in him emotions and thoughts before whose baseness and infamy he is horrified, then, in the moment of exhaustion, when judgment is stronger than impulse, the dread which woman inspires him withal will be suddenly changed into aversion and savage hatred. (168-69)

One immediately recalls the parallel motifeme of the "wretched wight" (line 1) in John Keats' "La Belle Dame Sans Merci" who was put under a spell by a lady "full beautiful-a faery's child" (14). Released on the "meads," in contrast to Prince Rilian, his soul was still in thrall to the lady, possessed by her. Then there is Lamia, the Serpent/Bride, in another poem by Keats, who destroys the Corinthian youth after a night of love. Admittedly, the erotic element is not as clear and strong in Lewis's version. But the motifeme is there, and metamorphosis is at work in all these versions, from human to beast or beast to human.

The giants and their localities—in the "north" of Narnia, Ettinsmoor, the Castle of Harfang, and their Ruined City—all have ominous associations as mentioned earlier. "The mere mention of the ruined city of giants seemed to have damped the spirit of the owls," Lewis writes (*SC* 62). It is here in the land of giants that Lewis introduces another Dantean image of evil. As the children and Puddleglum are walking across the frozen wasteland, they see in the distance what seemed to Jill to be huge rocks, which turn out to be giants. Lewis writes, "There were forty or fifty of them, all in a row, obviously standing with their feet on the bottom of the gorge and their elbows resting on the edge of the gorge" (*SC* 81). In his own journey into Hell, Dante also mistakes giants standing in the abyss for towers at the entrance of the ninth circle of the *Inferno*. As in the *Inferno*, the giants represent might without conscience, force without morals, brute Nature without Grace, and, therefore, without the possibility of salvation. But Lewis's giants are ridiculous and lack intelligence, travesties of the classical giants who opposed Zeus, used more for comic relief than establishing a horrific scene. They fight with hammers but instead hit their fingers. Their words are gibberish: "They stormed and jeered at one another in long, meaningless words about twenty syllables each" (83). Their Ruined City in *SC* is obsolete now, only a landmark of Aslan for voyagers to follow. Like the city of Charn in *MN*, it suggests the impermanence of evil.

As the travelers approach the Castle of the Giants, the country begins to change, for they are approaching Underland. Their trek over dark precipices is becoming dangerous. Snow is beginning to fall. The stones of the bridge they cross are cracked and crumbled and there are ominous pictures carved on them: "mouldering faces and forms of giants, minotaurs, squids, centipedes, and dreadful gods" (87). All of these carvings represent creatures of violence or low types of life, and even of Hell, connected with the worm (serpent), but here they are immobilized in pictures, made impotent. They suggest evil, but they are restrained from actual violence which would add an element of danger that would not be palatable to Lewis's readers. It would distract them from focusing on the mental/spiritual horror inside Underland. Puddleglum does not trust the bridge (87-88). It is in this bleak and desolate wasteland not too far from Harfang, symbolic of brutality, as we shall see, that the Witch appears again in the form of a beautiful lady in a "long, fluttering dress of dazzling green" on a white horse "so lovely that you wanted to kiss its nose and give it a lump of sugar at once" (89). Beauty and Evil melded into one. She encourages the tired and hungry voyagers to go to the burgh and Castle of Harfang, "where dwell the gentle giants," and where they will have "steaming baths, soft beds, and bright hearths" (90-91). The temptation is too strong for the children, but not for Puddleglum, who figures out that the lady is "[u]p to no good" and, more importantly, reminds them that "Aslan's signs had said nothing about staying with giants, gentle or otherwise" (92, 93).

After an evening of food and warmth in the castle, the children and Puddleglum learn that they are on the menu for the giant's feast and they manage to escape. They are back at the rocky, desolate wasteland, the flat plateau on which Harfang and the Ruined City are all constructed, and the surrounding gray landscape of high mountains, precipices, and valleys are, as had been mentioned earlier, reminiscent of the entrance to Hades/Hell in literature as book 11 of the *Odyssey* and 6 of the *Aeneid* show. The children and Puddleglum descend through a crack in the stones, following the sign UNDER ME. Inside, there is a labyrinth of caves differing in size and lighting, peopled by Earthmen (gnomes) under the control of the Green Witch. If we continue to see the trip to Underland as a traditional trip to the Underworld, we will discover several traditional motifs of Hell woven into its description: 1) As in Dante's Hell (which is guarded by Minos), there is a guardian at the entrance who shouts, "Tell me quickly who are you and what is your errand in the Deep Realm?" (145). When Puddleglum answers that they fell by accident, the Warden replies, "Many fall down and few return to the sunlit lands" (145)—a statement that recalls the inscription on the gate of Dante's Hell (canto 3); 2) Lewis's Deep Realm also has a ruler, the Green Witch, like Pluto (Hades in Greek mythology), who belongs to the realm of the dead (Silva 91, 94); 3) The lighting is also strange and sickly, and ranges from total absence to a desolate olive/gray, to the yellow lighting of a lamp in the Witch's chambers, and to the fiery red of the earthmen's lower world (Brism), all opposite motifs of Aslan's natural bright light associated with the sun and moon; 4) The caves are arranged one lower than the other, somewhat like Dante's circles of Hell, but with no order or degree of sin; and 5) There is a city proper of Hell inside this vast realm, with walls like the walls of Dis in Dante.

However, there are some differences between this Deep Realm and other versions of Hell that make it less terrifying to readers: 1) the inhabitants of Lewis's Underland are not punished individually, or in groups, according to a system as in Dante's Hell, but are lumped together under the spell of the Green Witch. 2) beneath these cocoons of caves lies the cheerful land of Brism, the original land of the Earthmen before they were captured and enslaved by the Green Witch. These potentially harmless gnomes are of all sizes and shapes, and are now made to appear like devils carrying three-pronged spears in their hands: some had tails; some had great beards; some had round, smooth faces, big as pumpkins; some had horns in the middle of their foreheads; and some had ten or twelve toes. (Lewis seems to be having fun describing them.)

Then comes the time to enter Hell proper and arrive at the City of Hell. From the main entrance to the Deep Realm, a little dark crack, functioning like Hell's gate in Dante's *Inferno*, or Hell's mouth in early English drama—and also a parody of the small entrance to Heaven in Lewis's *Divorce*—the travelers alight into a large cave full of drowsy radiance which has strange shapes growing out of its mossy floors. There are some creatures inside more caves that have unnatural shapes of trees and animals "of a dragonish and bat-like sort" (149). Lewis seems trying hard to show that hybridity is a motif of Hell, as has been discussed in chapter 1. However, although strange looking, these creatures are a far cry from the distorted, perverse, and depraved monsters of Homer's, Virgil's, or Dante's Hell. Lewis's Deep Realm is a sad, sleepy place, bereft of any joy: "There was no wind, there were no birds, there was no sound of water. There was no sound of breathing from the strange beasts" (151), another scene of the landscape of the City of Death. Passing through an arch they go into a smaller cave, like a cathedral, where an iconographical figure of Father Time is fast asleep. He is the giant who will wake up and blow the horn to effect the end of Narnia in *LB* in the final apocalypse of flood and fire and the journey to the Real Narnia (see ch. 9). After going through many caves, there is a body of water to cross (like Virgil's Styx or Dante's Acheron), but not threatening, leading to the city proper of Hell (like Homer's Tartarus or Dante's City of Dis in *Inferno*). Hellish surroundings begin to work on the travelers.

They get on a ship on which they spend a long time drowsing off and dreaming, a foreshadowing of their later state of sleep induced by the Green Witch's powder: "[They] began to feel as if you had always lived on that ship, in that darkness, and to wonder whether sun and blue skies and wind and all birds had not been only a dream" (154). The beauty of Narnia, experienced earlier in the story by the children, especially by Jill, is in danger of being forgotten, despite its intense colors and vivid imagery. Memory, the agent of positive transformation and self-discovery through remembering God (Aslan in Narnia) is weakening.

Then they see the City with its walls and pillars, which suggest palaces and temples, eerily quiet as the Ruined City of Charn in *MN*, the snow-covered Narnia in *LWW*, and the frozen lake of Dante's *Inferno*. All gnomes who are enslaved by the Witch are busy and sad. These images suggest the Green Witch's power in transforming those usually perky gnomes into insect-like creatures. At last they come to a great castle. The children and Puddleglum cross a courtyard and enter into a murky hall lit by a yellowish, warm light from human lamps, recalling the sickly, yellow color of the City of Charn. After another solemn ritual, they go up the stairs and enter a beautiful, well-furnished room with rich tapestries and a bright fire, lit by a yellowish lamplight and with red wine and glass on the table. Surrounded by these motifs of domesticity, unexpected in Underland, there was handsome Prince Rilian, dressed in black and looking "a little bit like Hamlet" (158) (and speaking like him, too). He, like all the inhabitants in this Diabolic City, has been enslaved by the Witch, in his case for ten years. Under this long enchantment, he has come to believe that the Green Witch is a "heavenly Queen" (163) and "a nosegay of all virtues, as truth, mercy, constancy, gentleness, courage, and the rest" (158). He cannot pick up mnemonic signs about who he is, for he has lost all memories. He asks carelessly, "Rilian? Narnia?... What land is that? I have never heard its name.... Billian? Trillian? ... Indeed to my certain knowledge, there is no such man here" (159).

In this magic-induced stupefaction, the Prince challenges the travelers' convictions and creates doubts in them that Aslan is only "a long liver" (ancient being) (160) and the sign UNDER ME is simply not addressed to them, but part of the inscription of an ancient giant buried in the Deep Realm. The facts—that the Green Witch is of a divine race, actually a long-liver herself, who will make him King of Narnia (when he is already the heir to the throne) and who will be joined in marriage to him (in spite of a great difference in their ages)—do not register at all in his mind. However, to complicate the strands of myths that are woven here, there is a dark side to his relationship with her, suggesting a type of mother-child relationship with a devilish creature. He defends his relationship with her, comparing her to a mother, saying, "I am well content to live by her word, who has already saved me from a thousand dangers. No mother has taken pains more tenderly for her child, than the Queen's grace has for me" (166). Later, when the Green Witch appears, she speaks to him in a "soothing voice as if humoring a child" (183). It is no wonder that the children and Puddleglum look at him with disgust. They call him fool, immature, and selfish (167).

Because Prince Rilian's mind is under the Witch's spell and a prisoner of illusion, several critics have seen parallels between Lewis's Deep Realm and Plato's Allegory of the Cave.[9] Prince Rilian's enchantment has led him to believe in false truths, inversions of reality, like the prisoners in Plato's cave, who believe that what they see and hear in the cave is real, all the stories told by narrators and enacted by puppets whose shadows are reflected on a screen. Rilian reverses the scriptural advice to open hearts and ears (Hinten 53). Like the prisoners of Plato's cave, Rilian is a victim of false consciousness, since this is the only reality represented to him, and he will have to leave the cave and go to Overland to see the pure light of the sun—the transparent, translucent, and transcendent Reality. So the Prince believes the Witch's story that because he is bound by a spell, at a certain time of the day he becomes wild and turns into the likeness of a serpent, and so he has to be bound to a silver chair. Of course the reverse is true. When he is bound to the chair, he is actually free from enchantment and therefore clear sighted. When the moment of disenchantment arrives in his rescuers' presence, we get facts about his relationship with the Green Witch. He begins to remember Narnia: "Let me feel the wind and see the sky . . . .and the trees growing upside-down in the water, all green, and below them, deep, very deep, the blue sky" (171). Finally, he recognizes that the Witch dragged him down and enslaved him for ten years and that she is "the most devilish sorceress" (173).

When he utters the name of Aslan, the children and Puddleglum remember Aslan's last sign and decide to rescue him as if he were one of Plato's prisoners. If they had muffed the last sign, they would all have been victims of the Green Witch, forever bound by her spell in Underland. When the Green Witch returns and finds he has awakened from her spell, has broken the silver chair, and is conversing with his rescuers, she turns white in anger and confronts him, "Why stand you here unbound?" (180). Prince Rilian declares, in answer to her question, "I am the King's son of Narnia, Rilian, the only child of Caspian, Tenth of the name" (181). The disenchanted prince has discovered his identity through remembrance of Aslan and with the help of the others. Memory is an agent for discovering the true Reality and the true self as we have seen happen in *PC*.

The Witch does not give up. She tries to seduce all of them through soft talk, soft music, and a peculiar green powder that burns in the fire like incense. She tries to brainwash them, as she did the Prince for so long, into believing that the world outside is an illusion, unreal, and that this world in Underland is the only real world. She tells them that there is no Aslan, no Narnia, and no sun; only her room and her lamp are real. We see another example of *goeteia* here. Jadis in *MN* and the White Witch in *LWW* had used this technique with Digory and Edmund, to persuade them that their senses are all that matters, and that eating the fragrant apple and Turkish Delight, respectively, supersedes all promises or obligations. All these witches try to reduce the whole world into material causes, inverting Plato's belief that matter is only a copy, a shadow of the divine original. Satan had also played this game with Eve, seducing her into focusing on the delicious fruit and its attributes rather than on God's commandment. None of these diabolic figures is to succeed in the end. Lewis makes this point in *Problem*: "A man can no more diminish God's glory by refusing to worship Him than a lunatic can put out the sun by scribbling the word 'darkness' on the walls of his cell" (53).

However, in *SC* one by one they fall under the influence of the burning green powder, except Puddleglum, who remembers Aslan's words and is empowered to squash the fire with his webbed foot, allowing all to return to rationality and clear mindedness. Puddleglum remarks, ironically, that what the Witch terms "made-up things" seem a good deal more important than the real ones: "Suppose this black pit of a kingdom of yours is the only world. Well, it strikes me as a pretty poor one. . . . I'm on Aslan's side even if there isn't any Aslan to lead it" (190-91). Defeated, the Green Witch slowly metamorphoses in slow motion in front of their eyes into her original form, a writhing green serpent, the same shining serpent that fatally stung Rilian's mother:

> The instrument [mandolin] dropped from her hands. Her arms appeared to be fastened to her sides. Her legs were intertwined with each other, and her feet had disappeared. The long green train of her skirt thickened and grew solid, and seemed to be all one piece with the writhing green pillar of her interlocked legs. And that writhing green pillar was curving and swaying as if it had no joints, or else were all joints. Her head was thrown far back and while her nose grew longer and longer, every other part of her face seemed to disappear, except her eyes. Huge flaming eyes they were now, without brows or lashes. . . .Long before there was time to do anything, the change was complete, and the great serpent which the Witch had become, green as poison, thick as Jill's waist, had flung two or three coils of its loathsome body round the Prince's legs. (191-93)

This scene of negative metamorphosis is powerful and vies with scenes of metamorphoses by other great writers. There is Ovid who describes the metamorphosis of Cadmus into a serpent:

> Over his coarsened skin
> He felt scales form and bluish markings spot
> His blackened body. Prone upon his breast
> He fell; his legs were joined, and gradually
> They tapered to a long smooth pointed tail. (4.578-82)

This is similar to Lewis's "Her legs were intertwined with each other, and her feet had disappeared." Then there is Dante's description of the thieves' transformation into serpents as punishment in circle 7 of the *Inferno*. One of Dante's sinners, bit by a serpent,

> drew his feet together;
> the legs, with both the thighs, closed in to join
> and in a short time fused, so that the juncture
> didn't show signs of ever having been there. (lines 105-08)

This is quite similar to the "interlocked legs" of the Witch, which "had no joint, or else were all joint." Dante's sinner "strains his face out long / and makes his ears withdraw into his head" (130-31) and the Witch's neck was "thrown far back and her nose grew longer and longer" (191). In *Inferno* the sinner's "tongue, / that once had been one piece and capable / of forming words, divides into a fork" (132-34) matches the Witch's "forked tongue [that] flicked horribly in and out" (*SC* 192). Milton also describes in similar images Satan's transformation into a serpent:

> His [Satan's] Visage drawn he felt to sharp and spare,

> His Arms clung to his Ribs, his Legs entwining
> Each other, till supplanted down he fell
> A monstrous Serpent on his Belly prone. (*PL* 10.511-14).

Lewis uses the same image of the "intertwining" legs, a modern spelling of Milton's "entwining" legs.

Then there follows in *SC* the heroic motifeme of Slaying the Dragon. Spenser's Redcross Knight beheads the Serpent of Error in *FQ* (1.1.18-19, 24); so did Christ slay the dragon in the Book of Revelation. Lewis absorbs this tradition of the Dragon Slayer to make Rilian a type of this hero. The Narnian hero strikes the Witch/Serpent, and the whole Underland collapses into apocalyptic fire and flood, which is the only way to bring the world of illusion and reality together. The light reflected from the fire itself is described as a sinister "great red glow" which with the flood will destroy the evil city. There is no mediation, only a cataclysmic moment of the transcendence of the good. As a corollary of this huge negative metamorphic incident, human-to-serpent, and Rilian's heroic act, the shield from Rilian's armor turns silver and on it, "redder than blood or cherries, was the figure of the Lion" (200), showing the returning faith of Rilian in the Lion, who is inscribed in blood in his heart but had been blackened by enchantment. Also, the image of fire lights up the surroundings into different colours like a "stained-glass window with the tropical sun staring right through it" (216), suggesting a Christian experience of salvation.

The Witch/Dragon/Serpent Slayer theme is at the heart of fairy tales (Silva 85). We will see this theme played out in *VDT* in the killing of the sea serpent. The motifeme of Descent Underground and Ascent represents death and rebirth (99). According to Scandinavian mythology, a renewed world will be born from the destruction of a Midgard serpent by Thor (see ch. 9), and a princess kidnapped underground, a myth paralleling the myth of Persephone, who was kidnapped by Hades but emerges to awaken all nature. In *SC* after the process of disenchantment in the slaying of the Green Witch/Serpent, Prince Rilian and his three rescuers are released into a celebrating Narnia in the middle of a moonlit snow dance. While the serpent in Genesis granted Adam and Eve knowledge of evil, thereby robbing them of their identity as God's children, this serpent does something similar, but only succeeds temporarily.

Underland is a city of illusion, of forces not controlled by reason and lacking Aslan's authority. It is demonic, housing a serpent in the tradition of Dante's and Spenser's serpents and dragons, and Milton's Satan. Fire burns in it and water floods its caverns. It is an unreal city like T. S. Eliot's London in *The Wasteland*, but it is unredeemable. Aslan does not intervene directly as he did in the White Witch's City to free the petrified Narnians. He achieves his metamorphosis through the travelers' remembrance of his sign (to "help the one who utters his [Aslan's] name") and, through them, liberates the victims of the Green Witch from the shadowy realms. It is interesting that Plato's sun, the light of knowledge, which became later a symbol of Christ, the lion, and the king, is also a symbol of Aslan in all the chronicles (see ch. 2). Prince Rilian needed human helpers, like the prisoners in Plato's allegory, and needed to face Reality like the prisoners also. However, unlike Plato's allegory, *SC* omits the need for the freed prisoners to return to the cave to liberate others because all prisoners are liberated with Rilian and the three rescuers. The liberated Earthmen, who are not evil, go back to their land of Brism in the bottom circles of the Deep Realms, and the children, Rilian, and Puddleglum ascend to sunlit lands.

Underland, the city of shadows, a type of Hell like Dante's, Virgil's, and Homer's, is posited structurally and conceptually against Cair Paravel, the city of beauty and all that is good—a common technique of Lewis in the *Chronicles* that involves weaving the plot across two polarized binary structures. The scene in Underland is the nadir of the plot line, a descent into decay, distortion, and negative metamorphosis, from human shape to beast, an inversion of human growth and identity. As Leonard Barkan explains, sinners in hell (like Dante's, I would add) are metamorphosed into beasts to express the decayed state of their moral condition (141). This type of metamorphosis is not an organic one since it disrupts spiritual growth; it has rich meaning when applied to our world. It is the "desecration of the image of God," since the serpent's transformation from a human form and back illustrates the elevation of the serpent into the image of God and thus, the degradation of His image and the destabilization of the human form and identity (see ch. 1). The Satan/Serpent of Genesis suggest the extent of sin's power on form, angelic or human. Instead of discovering identity and self-knowledge by obeying God, both Satan and his victims lost them by disobeying Him.

However, Lewis's mythopoeic aesthetics also paints a path for physical and spiritual ascent from such a corrupt state, a path for salvation through positive metamorphosis. As Roger Huard maintains in his analysis of Plato's Allegory of the Cave, "Whatever the ontological status of one world is for the Christian, it is clear that another (more perfect and complete) world exists apart from this one, and that the only way to get there is by the divine intervention (revelation, redemption, salvation) and certainly not by knowledge gained by human reason" (50). Because there is no mediation between the two opposing polarities of Aslan/Cair Paravel vs. Green Witch/Underland, there is only the collapse of the latter to be subsumed by the former. "To completely get at the reality behind the shadows would require . . .that the cave collapse unto itself, that appearances and reality become one and the same" (Huard 172). That is what happens at the end of *SC*, but only after the children learn to remember and follow Aslan's signs, albeit not without some dangerous lapses. Their education consists of a redirection or metamorphosis of their souls away from fear, sloth, and weakness to the Truth of Aslan.

In the *Chronicles* Lewis adheres to traditional concepts of the city, in general, as inseparable from the city of death (Lehan 181), although in its highest form it can replicate the City of God. In its worst form, the city is "a troubling territory, a place of loss, alienation, and corruption of the soul, a place of dangerous distancing from the natural world, the home of all beginnings" (21)—in other words, a Satanic City.

Moreover, Charn is a type of the City of Satan, destroyed by a non-human, tyrannical magician bent (later) on destroying or enslaving citizens. She, like Satan in his rebellion against God, represents Augustine's inordinate *libido dominandi* (lust for power). She will later create perpetual winter in *LWW* and turn many Narnians into stone. Not answering to any law, she instructs Digory, "[W]hat would be wrong for you or for any of the common people is not wrong for a great Queen such as I. The weight of the world is on our shoulders. We must be freed from all rules. Ours is a high and lonely destiny" (*MN* 71). In this speech she reiterates the tyrant's plea.

As Lewis writes about Jadis and her type, "They are not interested in things or people unless they can use them; they are terribly practical" (*MN* 86). They exercise their power in forms of entrapment and domination based on fraud and mind games. They do not fight open and ethical wars like Aslan's followers and allies; they attempt to subdue reality to their own wishes. They try to seduce their victims into believing that the world they experience with their senses is the only one there is, thus standing the Platonic psychology of the soul on its head. What Lewis writes about the White Witch also applies to Jadis and the Green Witch as well: "She would make things look like what they aren't" (*LWW* 152). The rulers of these corrupt cities (Cities of Satan) are tyrants and materialists, "besotted" with their own desires, "self love reaching the point of contempt for God" as Augustine would say (*City* 14.28). Evil cities, like Charn, provide for their citizens opportunities to sin, as we find out from Jadis's description of Charn before its devastation. The other two Satanic Cities enslave and rob their victims of the power of choice, but only temporarily.

Endnotes

1. What solidified the grim view of biblical cities for later writers was the classical pastoral tradition that always pitted the country against the city, the farm against the town, honest agricultural communities versus corrupt industrial ones. James Dougherty perceives the pastoral tradition to be based on Christian teaching: "The parables present a world which, with some exceptions, divides into 'a benignant countryside of good shepherds, generous vineyard owners, and abundant harvests, and a hostile urban scene of vengeful kings with armies and torturers, conniving stewards, and locked and guarded doors" (16). Later on, the Romantic writers generally saw the city as a "desert" devoid of spirituality, like William Blake's "London," (1740-92), the bleakest of city poems, and thus conflated the two earlier biblical views of cities and wastelands as metaphors of degeneration. Likewise, the modern city is generally viewed negatively in metaphors like a "jungle," a "sea," an "ocean," a "monster," a "volcano," although sometimes celebrated as a symbol of achievement, a "supreme expression of wealth, of energy, of the amalgam of living styles" (Von der Thusen 2). Witness Carl Sandburg's Chicago of 1914 in "City of the Big Shoulders" and Whitman's "Manhattan" as opposed to T. S. Eliot's *The Wasteland* (1922) about man as a dweller in a spiritually desolate city.

2. Compare Lucifera's throne (symbol of Pride) in Spenser's *FQ*:

> High above all a cloth of state was spred,
> And a rich throne, as bright as sunny day;
> On which there sate, most brave embellished
> With royall robes and gorgeous array,
> A mayden Queene, that shone, as Titans ray,
>   In glistring gold and perelesse pretious stone. (1.4.8.1-6)

And Satan's throne in *Paradise Lost* (2.1–5)

3. David Downing has studied this unpublished work in "'The Dungeon of His Soul': Lewis's Unfinished 'Quest of Bleheris,'" *Seven: An Anglo-American Literary Review* 15 (1998): 37-54. However, he does not include the passage that I quote from the original manuscript which I read at the Bodleian in Oxford.

4. Bodleian MS English let. c220/5, published with permission from The C.S. Lewis Company Pte. Ltd. See also Lewis's letter to Arthur Greeves on October 1916 and Chad Walsh, *The Literary Legacy of C.S. Lewis* (NY: Harcourt Brace and Jovanovich, 1979) 128.

5. To further understand Lewis's views of such a city of the past, one must look for some other possibly non-biblical / non-medieval influences. These may lie in his early readings of contemporary fiction. Crago states that Charn is a literary palimpsest "on which can be discerned, faintly, the images and phrases and texts from which [Lewis] drew his inspiration life long" (42). Crago also lists Oscar Wilde's *The Picture of Dorian Grey* and Rudyard Kipling's *The Jungle*

Books, not among Lewis's favorite fictions, as possible sources; for further discussion on the influences of E. Nesbit's and Rider Haggard's novels, especially *Ayesha*, on the *Chronicles*, see Mervyn Nicholson. See also Salwa Khoddam, *Truths Breathed Through Silver: The Inklings' Moral and Mythopoeic Legacy*, eds. Jonathan B. Himes, Joe R. Christopher, and Salwa Khoddam (New Castle, UK: Cambridge Scholars Publishing, 2008) 27-50.

6. One can speculate that Lewis's attraction to this archetype stemmed from his love of Wagner's operas, which often portray such female characters, as well as from Authur Rackham's illustrations of these characters (*Surprised* 76). See chapter 9 for further discussion on his enchantment with Nordic myths.

7. For information on Lewis's views on the Theory of Evolution, see "The Funeral of a Great Myth," *Christian Reflections*, ed. Walter Hooper (Grand Rapids, MI: Eerdmans, 1967) 82-93, where he writes, "for my own part, though I believe it no longer, I shall always enjoy it as I enjoy other myths" (93). His ideas on evolution in *Mere Christianity*, 218-27, support my discussion in the text.

8. See A.R. Cirillo, "Noon-Midnight and the Temporal Structure of *Paradise Lost*," *ELH* 29 (1962), 372-95. I'm indebted to David Shelley Berkeley for this information: Eve's temptation in *PL* occurs at noon (9.401).

9. On Plato's Allegory of the Cave see Roger L. Huard, *Plato's Political Philosophy: The Cave* (N.Y.: Algora, 2007), and Julia Annas, *An Introduction to Plato's Republic* (Oxford: Clarendon, 1981).

CHAPTER FIVE

A Tale of Two Cities of Man in Narnia:
Tashbaan and Anvard in The Horse and His Boy

CONTRACLEON: *O for goodness sake! Everything's a "conspiracy" or a "tyranny" with you lot. If anyone disagrees with you over even the slightest little thing, then it's a "tyranny." That particular coinage hasn't been used in Athens for the last fifty years, and now it's cheaper than a tin of fish.*
Aristophanes Wasps (487-492)

CHORUS: *And the furious leader the herd*
Of populous Asia he drives,
Wonderful over the earth,
And admirals stern and rough
Marshals of man he trusts:
Gold his descent from Perseus,
He is equal of god.
Aeschylus The Persians (72-80)

An offshoot of the plot of *LWW*—when Peter, Edmund, Lucy, and Susan are still Kings and Queens of Narnia—the plot of *HHB* resembles that of *LWW* and the earlier *MN* in that it is founded on two polarized structures. While the city of Charn is pitted against the Created Garden of Narnia in *MN*, and the Castle of Ice against Cair Paravel in *LWW*, the city of Tashbaan, the capital of the Calormene empire south of Narnia, is pitted against Anvard, the north city of Archenland, an ally of Narnia, in *HHB*. Thus the binary opposition in the story is between North and South, Narnians and Calormenes. In all these stories, the plot progresses from one end of the spectrum to the other to reveal the characters' spiritual regeneration. Of all the cities in the *Chronicles* the city of Tashbaan is the most fully and realistically described, having close links with cities in our Primary World. With its detailed topography and imagery, this exotic non-Narnian city takes hold of the reader's imagination and functions as the center of the story, although the plot moves away north to Anvard, which is merely sketched in comparison. Also, there is an unrelenting process of juxtaposing scenes, images, and customs from Tashbaan with such from Narnia and Archenland, toward the end, in a manner that always favors the Narnians/Archenlandians over the Calormenes. These stark cultural differences, with a focus on political/social issues like tyranny, freedom, and justice, take away from the sacramental vision normally associated with Aslan in *Chronicles*, and also from the fairy tale atmosphere with universal motifemes and motifs. *HHB* is more of a tale of two polarized Earthly Cities—Tashbaan and Anvard—notwithstanding the appearances of Aslan to punish Rabadash and regenerate and transform Aravis, the two Talking Horses, and the overwhelmed Shasta.

After a historical survey of tyranny and tyrants of Greece and the Near East, I will discuss in this chapter two typical qualities associated with them that exist in the Calormenes of *HHB*: opulent living and isolation from *philoi* (associates). Both lead to abuses like cruelty to social inferiors and conspiracy. Marvin D. Hinten, notwithstanding other critics' opposing views, states that "'Arabian' was a term of disdain with the context of the Chronicles" (67). For Europeans "the Arabs were the feared villains from the South who nearly conquered Europe in the eighth century, and the Turks were infidels who had taken the holy city of Jerusalem and spilled so much Christian blood during the Crusades" (14). One of Lewis's defenders on the issue of anti-Arab racism, Devin Brown, states that the Calormenes could not represent Muslims because they are polytheistic while Muslims are not" ("A Dark Queen" 5). If not representative of Arab Muslims, the Calormenes certainly represent races in the Near East in the Primary World like the ancient Persians, or some form of European stereotypical depictions of them, culled from Lewis's readings and stored in his memory. These views are reflected in *HHB* and supported by a close reading of the story.[1]

I. City of Man: City of Tyranny

To understand these sociopolitical distinctions between Tashbaan and Anvard, and their peoples, we will examine them as types of the City of Man. Lewis constructs his Earthly Cities in the *Chronicles* using mainly biblical/Augustinian ideas (as discussed in chs. 1 and 4), but also Platonic thought and imagery. Ideal cities on earth, as opposed to transcendent ones, can be defined by Platonic or gospel visions as places of creativity in industry and the arts, or places of law, justice, and equality (Jacobson 400). In Plato's opinion, the just Earthly City is the paradigm of the just man: If its citizens are wise, the city is wise, too (Charbit 14). In the ideal City of Man, which is close to the City of God, there are no distinctions among people (Gal. 3.28), and women participate in the affairs of the city (Charbit 13, 16). The goal of this city, according to Plato, is to achieve political virtue and justice (*Rep*.434^d-435^a). For Lewis, some of the sought-after virtues in the Earthly Cities are classical and Christian virtues: fortitude, patience, pity, and forgiveness (*Problem* 111). "One looks first for justice in a city that *is* wise, brave, temperate and just, in order to search more profoundly thereafter" (Ferguson 9). These qualities are found in the City of Cair Paravel, which will be discussed in chapter 6.

A. Paragon of Tyrants

To the classical Greeks tyranny was a major theme among writers and thinkers in the fifth-century BC. After defeating the Persians and before its own defeat in the Peloponnesian War, Athens was enjoying a form of democracy. However, the Athenians on the fringe of the Greek world were afraid of reverting back to tyranny (Seaford 104; Raaflaub 71), which abounded in the regions of early tyrants like Midas (738-696 BC) and Peisistratus (560-527 BC). In Syracuse and other regions from the fifth to the third centuries BC, tyranny was still a serious issue (Ober 226). This concern about tyranny was reflected in the subject matter of classical Greek tragedy (Seaford 96). In pre-Greek times and in the Asiatic mode, people "invested sovereign power in the single pre-eminent individual, whereas democratic Athens embodied sovereign authority in the institution of collective government" (Munn 318).

In non-Greek societies, people confused the relationship between men and gods (43), and saw tyrants as representatives of divinity on earth (354), actually as sons of the Mother of Gods who perfected their development (167). In *The Persians*, the leader of the Persian army against the Greeks is referred to as "equal of god" (80). This form of government was so abhorrent to the free-thinking classical Greeks (Raaflaub 64) that it was considered the civic duty of citizens to be haters and even killers of tyrants (72), for which they were praised as heroes (226).

Plato defines the tyrant as one who does not restrain himself from the base appetites, the lowest level of the soul's constitution, and as exhibiting the opposite of the intellectual virtues that lead to wisdom. Aristotle agrees: he writes that the tyrant possesses an "innate baseness" (*Politics* bk. 5 ch. 10). Thus, he is open to all temptations and vices, notably greed, so he seizes kingship and perverts it for his own benefit (Hooke 23). Indeed, the association of tyranny with wealth is very common and is further developed by Aristotle (ch. 10). As Lisa Kallet writes, the tyrant is a man with means, notably to raise an army (122). Plato's tyrant thinks of disgraceful gain and redistributing land (*Rep.* 566^a) and in general looks to his personal comfort and power (Dewald 27). His wealth leads his desire for more wealth and intensifies lust for goods. As a result, according to Plato, the tyrant is left with no friend, no *philoi* (whether friend, relative, or his subjects) (576^a). He is willing to commit parricide, the most egregious of sins, to keep his wealth (569^b). No *philoi* over personal power for him. This extreme isolation from *philoi* renders him willing to shed fellow citizens' as well as relatives' blood or banish these people (*Rep.* 566^a). Another trait of the tyrant is paranoia. This is seen in his suspicious attitudes toward people, even his own relations (Henderson 162-67). Conspiracy and having spies is a way of life for him and his society. Freedom of speech is non-existent in his city. For example, Periander of Corinth did not allow any leisure discussion (Aristotle bk. 5. 11).

According to Jeffrey Henderson, tyrants are bellicose, high-minded, harshly primitive, admiring of barbarians, paranoid, and indulging in flattery (161; Aristotle bk. 5.11). In brief, the tyrant draws all meaning to himself as the center of the providence, power, and wisdom (Munn 353). In Aeschylus's *Prometheus Bound*, Zeus exemplifies the character of a tyrant: he is harsh, a law unto himself, suspicious of his friends, implacable, and violent.

Plato and Aristotle distinguished between tyrants and kings. According to Plato, tyranny is opposed to kingship as evil to good (*Rep.* 576^d). Plato's ideal leaders are the guardians who possess wisdom through the exercise of the intellect and participation in an extensive program of training and education. For Plato, the ideal leaders, the philosopher-kings, are those who lust after truth—not appetites—and are governed by the rational soul, while tyrants lust after base appetites and passions. It is the human will that can drive a person toward evil within himself or toward good beyond himself, Augustine asserts. Both Plato and Aristotle agree that tyrants arise from the multitude, but ideal rulers are carefully selected. Aristotle believes that kings must be selected on the basis of pre-eminence in virtue or family (*Politics* bk. 5.10). Peace is paramount to the ideal king (Munn 346).

While the Asiatic mode of kingship invested sovereign power in the single pre-eminent individual, democratic Athens embodied sovereign authority in the institutions of collective government (Munn 318). For the Ancient Greeks and Europeans in general, Eastern tyrants, and the

Ionian tyrants that they backed, were models of tyranny that Plato and other Western writers attacked in their works. The primary purpose of the Greeks was to charge the Persians with all types of corruption that is associated with tyranny (Briant 789), in order to denigrate them and proclaim their own rights to rule over the Persians (Hooke 24). Dante places Dionysius of Syracuse in the seventh circle of Hell, reserved for the violent, punished in the river of boiling blood. With him are Alexander and Attila (12. 103-05). The sixteenth-century English playwright Christopher Marlowe was entranced by the figure of Mongolian Emperor Tamburlaine and wrote two plays about him. Tamburlaine exhibits all the characteristics of a tyrant in his rebellion towards all authority and exerting his own will: "This is my mind, and I will have it so" (*Tamburlaine* 1: 4.2.91). He believes he is so powerful that he can "move the turning spheres of heaven" (4.1.120). He treats his prisoners with cruelty and makes a footstool out of the captured Turkish king Bajazeth.

In *A Preface* to *Paradise Lost*, Lewis expresses his belief in hierarchy within a state and that order can be destroyed by tyranny, which he defines as the ruling of natural equals (76). We find this tyrannical way of governing among the Witches in Narnia and the rulers of Tashban.

B. Tyrannical Cities

The Greeks used the term "tyrant" to describe not only an individual but also a city (Morgan 274). Consequently, the tyrannical city (which stands for the tyrannical soul, indeed a macrocosm of it) is far from the city of justice. It is most wretched (*Rep.* 577^e) and does not provide the happy life that Thrasymachus envisions for the tyrant (344). The tyrannical city is enslaved (577^c), like the tyrant, mastered by a wicked, insane master (577^a), poor, and full of disorder, fear, and pain (578^a). Therefore, the only way to be safe under the rule of a tyrant is to submit to him (Plato, *Gorgias* 510^d). The tyrannical city is not based on law, equity, and what is right, but on legal positivism, i.e., laws enacted by the rulers are just *per se* (Majeske 17). "The city that seeks fulfillment within itself will disintegrate, as did the old Jerusalem, as did Babylon, as did Rome; the city which, though imprisoned within another city, maintains its faithful vision of a city elsewhere, a 'center' beyond itself, the new Jerusalem, finds in that self-denial a source of unity and endurance" (Dougherty 37). Lewis attributes this basic Augustinian belief in free will to citizens. He writes in *Problem*: "It is men, not God, who have produced racks, whips, prisons, slavery, guns, bayonets, and bombs" (89). He also states, "Every vice leads to cruelty" (65). Thus a "good" city for these writers would be one where virtue is nourished, whether classical or Christian, Platonic or Augustinian.

II. The Calormene versus the Narnian/Archenlandian Peoples and Cultures

The binary opposition between Greek and Persian cultures in the fifth century BC can be used as a framework to illustrate the antagonism between Narnian and Calormene cultures and peoples at the heart of *HHB*. Like the historical antagonistic relationship between the Greeks and the great kings of Persia, the relationship between the Narnians (along with their allies the Archenlandish people) and the Calormenes was based on enmity and struggle over power. What is revealed through these struggles between these hereditary foes is a dialectic involving the ancient topic of tyranny and the social elements that this term embraces, a sensitive topic to the Greeks of the fifth century BC and later to the English in the Renaissance. Here again Lewis draws on his "scholarship of imagination" from sources in his memory to construct this story.

At the outset, *HHB* presents us with a negative view of the Calormene empire and its culture, before taking us inside the Calormene capital city, Tashbaan. Shasta, the hero, actually a young prince of Archenland who was separated from his father and twin brother and has been brought up by a Calormene fisherman named Arsheesh, is exposed to all types of abuse in Calormene. He is often beaten and his ears boxed by his father who, we are told, has "a very practical mind" (3), a phrase which aligns Arsheesh with all evil characters in the *Chronicles* who happen to be also "practical": Uncle Andrew in *MN*, the White Witch in *LWW*, and Nikabrik the black dwarf in *PC*, the first two being magicians. In general, the Calormenes are unattractive, as the first portrait of them suggests: the men have "long, dirty robes and wooden shoes turned up at the toe, and turbans on their heads, and beards, talking to one another very slowly about things that sounded dull" (2).

To tip the scales in favor of the Narnians, after describing the Calormenes, Lewis juxtaposes a description of Narnia and Narnians as a contrast. We are given the testimony about Narnia's loveliness by Bree, the horse, a Talking Animal from Narnia who was kidnapped, stolen, or captured by a Tarkaan (a lord) of Calormen. However, the horse can still remember the joy he had in Narnia. "The happy land of Narnia—Narnia of the heathery mountains and the thymy downs, Narnia of the many rivers, the plashing glens, the mossy caverns and the deep forests ringing with hammers of the Dwarfs. Oh the sweet air of Narnia! An hour's life there is better than a thousand years in Calormen" (10), reminisces Bree (who has seemingly adopted the flowery language of his kidnapper). This evocative pastoral scene, which suggests the pristine Narnia after it has been thawed by Aslan and liberated from the White Witch in *LWW*, is a powerful contrast to the above-mentioned depressing scene from Calormen.

The Calormene soldiers also have weaponry that is associated with the Middle East: "The spike of a helmet projected form the middle of his [the soldier's] silken turban, and he wore a shirt of chain mail. By his side hung a curving scimitar... His face was dark... the man's beard ... was dyed crimson, and curled and gleaming with scented oil" (3-5). This soldier has the attributes of a warrior from ancient Persia. More importantly, however, Shasta is up for sale as a slave to a Tarkaan which introduces us to the custom of owning slaves in Calormen, much like in ancient Persia. Shasta finds himself fantasizing over becoming a slave of the Tarkaan so he can "wear lovely clothes" and own a palace and a chariot when the Tarkaan died (9), a first indication of the Calormene luxury that Lewis will target in describing Tashbaan. Then follows the bargaining over Shasta's price, bargaining being common practice still in the Middle East. In contrast to this negative view of the Calormenes, Lewis hastily inserts another speech by Bree in praise of a free Narnia. The horse says that he had fought as a slave and dumb beast in the Tisroc's (the Calormene ruler's) Wars, but he would rather fight as a free horse in Narnia.

In the conversation between Arsheesh and the Tarkaan, we have initial examples of the Calormene flowery language, with its strong rhetorical powers associated with the great kings of Persia, and in fact other parts of Middle Eastern culture. As will be discussed later, the Calormenes speak and write in formal and proverbial language—albeit exaggerated to the point of parody by Lewis. When the Tarkaan asks to buy Shasta, Arsheesh answers, "Has not one of the poets said, 'Natural affection is stronger than soup and offspring more precious than carbuncles?'" (5-6), and so on. Parodied maxims and flowery expressions litter *HHB* to denigrate the Calormenes further, as we shall see in the Calormene conversations inside the city of Tashbaan.

III. Inside the City of Tashbaan (1): The Calormene Sin of Luxury

Greeks compiled sources to condemn the Persians' manifestation of luxury, even though they (the Greeks) were overwhelmed by the image of the great king of Persia from Cyrus the Great to Darius. According to Greek sources, the first men in history to become notorious for luxurious living were the Persians (Athenaeus XII.513 e-f qtd. in Briant 299). In *Panegyrics* (380 BC) the Hellenist Isocrates portrays the Persians as dishonorable in their fight against Greeks and accuses them of "degeneracy" (148-51), fit only to be slaves. These traits are due to "natural causes" for "it is not possible for people who are reared and governed as are the Persians either to have a part in any other form of virtue or to set up on the field of battle trophies of victory over their foes" (148-51). He continues his attack on the Persians, stating that "most of their population is a mob without discipline . . . and has been trained more effectively for servitude than are the slaves in our country" (148-51). The Persians pamper their bodies but have "cringing" souls, "prostrating themselves and in every way schooling themselves to humility of spirit, falling on their knees before a mortal man" (151-54). He also accuses them of "effeminacy and [being] unversed in war and utterly degenerate from luxurious living" (*Phil.* 122-25).

Plutarch, however, even though he acknowledged that the labors of the Persian King Artaxerxes II (c. 436-358 BC) in battle were "not a whit inferior to those of the meanest persons in his army" (*Artaxerxes* 24.9-10 qtd. in Briant 301), he still condemned him for sumptuous living. Quintus Curtius, who was on a mission to de-legitimize the next king Darius III (336-330 BC) as a cowardly king, stated that the barbarians (i.e., Persians) are ostentatiously clothed "like women" (*History of Alexander* III 3.14 qtd. in Briant 798). Others mention the expensive perfume used to do the great king's hair, the footstool and the carpets that were reserved for him to tread upon, the royal throne made of gold and jewels, the concubines, and eunuchs, and locked treasuries in rooms (Briant 300). Greek playwrights also alluded to the Persians' sumptuous living. In Aristophanes' *Wasps* (422 BC), Contracleon tries to bribe his father with a very expensive Persian cloak that to the Greeks is symbolic of Persian vanity (1136-54). In *The Persians* (472 BC), which is about the defeat of the Persian King Xerxes (486 BC) by the Greeks at Salamis, the herald refers to Persia as "wealth's great anchorage" (249). Also, the ghost of the Persian emperor Darius asks his queen to "gather up rich and brilliant cloths" (843) to meet their son Xerxes who is returning from battle.

Clear indications of such sumptuous living and "degeneracy" are found in the city of Tashbaan. At first glance, the walled city of Tashbaan in *HHB* suggests an Edenic image. After all, it is "one of the wonders of the world" (53), situated in a non-specific Middle Eastern location on an island between two streams. However, this phrase has negative connotations because it suggests man-made artifice, used earlier by Lewis to describe Charn, the ruined city of Jadis, in *MN*. Tashbaan is described in the following passage:

> Round the very edge of the island, so that the water lapped against the stone, ran high walls strengthened with so many towers that he [Shasta] soon gave up trying to count them. Inside the walls the island rose in a hill and every bit of that hill, up to Tisroc's palace and the great temple of Tash at the top, was completely covered with buildings—terrace above terrace, street above street, zigzag roads or huge flights of steps bordered with orange trees and lemon trees, roof-gardens, balconies, deep archways, pillared colonnades, spires, battlements, minarets, pinnacles. (53-54)

This is a powerful scene in its vivid and concrete details. The reader is offered a plethora of sensual delights that appeal to the eye and the sense of smell. There is an overabundance of sensual beauty here, too lavish, like Milton's Garden of Eden—a dazzling scene of great imagination. The city also has a great silver-plated dome on the temple, dazzling when the rising sun shines on it. In some cities of present Iran as well as Iraq there are shrines with domes that are gold plated. This ornamented, artificial beauty recalls Satan's heavily ornamented throne in *Paradise Lost* (2.1-10), as well as Lucifera's palace in *FQ* (1.4.8ff), a point that reveals English Renaissance views of the ancient Near East. Up the hill there are more instances of luxury: there are finer streets decorated with great statues of the gods and heroes of Calormen, pillared arcades, palaces, fountains, and smooth lawns that could be seen through the gateways (58). Lewis makes it clear that everything in Tashbaan, even its beautiful pleasure gardens, planted for the rich, and its splendid external appearance connote a social evil.

Extravagant beauty among the aristocratic class in *HHB* is conveyed in the mass of pleasure gardens with delicious smells that are found only in rich people's houses. This detail here is an interesting and relevant allusion to the royal pleasure gardens of Ancient Near Eastern kings, which were not only sources of pleasure, but also of produce, since they were planted with choice fruit trees of all kinds as well as spice plants. Such gardens existed in Egypt, Assyria, and Persia. Leo Oppenheim states that the garden became "an essential feature of the palace of Assyrian kings, beginning with the Sargonids" (331). A type of these royal gardens was known as the "hanging gardens" and ascribed to the Babylonian King Nebuchadnezzar (605-562 BC), who built high stone terraces which looked like mountains planted with all kinds of trees to please his mountain-bred queen (Wiseman 139).

Lewis was familiar with the Hanging Gardens from reading Herodotus, who, as Lewis wrote to his father on May 1, 1920, with "no knowledge of a language but his own . . . had yet penetrated to Babylon and seen the Hanging Gardens and the Temple of Bel-Baal [the Near Eastern version of Zeus]" (*CL* 1: 486). This allusion to Nebuchadnezzar is particularly useful here to support the themes of luxury and tyranny in this story, since he was known to be a tyrant.[2] The walls of Tashbaan are so high that the houses are exclusive like the "inner ring" that Lewis discusses in *The Weight of Glory* and *That Hideous Strength*. There is a hill, a motif of the Edenic garden, but it is topped by a tyrant's (the Tisroc's) palace, and the Temple of Tash, Aslan's competitor in the world of Narnia. A similar scene of a Near Eastern city appears in *VDT* under water, but in that context, Lewis is noncommittal and the non-European culture suggested by the buildings remains neutral (see ch. 8).

As one enters the "inner ring" of the City of Tashbaan, one finds numerous examples of the wealthy, sumptuous living associated with a tyrant and his court, which is clearly contrasted with the life of the poor and the slaves. The Tisroc makes his entrance into a palace room where Aravis, the Calormene girl who is running away, and Lasarleen, the rich Calormene woman and friend of Aravis, are hiding. Aravis, behind a sofa, could see everything. Two slaves (deaf and dumb) were walking backwards in front of the Tisroc, holding candles. Then came the Tisroc, "an old man, very fat, wearing a curious pointed cap . . . The least of the jewels with which he was covered was worth more than all the clothes and weapons of the Narnian lords put together: but he was so fat and such a mass of frills and pleats and bobbles and buttons and tassels and talismans that Aravis couldn't help thinking the Narnian fashions . . . looked nicer" (115).

Lasarleen herself also exemplifies the rich, vain Calormene lady.

She is worried about her clothes and would like to show them off in the litter, so she objects to the curtains being drawn by Aravis. In the midst of Aravis's tragic story, Lasarleen interrupts, "But you haven't even told me yet what you think of the dress" (105). As the narrator continues, "She insists on Aravis having a long and luxurious bath . . . and then dressing in the finest clothes" (106). Her own rooms as well as those of the palace are expensively furnished. The palace itself is composed of halls within halls, with colonnades and great copper doors through which they go to the throne room. "It was all magnificent beyond description" (112).

IV. Inside the City of Tashbaan (2): Isolation, Violence, Class Consciousness, and Rhetoric

Eastern tyrants, whom the Tisroc and his associates resemble, were also thought to be isolated from their citizens as well as their own family members as has been discussed earlier. Their society was based on a strong sense of class consciousness and inequality, which bred violence. Their isolation also led to cruelty in the treatment of inferiors like slaves or eunuchs, as well as their own citizens. As Carolyn Dewald states, "Eastern tyrants were marked by violence, lies, fraud, and dishonesty" (48). Paraphrasing Plato in the *Republic* (549-61), Julia Annas writes, "Reason and spirit are made to squat like slaves before the Persian king and carry out the orders only of desire" (134). Conspiracy, even among family members, was common. Cruelty was thought to be a common practice in the Persian Achaemenid court. Artaxerxes III (358-38 BC), who wiped out his family, was held to be "hot, violent, no less treacherous than bloody" (Plutarch qtd. in Briant 776). Thus Persian subjects were described as prostrating themselves before the king, an act that was called *proskynesis* (Briant 222-23), which Aristotle writes about (*Politics* 5.11). In Euripides's play *Orestes* (408 BC) one of Helen of Troy's Phrygian slaves escapes Orestes' sword saying, "I bow down, yessir. / I kiss the ground, lord. Is Eastern custom, yes" (line 1508), to which Orestes replies, "This is Argos, fool, not Troy" (1509). The Phrygians and Lydians were associated with Eastern tyranny.

Calormen is clearly a slave-holding society with a deep sense of class consciousness that leads to violence, cruelty, and abuse of "inferiors," just as Shasta experienced. Educated in a class-conscious society, Lasarleen tells Aravis that Shasta is "a peasant boy" (*HHB* 110). This way of life, fostered by the tyrant, the Tisroc, and his cabinet, is evident as we examine the lifestyle in the Calormene city. As Shasta, Aravis, and the two horses cross the bridge of many arches, an optical illusion greets them in this "artificial city": "the brazen gates stood open in the gateway which was really wide but looked narrow because it was very high" (56). The word "brazen" suggests lack of nobility, baseness, and the word "high" suggests exclusiveness. But Shasta is tempted by the illusory Edenic façade: "It must be nice inside, he thought" (58). However, at the gate, soldiers greet them with spears, cruel and taunting as one of them throws a carrot at Shasta and gives him a box on his face, mistaking him for a slave (57). Inside the gate, social violence exists in the form of a rigid class system: litters carried by slaves, beggars and peasants, poor ragged children, stray animals, and other signs of deprivation: "There were the smells, which came from unwashed people, unwashed dogs scent, garlic, onions, and piles of refuse which lay everywhere" (58). Tarkaans and Tarkeenas, Viziers (ministers) and ambassadors, loll upon litters gigantic: "For in Tashbaan there is only one traffic regulation, which is that everyone who is less important has to get out of the way for everyone who is more important" (59). A little later, Lasarleen herself appears in a litter in a type of royal pageant:

> [I]mmediately, following the crier, came four armed slaves and then four bearers carrying a litter which was all a-flutter with silken curtains and all a-jingle with silver bells and which scented the whole street with perfumes and flowers. After the litter, female slaves in beautiful clothes, and then a few grooms, runners, pages, and the like. (102)

Such blatant class differences are inadmissible in Narnia, where no one is a slave nor forced to do anything against his/her will, except under the White Witch's reign and the tyrant Miraz. To bring out the differences between Calormen and Narnia, Lewis deftly juxtaposes these scenes of Tashbaan with an earlier scene of Narnians passing through (described from the point of view of Shasta):

> There were about half a dozen men and Shasta had never seen anyone like them before. For one thing, they were all as fair-skinned as himself, and most of them had fair hair. And they were not dressed like men of Calormen. Most of them had legs bare to the knee. Their tunics were of fine, brighter, hardy colors—woodland green, or gay yellow, or fresh blue. Instead of turbans they wore steel or silver caps, some of them set with jewels, and one with little wings on each side. A few were bare-headed. The swords at their sides were long and straight, not curved like Calormene scimitars. And instead of being grave and mysterious like most Calormenes, they walked

with a swing and let their arms and shoulders go free, and chatted and laughed. One was whistling. You could see that they were ready to be friends with anyone who was friendly and didn't give a fig for anyone who wasn't. Shasta thought he had never seen anything so lovely in his life. (60-61)

As he meets more Narnians, he says that they "had nicer faces and voices than most Calormenes" (67). King Peter would later refer to Susan's supposed Calormene fiancée, Radabash, as "dark faced" (67), a clear contrast to the fair-skinned Narnians. The contrast between the two races is sharp and clear—the comparative *er* and *instead of* are used repeatedly to favor the Narnians: their tunics are of bright*er* colors; they had nic*er* faces and voices; *instead of* curved scimitars they had straight swords; *instead of* being grave and mysterious, they chatted and laughed; *instead of* turbans, they had steel or silver caps on.

Those who best represent Tashbaan—the Tisroc, the ridiculous Prince Rabadash, and the Grand Vizier (Prime Minister)—are soon described. Rabadash is clearly described by King Edmund as a "most proud, bloody, luxurious, cruel, and self-pleasing, tyrant" (68). Tyranny is seen not only in the blatant class differences and the luxury of aristocrats in the city, but also in the obsequious behavior of inferiors towards superiors as has been mentioned earlier. The first vivid instance of this humiliating behavior is noted early in the story when Arsheesh bowed down before the Tarkaan. Inside the palace of the Tisroc, however, the slaves, as noted earlier, walk backwards before the Tisroc. The Grand Vizier completely prostrates himself before the Tisroc in the council: "Last of all came a little hump-backed, wizened old man," whom Aravis recognized as the Grand Vizier and her betrothed husband (116). As soon as the Tisroc seated himself on the throne, "the Grand Vizier got down on his knees and elbows and laid his face flat on the carpet" (116). He maintains this painful position during the whole council, in spite of insults from the prince and "a series of well-aimed kicks at [his] hindquarters" (118).

This humiliating incident is closely linked to other acts of injustice, conspiracy, cruelty, and abuse of power perpetrated in general by tyrants. As revealed in this council, the proud Prince Rabadash is little used to having his will opposed and is planning to take Narnia and Archenland and redistribute the land. He will later command his soldiers to "kill every barbarian male" (171), recalling biblical tyrants like Herod. After the council, the Tisroc reveals more of his cruelty. He commands the

Grand Vizier to "call back the pardon we wrote for the third cook," since he feels the manifest prognostics "of indigestion" (130).

The Tisroc also plots with the Grand Vizier to incite his own son Rabadash to fight the peaceful neighboring people of Archenland for Queen Susan and also to "make one mouthful of Narnia and Archenland both," as Edmund says (73), knowing that his son may not succeed in this misadventure. He would then blame Rabadash's defeat on rashness and violence. He tells the Grand Vizier, "No man will be more astonished than you and I to hear that Anvard [the city of Archenland] is in his hands" (124). The Tisroc confesses to the Vizier that he values nothing more than "the glory and strength of my throne" (129). He also refers to conspiracies by eldest sons to assassinate their fathers to get the throne. These actions exemplify the bona fide cruel tyrant in Plato's opinion. There are other abuses of power that pertain to tyranny in Calormen: the selling of children, as has been mentioned before, and the enforced marriages of young girls, as shown in the enforced betrothals of Aravis to the Grand Vizier and Queen Susan to Prince Rabadash. The Calormenes are also polytheistic. Aravis prays to Tash, Azaroth [sounding similar to Ashtaroth the Near Eastern goddess of love], and Zardeenah "Lady of the Night" (32). Although Tash is the chief god, he does not appear in *HHB*, but will do so in *LB* when Narnia is taken over by the Calormenes (see ch. 9). Nancy-Lou Patterson remarks that Tash is like the Near Eastern god Baal ("The Bolt" 23). It is no wonder that Tumnus the faun from *LWW* hates "every stone" of Tashbaan (*HHB* 72). Edmund, also acquainted with evil like Tumnus, calls it "a devilish city" (74).

The peculiar writing and speaking style of the Calormenes, which also associates them with the Near East, is displayed and parodied in the conversations in Lasarleen's and the Tisroc's palaces. As Lewis writes, "In Calormen, storytelling (whether the stories are true or made up) is a thing you're taught, just as English boys and girls are taught essay writing" (*HHB* 36). The Vizier himself comments on the Calormene language: "For the gods have withheld from the barbarians [Narnians] the light of discretion, as that their poetry is not, like ours, full of choice apothegms and useful maxims, but is all of love and war" (126). In a Near Eastern style, Aravis begins her story by giving a long list of her ancestors. Her narrative is dotted with formal expressions of reverence for the Tisroc ("may he live forever") and her dead mother ("on whom be the peace of the gods") every time the Tisroc or her mother is mentioned. Metaphors and similes are abundant in their language. The expression "and the sun appeared dark in her (or his) eyes" is used several times in *HHB* to show anger or sadness (38, 73). Aravis addresses her father, "O my father and O the delight of my eyes, give me your license and permission to go with one of my maidens" (41), and he responds, "O my daughter and O the delight of my eyes so shall it be" (41). The Grand Vizier gains the Tisroc's favor and his position through verbal flattery and evil counsel (38). He addresses the Tisroc, "The praise of my masters is the light of my eyes" (127). Later, he even goes further in his exaggeration: "O impeccable Tisroc . . . In comparison with you I love neither the Prince nor my own life nor bread nor water nor the light of the sun" (129).

Further hyperboles and maxims illustrate the Calormene language. Aravis says, "[N]one of my lineage ought to fear death more than the biting of a gnat" (39). The oldest slave loved her "more than the air and the light" (41). Inferiors always mutter, "To hear is to obey." In the war council, the Tisroc and the Vizier each proffer an unsolicited proverb as advice to Rabadash who is inflamed by the beauty of Susan. The Tisroc says, "Compose yourself, O my son . . . For the departure of guests makes a wound that is easily healed in the heart of a judicious host" (118). The Vizier says, "How well it was said by a gifted poet . . . that deep drafts from the fountain of reason are desirable in order to extinguish the fire of youthful love" (118). Lewis seems to be having fun in these passages. Lewis strengthens the link between the Calormenes and Middle Eastern people also by providing places and characters with proper names that sound authentic to Middle Eastern/Persian/Arabic/Turkish cultures. First and foremost, "Aslan" sounds like Alp Arsalan (Persian shah AD 1064-72). "Tisroc" shares some phonetic sounds with "khosrow" ("king" in Persian). "Tashbaan" rhymes with Isfahaan, Ecbatan, Hamestan (cities in Persia) and with Sha'aban, Ramazan (holy months in Islam); "Rabadash," "Chalamash," "Alimash" certainly rhyme with "Shamash" ("sun" in Persian), "Habash" ("black" in Persian), and "Khoshbash" ("be happy" in Persian), "Ali" being the nephew of the Prophet Mohammed; "Lasarleen" (46) has the same suffix as "Shireen," "Parveen," "Simeen" (all Persian feminine names); others like "Jikeen" (108), "Ilgamuth," the flowery "Valley of the Thousand Perfumes" (46), to name a few, also sound Middle Eastern.

VI. Anvard: The City of Laws and Justice

The only other kingdom in the *Chronicles* that comes close to Narnia morally and spiritually is Archenland to its south, whose capital is Anvard. This city is an example of the ideal City of Man. Not only are the two countries on friendly terms, but their royalty are also related through intermarriage. King Lune of Archenland is the kindest-hearted of men. When Shasta, who is actually King Lune's kidnapped son Cor, first sets eyes on the King, he observes that he was "the jolliest, fat, apple-cheeked, twinkling-eyed king you could imagine" (165). He had grey eyes (167), a mark of nobility in European culture. Contrary to the Tisroc, King Lune is a loving father, affectionate toward his people. He is hospitable to the Calormene Aravis, who is seeking refuge in his kingdom. He is also unpretentious and an animal lover, politely conversing with the two horses, Hwin and Bree, who are a little taken aback, as he does with people.

Most importantly, however, King Lune is an ideal king and courteous warrior. His government is based on the rule of law and virtue through knowledge, which are Platonic ideals, and as such he is an example of the guardians in Plato's Kallipolis, the ideal city. He instructs his son, saying, "The king's under the law, for it's the law makes him a king" (239). He follows the law of inheritance by appointing Shasta (Cor) as his heir and the law forbidding killing except in battle. He prevents Edmund from fighting the Calormene Prince Rabadash because the latter is a traitor and consequently "rather to be whipped by the hangman than to be suffered to cross swords with any person of honor" (208); he admonishes his young son Corin for fighting in the battle against the Calormenes, but at the same time he is secretly proud of his courage; and he forgives his chancellor for embezzling, though he puts him to death when he discovers he is also a Calormene spy who had kidnapped his son, since treachery for him is, as it is for Plato and Dante, the worst sin. After capturing Prince Rabadash, King Lune provides him with food and tells him that he will not follow the law of nations as well as prudent policy to legally execute him: "[I]n consideration of your youth and the ill nurture, devoid of all gentleness and courtesy, which you have doubtless had in the land of the slaves and tyrants, we are disposed to set you free, unharmed, on these conditions," only to be answered by the vengeful Rabadash with "Curse you for a barbarian dog" (231), a tyrant's curse, and with "The bolt of Tash falls from above!" (232). As a result he receives a humiliating punishment by Aslan, i.e., metamorphosing him temporarily into a donkey á la Apuleius. (See fig.9).

FIG. 9 THE UNFORTUNATE LUCIUS, WHO WAS TRANSFORMED INTO AN ASS, AT LAST REACHES THE ANTIDOTE—A BUNCH OF ROSES—AND BEGINS TO TURN BACK INTO A MAN (FROM APULEIUS, *THE GOLDEN ASS*) (WARNER, FIG. 19).

He does become more peaceable following this ordeal, but mainly for selfish reasons, since he cannot travel ten miles away from Tashbaan.[3]

This Kingdom of Archenland, with its little reddish-brown castle, is a city of law and justice in the tradition of Plato's Kallipolis. There is also mercy in it because Radabash is granted a second chance to reform himself. It is a type of the ideal Earthly City, the Augustinian City of Man, which is based on law, justice, and mercy as evidenced in its antitype Cair Paravel. The *eucatastrophe* is signaled by a feast, the installation of Cor as heir to the throne or Archenland, and his later marriage to Aravis.

The brutal tyranny at the foundation of Tashbaan contrasts sharply with law and justice in the egalitarian government of Archenland, fulfilled in Narnia's Cair Paravel. The damaging effect of slavery in Calormen is, as Lewis writes, "that when there is no one to force you any more you find you have almost lost the power of forcing yourself" (*HHB* 146). Tashbaan comes close to the "bad" cities discussed in Plato's *Republic*, the cities of tyrants and also St. Augstine's corrupt City of Man. Anvard, on the other hand, is a city based on freedom from servitude, physically and mentally, which is at the foundation of Plato's ideal city and all cities that oppose tyrants. Tyrants, Plato says, are slaves of their own appetites, particularly Passion itself, so they live their own lives without having any relationship except that of master/slave (*Rep.* 576^a, 577^d).

Rabadash's hot-tempered and forceful attempts at getting Susan to marry him and the Tisroc's threatening and cunning manner powerfully illustrate tyranny. The Calormenes, with few exceptions like Emeth in *LB* and Aravis in *HHB*, represent a culture that is obviously inferior in the mind of Lewis to the Narnians and the Archenlandian peoples. One may conclude that just as the Greeks had focused on denigrating the Ancient Persians, not acknowledging their various great achievements, Lewis offers a dismal picture of the Calormene culture, a culture that may be linked indirectly to one of the Primary World's. It is also interesting to note that in a subtle manner, Lewis in *HBB* shows his preference for the country over the city by elevating those who love the former over the latter, like Aravis "who had always lived in the country and hated every minute of her time in Tashbaan" (134). Another thing to note is that, in contrast to other Earthly Cities in the *Chronicles*, Tashbaan alone is left unredeemed and untransformed until the apocalypse in *LB*, in which it is included in the Real Narnia. Maybe there is something good about the Calormenes after all. Aslan does not seek its welfare in *HHB*, but is content to punish its prince, Rabadash. The rulers of Tashbaan, for the moment at least, represent the type of "a bad man, happy, [who] is a man without the least inkling that his actions do not 'answer,' that they are not in accord with the laws of the universe" (*Problem* 93).

Endnotes

1. Lewis's denigration of the Calormenes at the same time as he aligns them with Near Eastern people in our world works against his purported view of inclusiveness. He could be using stereotypical characterizations and descriptions to formulate the polarity between good and evil (Ford 363), but his insensitivity to Near Eastern culture and characters represented by the Calormenes in *HBB* (passing Emeth and Aravis) is certainly regrettable. There is a plethora of critics who perceive racism in the description of the Calormenes: David Colbert, *The Magical Worlds of Narnia*, believes Lewis's writing is filled with bigotry (166); Gregg Easterbrook notes Lewis's use of the word "darkies" in reference to the Calormenes, who are "unmistakable Muslim stand-ins"; Philip Pullman has attacked the Narnia books as racist and sexist in *The Guardian* (Oct. 1998, June 3 2002). Lara Miller, in *The Magician's Book: A Skeptic's Adventures in Narnia*, also believes there is racism in the description of the Calormenes. In his published writings, Lewis showed some respect to Islam as a noble, monotheistic religion, but "wrong." He referred to it as a "Christian heresy" and failed to include it in the appendix on the Tao in *The Abolition of Man* (see Eugene McGovern, "C.S. Lewis and Islam," *CSL: The Bulletin of The New York C.S. Lewis Society* 41.5 (Sept./Oct. 2010): 1-8. However, I believe the Calormenes represent a race or an ethnic group rather than a religion.

2. Other examples of pleasure gardens are those of the Assyrian rulers Sennacherib (704-681 BC) and Ashurbanipal (660-626 BC) in Nineveh, the first place in Dante's *Purgatorio* in the terrace of Pride (12.34).

3. For a contrasting opinion on Rabadash's transformation see James F. Sennett, "Worthy of a Better God: Religious Diversity and Salvation in *The Chronicles of Narnia*," *The Chronicles of Narnia and Philosophy: The Lion, the Witch, and the Worldview*, eds. Gregory Bassham and Jerry L. Walls (Chicago: Open Court, 2005) 245-46.

CHAPTER SIX

THE CITY OF GOD IN NARNIA: CAIR PARAVEL

*If I forgot thee, O Jerusalem, let my right hand lose her cunning.
If I don't remember thee, let my tongue cleave to the roof of my
mouth; if I prefer not Jerusalem above my chief joy.*
(Psalm 137. 5-6).

Some cities (and metonymically castles, temples, monuments, cathedrals, minarets, and other man-made structures) accrued sacred meanings over time to become *axes mundi*, "centers of the world." As Mircea Eliade explains, "Every consecrated place, in fact, is a 'centre'; every place where *hierophanies* [holy revelations] and *theophanies* [divine revelations] can occur, and where there exist the possibilities of breaking through from the level of the earth to the level of Heaven" (*Patterns of Comparative Religion* 371-72). Thus a city can become a "Centre" that

> represents an ideal point which belongs not to profane geometrical space, but to sacred space; a point of communication with Heaven or Hell may be realized; in other words, a 'Centre' is the paradoxical 'place' where the planes intersect, the point at which the sensuous world can be transcended. But by transcending the Universe, the created world, one also transcends time and achieves *stasis*—the external non-temporal present. (*Images and Symbols* 75)

And cities can also be *axis mundi* in the *Chronicles* where Hell or Heaven (as they are supposed to be in Narnia) is tapped or transcended, and place, direction, or time is suspended. Stephen Scully, who has studied in depth the *polis* in Homer's *Iliad*, agrees with Eliade that the city, like Troy, can be a sacred place, built by the gods, a collective body of people with common interests, whose civilization partakes of the divine. The celestial archetype of the city is "a sacred enclave at the center of the universe, where earth and sky, human and divine, nature and social order are in harmony" (142).

Eliade's sacred city as a center of the world and Homer's Troy overlap with the pre-Christian belief regarding Jerusalem. It was considered to be the center of the world, which in future time would be ruled by the Messiah (Nathan 4). First-century historian Flavius Josephus referred to Jerusalem in similar terms (Nathan 4). Augustine's imprecision about the City of God may be deliberate to allow him to include both the Church *ecclesia* as an image of the city of God on earth as well as those outside the Church who might be good.[1] However, the matters of Jerusalem as a holy city and in what capacity are far from resolved. Resorting to biblical exegetes for help complicates this issue, since patristic authors are subject to their personal views. For instance, references to the "holy city" in Matt. 4.5 and Ga. 4.26 are explicated differently. St. Eusebius believed that while the heavenly Jerusalem is eternal, its earthly image, the Earthly City of Jerusalem, which he considered merely a physical place, was essentially irrelevant and was permanently destroyed by the Romans' attack in 70 A.D. However, later on, he came to believe that the monarchy of Constantine would bring forth the Kingdom of God (Cranz 220) and advocated Constantine's plan to build the Church of the Holy Sepulchre at the site of Christ's crucifixion as evidence of this understanding (Nathan 3).

On the other hand, St. Cyril of Jerusalem believed that Jerusalem is holy because it is a significant physical place, imbued by the holiness of God and thus the center of the world, eternal though temporarily destroyed by the Romans. Some conclusions about the holy city emerge from this brief review of Eliade, Augustine, and the Christian exegetes: while its full form is in Heaven (the City of God proper), its earthly form (as a City of Man in its highest sense) is unique because 1) major salvific events occurred in it (i.e., the resurrection, the temptation, the transfiguration) which united mankind with the city of God; and 2) God's people inhabit it, existing within His purposes and thus rendering it more than a temporary physical structure but as a mystical body of Christ in fellowship and existing in the individual's heart. These concepts, I believe, provide some insight into Cair Paravel, the sacred city of Narnia.

Lewis's personal beliefs about God's revelation come from his reason and intuition as well as from his wide readings in literature, religion, and ancient world myths, as discussed in the introduction. Lewis's inclusive type of Christianity, which appears to have roots in Hebraic, Christian, and ancient mythic cultures, enriches his fiction, especially the *Chronicles*. Cair Paravel in *LWW* is transformed through Aslan's holiness into a sacred place (an *axis mundi* to use Mircea Eliade's phrase), the antitype of all cities in Narnia. Analogously, Jerusalem was the antitype of Earthly Cities as explicated by St. Augustine of Hippo, St. Eusebius of Caesarea, and St. Cyril of Jerusalem.[2]

Built by the great-great-grandfather of Prince Caspian in the period between *MN* and *LWW*, Cair Paravel is imbued with Aslan's holiness and permeated with his glory. Before any view of Cair Paravel is offered to the children (and to us readers), Mr. Beaver informs them of the prophecy attached to the coronation at the Castle. Later, he describes Cair Paravel as

> the castle on the seacoast down at the mouth of this river which ought to be the capital of the whole country if all was as it should be—down at Cair Paravel there are four thrones and it's a saying in Narnia time out of mind that when two Sons of Adam and two Daughters of Eve sit in those four thrones, then it will be the end not only of the White Witch's reign but of her life. (89)

Later in the story, the description of Cair Paravel includes spiritual/ontological associations in Narnia which make it a type of the heavenly Jerusalem, the City of God described at the end of the Bible, prophesied about by Zechariah: "And I will bring them [my people], and they shall dwell in the midst of Jerusalem: and they shall be my people, and I will be their God, in truth and in righteousness" (8.8). Cair Paravel is presented by Aslan to Peter, who will become High King of Narnia. As if understanding a pilgrim's need for physical evidence, Aslan takes him to the eastern edge of a hilltop:

> There a beautiful sight met their eyes. The sun was setting behind their backs. That meant that the whole country below them lay in the evening light—forest and hills and valleys and, winding away like a silver snake, the lower part of the great river. And beyond all this, miles away, were the sea, and beyond the sea the sky, full of clouds which were just turning rose color with the reflection of the sunset. But just where the land of Narnia met the sea—in fact, at the mouth of the great river—there was a something on a little hill, shining. It was

shining because it was a castle and of course the sunlight was reflected from all the windows which looked toward Peter and the sunset; but to Peter it looked like a great star resting on the seashore.

"That, O Man," said Aslan "is Cair Paravel of the four thrones." (142)

This scene is full of apocalyptic imagery and motifs. Cair Paravel is pitted structurally and thematically against the Witch's Castle, good and bad forms of the image of the city: Jerusalem vs. Babylon again. It is also pitted against all evil cities in Narnia. What Lewis writes in *Spenser's Images* about the House of Busyrane and the Temple of Venus parallels this polarity here: "What is common to both . . . is that they are products of Art. The first is entirely Art, and the second Nature and Art in happy symbiosis" (45). The meaning of "Art," as explained earlier, is somewhat negative, including man-made objects and skills that can potentially be either cut off from Nature (Divine order) or perversions of it and thus having a close relation to *goetia* (black magic) (see chs. 1 and 4). Just at the place where sea, river and land meet, the major classical cosmic divisions, there is the shining hill. What comes to mind immediately is the celestial city of New Jerusalem on top of a mountain with great and high walls and the river of life proceeding from the throne of God and the Lamb. The castle is a complex symbol partly derived from the Bible and partly from the enclosed or walled city trope which "figure in medieval art as a symbol of the transcended soul of the heavenly Jerusalem" (Cirlot 38). Cair Paravel is flooded with sunlight, an iconic image of God (and in Narnia Aslan) as has been discussed in chapter 2. Aside from sunlight shining on the castle, the castle "looked like a great star," symbolizing the Spirit (Cirlot 309) or, in Christian terms, Redemption. According to Revelation 21.23, "And the city had no need of the sun, neither of the moon to shine in it, for the glory of God did lighten it, and the Lamb *is* the light thereof."

The traditional scriptural motifs used in this passage about Cair Paravel align it primarily with the heavenly city of Jerusalem, the City of God, although it might have other etymological derivations. The word "Cair" is an Old Norse word used for place-names (Hinten 15), which Lewis may be using to establish the atmosphere of "Northerness" that so deeply enchanted him. Another etymological derivation of Cair Paravel is "city in the valley" (Ford 126); however, the Castle of the city is situated on a little hill, though not the great mountain of Rev. 21.10:

"And he carried me away in the spirit to a great and high mountain, and shewed me that great city, the holy Jerusalem, descending out of heaven from God"; or Ezekiel 40.2: "In the visions of God brought he me into the land of Israel, and set me upon a very high mountain, by which *was* as the frame of a city on the south." Also, the psalmist says, "His foundation *is* in the holy mountains" (Ps. 87.1), the mountain being equated with the "loftiness" of spirit and in world mythology the center of the world (Cirlot 219), recalling Eliade's *axis mundi*. In medieval emblems, it is the mountain of salvation (221). According to Jacques Ellul, the whole vision of the New Jerusalem bursts with light: the stones of the city's foundation, with their brilliant facets, mentioned by Isaiah, the whiteness of the garments, the crystal waters, and the glistening gold (195-96). Though the Castle of Cair Paravel is not surrounded by walls of jasper and other jewels, or by streets of gold, like the heavenly Jerusalem, the roof of the Great Hall is made of ivory (*LWW* 194). Also, a castle is an enclosed place and like the city of Jerusalem, it represents harmony, order, balance, and protection from the external world of danger, an actual version of the city that neither comes to be in real time nor perishes. The psalmist entreats God to build the walls of Jerusalem so that the contrite people can be restored (Ps. 51.18). In Zechariah's visions, the Lord of Hosts speaks, "For I, saith the Lord, will be unto her [the city of Jerusalem] a wall of fire round about, and will be the glory in the midst of her" (2.5). Similarly, Aslan brings his people together under his protection. Above all, Cair Paravel is situated in a cosmic place where three cosmic regions meet (the land, the sea, the sky) at the mouth of a great river, an allusion to the river that proceeds from the throne of God and the Lamb. (See fig.10).

Furthermore, of particular importance, the Castle of Cair Paravel is situated in the East of Narnia, with its eastern door open to the sea over which Aslan would come, since he is the son of the Emperor-Beyond-The-Sea. Eusebius in *Martyrs of Palestine* 11.7-19 tells the story of Christian martyrs who described Jerusalem as "a city to be the homeland only of the righteous, for none but those should have a share in it; and it lay toward the east, toward the rising sun."[3] In Ezekiel's visions of the new temple, one of the gates faces east and "behold, the glory of the God of Israel came from the way of the east" (43.2). In Spenser's *FQ*, Una (the Protestant church) has a father who is emperor of the East, while Duessa (the Catholic Church) is queen of the West. Thus, in Milton's *Paradise Lost*, Adam and Eve exit Paradise from the West.

Fig. 10 St. John is Shown *The New Jerusalem*, woodcut by Albert Dürer (1498).

Throughout the centuries, the East has acquired a wealth of meanings and connotations that associate it with the spiritual focal point of life, as opposed to the West which is associated with death.[4] According to John A. Wilson, in the theology of the early Egyptians, the East was considered a place of religious significance, the region of birth and rebirth, indeed "God's Land," while the West was the place of the sun's setting (52). The early Christian churches oriented their altars to the East because, according to the tradition of the church fathers, the holy city is in the East (Berkeley 94). As David S. Berkeley writes, "Early Christians during private and liturgical prayer seem to have faced, Tertullian indicates in his *Apology*, the rising sun" (103). Judeo-

Christian literature is filled with allusions to Paradise as east of Eden, having an eastern gate and oriented to the sunrise. Also, the royal tribe of Judah set up its camp toward the East. Numerous scriptural passages and their interpretations associate the East with the Christian Heaven. In the traditions of the Church fathers, the holy city is in the East. In the *Gnostic Acts of St. Thomas* taken from the *Apocryphal New Testament*, the King's son comes out of his home in the high East, overcomes the serpent, and then returns home. Similarly, Aslan's Country is situated in the East, and Ramandu and his daughter will pray in the direction of the east in *VDT* (see ch. 8). Eusebius used the western course of the sun as an analogy to Christ's appearance on earth, his death, and resurrection. Jesus, during his crucifixion, turned west.

Clearly then the eastern rim of the Narnian universe is a place analogous to the Christian Heaven, awe-inspiring and holy. Aslan and the East are associated in other Narnia stories. In *MN*, Aslan makes a cameo appearance from the east in a vision-like tableau similar to the one witnessed by Eustace in *VDT*. During the creation of Narnia, Aslan appears to the children, and "when it [the lion] had passed them and gone a few paces further it turned, passed them again and continued its march eastward" (*MN* 128). In *PC*, Dr. Cornelius states that the Narnian usurpers fear the sea and do not look "toward Aslan's land and the morning and the eastern end of the world" (56). In *LB* Jill states that Aslan's Country is situated "beyond the Eastern End of the world . . . I've been there" (209), referring to her earlier experience with Aslan in *SC*. All Narnia is united as a creation of Aslan. All Narnia is potentially a part of Aslan's Country, as our world (in analogy) is open to "an incursion of the sacred" (Eliade, *Images and Symbols* 51) (see ch. 9).

Shortly before the Battle of Beruna and the defeat of Jadis the Witch in *LWW*, there is a scene of metamorphosis, which I call a pageant, which is both iconic and powerful, and so deserves close attention. As Aslan approaches from his home beyond the sea to usher in the spring and defeat the White Witch, "[s]hafts of delicious sunlight strike down on the forest floor" (131), and beautiful primroses and gold and purple and white crocuses sprout up from the soil, larches and birches are covered with green, the laburnums with gold, and the beech trees with transparent leaves. The chattering and chirping of the birds fill the air. "This is *Spring*," the Witch's dwarf explains. "What are we to do?" (133). Nothing, one might answer. The season of Aslan's spring will overcome the long rule of the Witch's winter, as Christ's resurrection has given humans eternal life and restored the world. Lewis is following the medieval tradition described in the introduction that associates seasons of Nature with Christian meanings. It foreshadows the last pageant in the story, the coronation of the children.

The coronation takes place in the shining castle on top of a green hill where land and sea meet, a place of cosmic significance, in

> the Great Hall of Cair Paravel—that wonderful hall—with the ivory roof and west wall hung with peacock's feathers and the eastern door which looks towards the sea. . . . And through the eastern door, which was open, came the voices of the mermen and the mermaids swimming close to the shore and singing in honor of their new Kings and Queens. (199)

The transformed world is represented in the motifeme of Coronation of the Rightful Kings and Queens of Narnia after the Witch is killed. Order and ceremony prevail over chaos and destruction, Joy over despair, the sacred rites over black magic. Lewis introduces the motifs of singing mermen and mermaids, representing divinity, their voices coming through the Eastern door like an angelic choir (199).[5] Tableau and narrative coalesce in this glorious finale, this metamorphic closure. In this Narnian setting, there is nothing more to tell. The journey of redemption in *LWW* is accomplished. The White Witch's Castle of Ice metaphorically melts into Cair Paravel, a sort of metamorphic pageant, an image of good.

However, this iconic castle will be destroyed for a while (as we saw in ch. 3) and will appear as a ruined structure in *PC* because of the usurpation of the Narnian kingship by Miraz, the uncle of the legitimate heir, Prince Caspian the Tenth, although at the end of *PC* the city is regenerated. In *SC* Jill visits the restored city and gets a good view of the Castle of Cair Paravel after it is inhabited again: "On the far side of the lawn . . . rose a many-towered and many-turreted castle; the most beautiful castle Jill had ever seen" (31). The green lawn is shining again, banners are fluttering in the air, bright clothes, swords, armor, and gold glittering in the sun, near a huge ship shining "like an enormous piece of jewelry—a true scene of splendor" (30). This is the scene of King Caspian the Tenth's embarking on the sea. There are beautiful people with willowy hair, rooms with views of the sunset, which made Jill "long for more adventures and feel sure that this was only the beginning" (42). This scene in Jill's imagination reflects the earlier Golden Age of Narnia, which represents Western Civilization, classical, medieval, and Renaissance Europe—all blended together in Lewis's imagination. This rich picture of Cair Paravel is a defense against the brute forces of chaotic and potentially evil civilizations, represented by Charn in *MN*, the Castle of Ice of the White Witch in *LWW*, Tashbaan in *HHB*, and the Castle of the Giants and the Underland City of the Green Witch in *SC*. After regeneration, Cair Paravel is taken by the Calormenes in *LB*, but will appear again in Real Narnia in *LB*.

However, Cair Paravel is not a physical building only. Like the heavenly city, it is a seat of divine glory. It is infused with Aslan's love, a haven for the British children who went through many struggles and temptations on the way to it in *LWW*: a journey through the snow, Edmund's temptation by the White Witch, Aslan's martyrdom, and the battle of Beruna, to name a few. They receive Aslan's glory when they are crowned as Kings and Queens of Narnia at Cair Paravel, to become the dearly beloved people of Aslan and wear clothes of glory as inhabitants of Paradise. Their successful reign is called "The Golden Age" (*PC* 55). One is reminded of James 1.12: "Blessed *is* the man that endureth temptation: for when he is tried, he shall receive the crown of life, which the Lord hath promised to them that love him." In discussing scriptural imagery in *Mere Christianity*, Lewis writes that crowns suggest that "those who are united with God in eternity share His splendour and power and joy" (137). We see in *LWW* the close bond of the children, especially Lucy, with Aslan. Cair Paravel is like the ideal city Kallipolis in Plato's *Republic*, which is an expression of hierarchy (Jonathan Smith 26). The four royal figures rule equally in their different capacities and are beloved by their followers, and, in that sense, the city also mirrors the heavenly Jerusalem to a certain degree.

Walter Hooper describes Narnia, in general, as "a monarchical society, one in which there is loyal and joyful obedience to those above one in the hierarchic scale of being" (*Past Watchful Dragons* 91). It is like Charles Williams' ideal city in *Descent*, hierarchic and republican (Moorman 37). Cair Paravel is thus a sacred city, like the heavenly Jerusalem, because it is an expression of Aslan, his commitment to his people (i.e., in the act of crowning), as the New Jerusalem is an expression of God's work. In it Aslan reveals himself as the Lord, establishing a community for his followers, a commonwealth led by the royal Kings and Queens, and uniting it with His Country, analogous in our world to the uniting of earth and heaven in a space made sacred by the presence of Christ, specifically his Transfiguration. Charles Williams' ideal city was the church and its authority, a type of kingdom of God, where ideal marriage, acts, love, and justice thrive (Moorman 37). Cair Paravel shares all these attributes. It is described as a "blessed place" (*PC* 55).

Reflecting on temples or churches (metaphors of the City of God on earth), Lewis often states that it is the heart rather than the buildings that ensures their sacredness, thus in agreement with Eusebius (Peter W. L. Walker 76) and Origen, both of whom state that Jerusalem was purely spiritual (Nathan 2). Eusebius paraphrases Jesus' teaching as follows: "The Law of Moses required all who desired to be holy to speed from all directions to one definite place; but I, giving freedom to all, teach men not to look for God in a corner of the earth, nor in mountains, not in temples made with hands, but that each should worship and adore him at home" (qtd. in Walker 73). In a speech to an assembly of Anglican priests and youth leaders during Easter 1945 titled "Christian Apologetics," Lewis stated that most people use the word "church" to mean "a sacred building" or "the clergy," forgetting about its most important sense as "the company of all faithful people" which is a phrase in the prayer of "thanksgiving" at Holy Communion (*God* 97).

In *Surprised* Lewis writes that God "cares only for temples building and not at all for temples built" (167), probably basing his statement on John 4.24: True worship of God was to be "in spirit and in truth"; and 1 Cor. 3.16: "Know ye not that ye are the temple of God, and *that* the Spirit of God dwelleth in you?" In *Reflections on the Psalms* (1958), he contrasts Judaism and Christianity: "Judaism without the Temple was mutilated, deprived of its central operation; any church, barn, sickroom, or field, can be the Christian's temple" (45). This statement is yet another evidence of Lewis's universe as dynamic and open to any intrusion of the sacred.

Cair Paravel is thus a blend of myth, patristic exegesis, and Lewis's own Christianity. It shares with Mircea Eliade's and St. Cyril's holy cities the focus on the city's centrality and holiness, and approaches Augustine's City of God. It is a physical place where the British children, called from faraway places, will find their identity, their citizenship. By analogy, Cair Paravel is also a place partly of heavenly citizenship for us on earth. "My kingdom is not of this world," Christ says (John 18.36). In that aspect it is a spiritual entity, more of heart than a building, like Augustine's and Eusebius's heavenly cities. However, Cair Paravel differs from the heavenly city in that it is not clearly Christian, though analogous to a Christian City, has no emperor's sacred throne, is not condemned by God (Aslan) even though it is abandoned for a while, and does not contain too many ornaments nor walls of jasper and streets of gold. Nevertheless, it remains the holy city of Narnia, timeless but also in time, as opposed to the vanished Charn, the White Witch's Castle of Ice that melts with the sun of Aslan, and the crushed Underland of the Green Witch. Cair Paravel will continue to exist in the Real Narnia as, analogously, the heavenly Jerusalem that will descend on a new earth in the Day of Judgment. Jerusalem "gave true meaning both to the text and to the land . . . she was the centre around which they [the people] had to revolve" (Peter W. L. Walker 344). One can say the same of Cair Paravel. In Lewis's *Chronicles*, all roads for Aslan's followers lead to or from Cair Paravel, and, metaphorically, all cities in Narnia find their antitype in this holy city. Cair Paravel is in the heart of every true Narnian as Jerusalem is in the heart of Christians.

Endnotes

1. Personal correspondence with John Starkey.

2. My ideas on Eusebius and Cyril come from Peter W. L Walker, *Holy Cities, Holy Places?* (Oxford; Clarendon, 1990). According to Dom Bede Griffiths, O.S.B., a long-time friend of Lewis, Lewis "showed very little interest in the Fathers of the Church" except for St. Augustine's *Confessions* ("The Adventure of Faith" 21). I might add that Lewis mentions Origen in *The Discarded Image: An Introduction to Medieval and Renaissance Literature* (Cambridge U.P., 1964), 155. As mentioned earlier in chapters 1 and 2, there is evidence that he was familiar with the Greek Orthodox community in Oxford. (See chapter 1 n. 14).

3. Cited by Ramsay MacMullen in *Enemies of the Roman Order* (Cambridge: Harvard UP, 1966) 91.

4. I am indebted for all the information in this section on the East to David Shelley Berkeley's *Inwrought with Figures Dim: A Reading of Milton's "Lycidas"* (The Hague: Mouton, 1974) 90-98; Berkeley's outstanding scholarly work includes much on the sacral meaning of the East in pagan thought and Judeo-Christian tradition. There is little work on the geographical symbolism of the East in Narnia. Both Glen GoodKnight's pioneering work in geographical criticism published in 1969 and J. R. Christopher's, which followed in 1971, briefly note biblical and Greek symbolism of the East in Aslan's Country, but they do not explore in detail the literary and Christian traditions associated with this direction in the narratives. See my article "The Significance of the East in C.S. Lewis's *The Voyage of the* Dawn Treader and Other Narnia Stories: Topos or Cosmos?" *CSL: The Bulletin of the New York C. S. Lewis Society* 29. 5-6 (May-June 1998): 1-10.

5. On the mermaids and mermen's relation to *goeteia* see John Donne's poem "Song: Go and Catch a Falling Star" (line 5); on their Romantic associations see Matthew Arnold's "The Forsaken Merman," *The Oxford Book of English Verse, 1250-1900*, ed. Sir Arthur Quiller-Couch (1919) and T. S. Eliot's "The Love Song of J. Alfred Prufrock," *The Complete Poems and Plays, 1909-1950* (San Diego,CA: Harcourt Brace Jovanovich, 1971) 7.

CHAPTER SEVEN

THE GARDENS OF NARNIA

A garden enclosed is my sister my spouse: A spring shut up, a fountain sealed.
      (Song of Sol. 4.12)

Here blossom bloom
Secretly, herbs grow vigorously, trees leaf profusely
Fruits abound, birds chatter, streams murmur,
and the gentle air warms all.
      Matthew of Vendôme (1.3.49-52)

The traditional motifs of the garden in its ideal form are trees, fruits, green hills, sweet odors and a well or fountain (see ch. 1). It is also set on a mountain, "a befitting spot of worship" (Porteus 45). Moreover, as Stanley Stewart writes, "Night cannot fall in the enclosed garden because the sun, who is the Son, has eternally risen" (110). However, this garden can also be a garden of loss, a type of Gethsemane, a moment of temptation or a place where temptation is actualized as in the biblical Garden of Eden.

As a place of testing, as in the Created Garden in *MN*, where the hero undergoes spiritual and moral tests in a locus set apart from society, it can contain peril in its beauty. The danger in this Edenic Garden exists in Jadis the Witch, who uses the fragrant silver apples to appeal to Digory's weaknesses. As a place of actualized temptation, again as in the biblical garden, where the self folds back, serpentine, on its own image (Gillespie 314), the garden metamorphoses into a wilderness, exposed to spiritual and physical onslaughts from the outside, a close relative of the City of Satan/Man. What has been the promised land is now occupied by the forces of evil, such as Acrasia "the foe of life" in Spenser's *FQ*

(2.11.48.4), whose bower is "infected by lust and overindulgence," which "seek to infect what surrounds them and bend it to their will" (Giamatti 275). The spoiled garden is a place of deadly plants and false dreams (*Od.* 1.9.562; *Aen.* 6: 843-96). All these are not common abodes for men (Corbin 2). In Lewis's own imagination, a spoiled garden harbors serpents in its midst, and also, a courtyard of petrified animals, a field of snow, a Witch from Charn, a White Witch, a Green Lady/ Serpent, and a shape-shifting Ape—all types of despair and isolation as has been discussed.

In describing his various gardens in the *Chronicles* Lewis draws heavily upon these traditional motifs of gardens in biblical, classical, and early Christian literature.[1] A close reading of the *Chronicles*, in canonical order, reveals that all these levels of meaning regarding the garden imagery operate to some degree in the three types of gardens that are vital in Lewis's larger narrative of the *Chronicles*, the Christian story of Temptation and Redemption: 1) the Created Garden (a type of the biblical Garden of Eden) in *MN*, which focuses on the inward personal struggle of the soul in the context of temptation; 2) the Garden of Restoration (a type of terrestrial paradise) in *VDT*, which focuses not only on the trials of the fallen soul but also on its restoration into a community that experiences rest and refreshment of the spirit (the church by analogy); and 3) the Celestial Garden (a type of a celestial paradise) in *LB*, which provides full perfection, open to all Aslan's followers, analogous to the Christian heaven.[2]

I. The Newly Created Garden in *The Magician's Nephew*

The newly created garden in *MN* is a composite of all versions of the garden transmuted by Lewis's imagination and fired by his classical, biblical, medieval, and Renaissance scholarship—his "scholarship of imagination." Also, motifs from Homeric and Miltonic epics, as well as from exegetical literature on the Song of Solomon appear in Lewis's depiction of the first garden in Narnia, the scene of an archetypal temptation. As Amphion, King of Thebes, built the walls of his city by moving stones into place through the music of his lyre, so Aslan creates Narnia through the power of his song in *MN*. Birth and creation are the great metamorphoses. Out of the darkness comes the blazing sun of creation, giving life and energy to the landscapes of Narnia and then to its creatures. Digory notices that it looks younger than the sun that rose above the ruins of Charn: "You could imagine that it laughed for joy as it came up. And as its beams shot across the land the travelers could see for the first time what sort of place they were in," writes Lewis (119). This statement aligns with Lewis's above-mentioned Platonic concept of light (see ch. 2) as the ultimate Christian Reality that we cannot see, but only through it we can see.

In a series of splendid tableaux, as if in a medieval painting, life in its multifarious forms bursts out from darkness: first light, then grass, then trees and animals. During the creation of Narnia, Aslan's voice raises the sun, and the landscape is filled with "a thousand points of light ... single stars, constellations and planets, brighter and bigger than any in our world" (117), something like the medieval light of the Empyrean irradiating the whole cosmos, making way for the creation of life. The aggressiveness of this act is obvious as it is in Genesis, when the Holy Spirit penetrated matter in our world (Gen. 1.3). Aslan also informs matter with a light that originates in the East. Watching him in the process of creating Narnia made the Pevensie children forget everything else. He is "huge, shaggy, and bright" and he stands facing the sun with his "mouth wide open in a song" (120). While all characters watch, "the eastern sky changed from white to pink and from pink to gold" (119), revealing the freshly created mountains and hills. Aslan's creation also suggests God's implanting of His image on the living substance of the universe as in Genesis, endowing the world and man with seeds of divinity. It is as if the Holy Spirit in our world has penetrated matter. These passages portray Aslan (and God/Christ) as the creator, the artist, shaping the world with music that suggests the classical concept of the music of the spheres. Aslan thus creates the Narnian world in *MN* and endows some creatures with the gift of speech: "Love, think, Speak," he says (116);[3] they are also given crowns and thrones.

In a letter to Sister Penelope C.S.M.V. on January 10, 1952, Lewis wrote that he pictured Adam physically as an anthropoid, "on whom, after birth, God worked the miracle which made him Man," an event that prefigures 1) God's call of Abraham to leave his home in Ur, Chaldea, and take his people to the promised land and 2) the regeneration that is possible in each one of us (*CL* 3: 157). In another letter to Reverend E. T. Dell on April 6, 1950, he wrote that St. Athanasius's theory in *On The Incarnation*, that God superimposed the Word or His image on the animal form (38) seems "sensible" (*CL* 3: 21). This "miracle," I would suggest, is God's granting of the power of speech to man in order to establish a covenant with him, which is reflected in this passage. This event suggests the ultimate significance of the power of words, based on 1 Cor. 15.46: "It is not the spiritual which comes first, but the animal, and after the spiritual." The power of language as an agent of memory and metamorphoses ties in with Lewis's ideas on *theōsis* (see chs. 1 and 3).

But the garden proper, the first created garden in the *Chronicles*, soon to be a place of temptation and healing for Digory, lies far beyond the edges of this bubbling Narnia. Interestingly, it is the only garden in Narnia that has the motif of evil in it. Like the biblical Garden of Eden and John Milton's garden in *Paradise Lost*, it includes the potential for evil, because the Witch is already lurking there. However, the two questors, Satan and Digory, have two different motives: Satan to destroy the Garden of Eden and its inhabitants, through the fruit as it turns out; and Digory to protect Narnia by fetching the seed from the apple tree to plant in Narnia. Although he does not know it yet, the apple from the tree will test his promise to Aslan and later cure his mother. Satan is motivated by disobedience to God, Digory by obedience to Aslan. In *PL*, the "questor" is also the tempter; in *MN*, Lewis reverses this by having the mortal "questors," Digory and Polly, travel to the Edenic garden, where the tempter is already waiting.

Milton's influence is evident in Lewis's use of traditional geographic garden motifs. One of these motifs is the garden's remoteness, albeit Milton's garden is situated in the east of Eden and Lewis's in the Western Wild, out of the land of Narnia. Like Satan, who has to fly across the vast expanse of the universe to reach Eden, Digory and Polly ride on Fledge, the flying horse, to cross the Western Wild to get to the Edenic garden of the silver apples. Fledge can be seen as Lewis's analogue to the classical flying horse Pegasus, symbol of inspiration and liberation. The grim and horrible mountains that they fly over, sometimes symbolic of sin in biblical tradition (Nicolson 43-45), parallel the realm of Chaos that Satan must cross. While Satan must go out through the gate of Hell, Polly and Digory must fly over various boundaries, one of which is a waterfall, which divides the lands of Narnia from the Western Wild later referred to in *LB* as "the Waterfall" (216, 218), which acts as a barrier between Narnia and the Real Narnia. There is also a lake encircled by mountains of ice—a motif of danger, death, and obstruction going back to *Hakluyt's English Voyages* (1.42) (see ch. 8; *PL* 10.290-93), and *The Lyfe of Saynt Branden*, a piece of medieval hagiography recounting St. Brendan's voyage, considered by Walter Hooper to have been in Lewis's mind when he wrote a rough sketch of *VDT* (*C.S. Lewis A Companion and Guide* 403) (see ch. 8).

Other traditional motifs from the medieval/Renaissance enclosed garden and Milton's appear in Lewis's garden in *MN*. These pertain to the terrain of the garden proper. The garden in *MN* is an enclosed garden on top of a green hill, traditionally a holy spot for prayer (Porteous 45), with a "high wall of green turf" (*MN* 186) as compared with the enclosed garden in Milton (4.133). In medieval and Renaissance Christianity, these walls were conceived to be God's protection of his people from natural and spiritual onslaughts through the dispensation of grace for those who enter the garden lawfully (Stanley Stewart 59). In Lewis's garden there are gates of gold "facing due east" (187), while in Milton's "one Gate there only was, and that look'd East" (4.178). The gates of Lewis's garden harken back to the wall of "bright gold" in the description of the Garden of Adonis in Spenser's *FQ* (3.6.31). Inscribed with silver letters, the Narnian garden gates warn visitors to

> Come in by the gold gates or not at all,
> Take of my fruit for others or forbear,
> For those who steal or those who climb my wall
> Shall find their heart's desire and find despair. (*MN* 187)

The Christian virtue of *caritas* suggested in the second line ("Take of my fruit for others or forbear") is an antithesis to the sin of *acedia*, spiritual sloth linked to despair brought about, as Lewis states clearly, by the satisfaction of the "heart's desires" (i.e., on the part of "those who steal or those who climb my walls," another Miltonic parallel [see introduction]). Lewis repeats this concept when Aslan says, "She [the Witch] has won her heart's desire; she has unwearying strength and endless days like a goddess. But length of days with an evil heart is only length of misery and already she begins to know it. All get what they want; they do not always like it" (208). Despair, according to Lewis in the above verses, is a consequence of such self-centered actions, whether the individual is aware of this consequence or not. The opposition here, to use other terms, between *agapé*, love of God (Aslan) that leads to grace, and *amor*, love of self, the foundation of the City of Satan, will become more apparent in the later temptation by the Witch.

The gates in Lewis's garden, like the gate in *PL*, suggest the exclusiveness of the garden, lawfully accessible only to those who follow Aslan in Narnia and God in Milton's garden. As he enters the garden, Digory immediately notices its exclusiveness: "You never saw a place which was so obviously private. You could see at a glance that it belonged to someone else. Only a fool would dream of going in unless he had been sent there on a very special business" (187). The doctrine of grace, available to those who can hear God's words (or Aslan's in Narnia), is represented by another common medieval and Renaissance garden motif—the fountain at the center of the enclosed garden, a marked contrast to the dry fountain in Charn. A ubiquitous image in medieval paintings as well, it has its basis in Genesis 2.10, the "well of living waters" from the Song of Solomon (4.15), and the spring of eternal life in John 4.14. Milton's garden also includes a "fresh fountain," which waters the garden and is divided into the four rivers of Eden (4.229-45). Finally, Lewis's garden also has a sweet odor that harkens back to the "native perfumes" in Milton's *PL* (4.158). Lewis mentions the "heavenly smell" (*MN* 185) and "the lovely smell" in the garden (188).

However, the central and most powerful garden motif in *MN* is the silver apple tree, situated in the middle of the garden beside the fountain. The silver apples resemble the fruits in earlier garden poetry, for example the garden of Alkinoös in book 7 of the *Odyssey*, as well as the fruits in the medieval and Renaissance enclosed garden. Although the fruit of the Tree of Life in Milton's garden is not silver or gold, it is "of vegetable gold" (4.220), and other trees in the garden have fruit "burnisht with Golden Rind" (249). The medieval poem *Pearl* describes a similar vision of paradise:

> As bornyst sylver the lef on slydez,
> That thike con trylle on uch a tynde.
> Quen glem of glodez agaynz hem glydez,
> Wyth schymeryng scheme ful schrylle they schynde. (77-80)

(*The leaves that quiver abundantly on every branch slide against each other as burnished silver. When the light from the glades falls on them, they shine dazzlingly with shimmering brightness.* –Thorlac Turville-Petre 476). The silver apple tree also has links to the apple tree in the Song of Solomon Over time, the apple image accrued a rich cluster of associations in Judeo-Christian literature, particularly because of its *locus amoenus* in the Song of Sol. as a provider of refreshment for the soul, as a few passages from this work might illustrate. The beloved is repeatedly compared to apples or the apple tree by the speaker: "As the apple tree among the trees of the wood so is my beloved among the sons. I sat down under his shadow with great delight, and his fruit was sweet to my taste" (2.3). The speaker then complains of lovesickness saying, "Stay me with flagons, comfort me with apples, for I am sick of love" (2.5). Such verses have given rise in some biblical commentaries to the metaphor of Christ as the tree of life and fruit as well as gardener, the refreshment and defender of mankind (Stanley Stewart 88). The parched soul, on one allegorical level, turns to the apple tree for refreshment and regeneration, "allowing a garden to spring where all had been desert" (Stewart 168). Stewart concludes, "Whether in poetry or painting, the fruit of the apple tree of the Song Solomon symbolizes [for Christians] the Eucharist" (85). (See fig.11).

FIG. 11. FRANCIS QUARLES, *EMBLÈMES* (1635). HENRY HUNTINGTON LIBRARY AND ART GALLERY (STANLEY STEWART, FIG. 31)

Lewis himself appreciated the Song of Solomon on both the literal and allegorical levels. In his commentary on Psalm 45 and the Song Solomon, he writes that to reject the mystical meaning "just because it does not appeal to our age is to be provincial, to have the self-complacent blindness of the stay-at-home" (*Reflections on the Psalms* 130). He also states, "The image of sexual union is . . . almost inevitable as a means of expressing the desired union between God and man" (129). As in the Song of Solomon he uses the apple in the garden of *MN*, with all its sacramental meanings, as Aslan's instrument of healing and regeneration—if plucked and eaten properly at the right time by the right person. When Digory enters the garden, "He knew which the right tree was at once, partly because it stood in the very center and partly because the great silver apples with which it was loaded shone so and cast a light of their own down on the shadowy places where the sunlight did not reach" (188). Lewis's phrase, "the shadowy places," seems to have its source in the Song of Solomon (2.3).

Through the ordeal of obtaining the apple, Digory discovers in himself strength to resist the Witch and keep Narnia safe. Another poetic rendering of the apple tree is one of Herman Hugo's poems *Pia Desideria* (1628), where he renders a verse paraphrase of the image of the apple tree as a healer of a soul caught in "the burning sand of spiritual wilderness." The soul hears the voice of God saying,

> I know you see *Jerusalem* above
> Thither your life and your endeavors move:
> But with the tedious *Pilgrimage* dismay'd,
> Implore refreshment from the *Apple's* shade.
> See, see, I come to bring your pains relief!
> Beneath *my shadow* ease your weary grief.
> Behold my arms stretch'd on the fatal *Tree*,
> With these extended boughs I'll cover thee.
> Behold my *bleeding feet*, my *gaping side*,
> In these free Coverts thou thy self maist hide
> This shade will grant thee thy desir'd repose,
> *This Tree alone for that kind purpose grows.*
>   (ll. 22-33 qtd. in Stanley Stewart 87-88)

Under one of his emblems, Hugo writes the following epigram: "'The *Tree of Life, to wit,* the *Apple,* is the holy Cross; its Fruit *is* Christ, its shadow the refreshment *and* defense of *mankind*'" (qtd. in Stewart 88). In this passage we find the same attribute that Lewis associates with the silver apple in his Edenic Garden: its refreshing shade and healing powers if eaten at the right time and in the right way by the right person.

Aslan's role as a healer, like Christ in the passages from the Song of Solomon, is clear in that he later uses the apple to heal Digory's mother. Aslan takes on Christ's role as a gardener in John 15, through the planting of the apple after Digory throws it toward the river soil. After the coronation of the cabby and his wife as the first King and Queen of Narnia, analogues to the blessed souls in the afterlife, the silver apple tree shoots up miraculously from the soil: "Its spreading branches seemed to cast a light rather than shade, and the silver apples peeped out like stars from under every leaf. But it was the smell which came from it, even more than the sight, that had made everyone draw in their breath" (206). A smell that breaks one's heart. In a passage that alludes to the apple tree in the Song of Solomon, Aslan tells Digory, who is a type of the soul in pilgrimage, "For this fruit you have hungered and thirsted and wept" (198) and, later, he commands the Narnians to "guard this Tree, for it is your Shield.... But while that Tree flourishes she [the Witch] will never come down to Narnia" (206). Aslan thus fills the roles of Christ as tree, fruit, and gardener. Accordingly, like Jesus in John 13.26, 38, he foresees his own martyrdom, which will occur later at the hands of Jadis in *LWW*. He tells his followers, "Evil will come of that evil [the Witch], but it is still a long way off, and I will see to it that the worst falls upon myself" (*MN* 161). But as long as the apple tree, the Tree of Protection, flourishes in Narnia, the Witch will stay away.

To clarify the Christian meaning of Lewis's garden and the apple tree, one must examine the scene of temptation by Jadis (*MN* 191-95) that occurs after Digory and Polly have been transported by magic rings from the Ruined City of Charn to Narnia. This temptation is the only one that occurs in a garden setting in the *Chronicles*, with the fruit becoming more central than ever as it is in Genesis. Jadis's tempting of Digory presents parallels to Satan's tempting of Eve in Genesis and *Paradise Lost*. In all three settings it is the eating (or not eating) of the fruit that matters, an action upon which hangs the destiny of Narnia and the world. Eating the forbidden fruit in the gardens of Genesis and *PL* leads to many catastrophes, including the introduction of evil in the minds of the inhabitants and their expulsion from the gardens; eating of the apple in *MN* by the wrong person at the wrong time transforms his/her perception of good into evil and leads to death (of Digory's mother, for example, if she had not been given the apple to eat in the right manner).

Both Jadis and Milton's Satan have already entered the enclosed garden unlawfully. Unlike Satan, however, the Witch has actually eaten of the fruit herself and tempts Digory to eat the apple, which he has picked for Aslan and put in his pocket, outside the garden—after she had vaulted over the gate. She proceeds to feed Digory's fancy with vain hopes and illusory dreams, cloaking evil with good, much as Satan does in tempting Eve in his signature move.[4] The Witch tempts Digory on many levels, playing on his false hopes and fears, on his love for mother and friend, and on his sense of security. First, like Satan in *PL*, she appeals to his vanity by describing the apple as "the apple of youth, the apple of life," (192) without telling him of the disastrous consequences of eating it. These words echo the words of Milton's Satan to Eve: "Ye shall not Die. / How should ye? By the Fruit? It gives you Life / To Knowledge" (9.685-87).

Next, the Witch targets Digory's loyalty to his master in hopes of creating a breach between the two by talking of Aslan's alleged tyranny and his plans to enslave Digory. Similarly, Satan tries to convince Eve that God is a tyrant who forbids her and Adam to eat of the fruit in order to intimidate them and "keep ye low and ignorant, / His worshippers" (704-05). Satan and the Witch both suffer from *acedia*, the result of satisfying their heart's desire in disobeying God and Aslan, respectively. In other words, obeying one's self-centered desires can never lead to final satisfaction. While the Witch does not directly manifest this despair, Satan does so very eloquently. Satan's soliloquy on Mount Niphates in book 4 of *PL* as he views the Garden of Eden, reflects a rare moment of self-understanding. The poet writes, "Now conscience wakes despair / That slumber'd, wakes the bitter memory / Of what he [Satan] was" (4.23-25). Later on in his soliloquy, Satan laments: "Me miserable! Which way shall I fly / Infinite wrath and infinite despair?" (4.73-74). Satan and the Witch both try to arouse the same despair in their victims which would then lead them to eat of the fruit.

When the Witch fails, she changes her strategy by appealing to Digory's concern for his mother, urging him to steal the apple to save her. As a last resort, she tempts him to abandon Polly in Narnia so that she would not tell on him if he were to steal an apple. His head clears at this mean and shocking suggestion to break a promise to a friend, and he confronts her with the question, "What's it got to do with you?" (195) recalling Jesus's words to Peter: "If I will that he tarry till I come, what is *that* to thee?" (John 21.22). Temporarily defeated, the Witch turns and skulks northward, in the direction of the evil country of the giants. Resisting this temptation becomes a rite of passage for Digory, who thus attains the classical virtues of temperance, continence, moral courage, loyalty, and the Christian virtue of *caritas*, albeit with some help from Aslan, who earlier had given him a Lion kiss to instill "new strength and courage into him" (169), an analogy to Christ's power working on individual souls to endow them with grace (John 20.22).

In the quest for the silver apple, Digory finds himself. On the other hand, Adam and Eve fail miserably. But then their temptation is more complex and perilous, and their tempter more subtle and guileful, appearing in the shape of a beautiful Talking Animal. While Digory is not of the same stature as Adam, nor was meant to be (although Aslan occasionally calls him "son of Adam"), his resistance to the Witch is heroic and acquits him of his error in Charn. When one next sees him in *LWW,* he is a mature and compassionate professor in England (if not also a bit eccentric). Digory's spiritual metamorphosis is a continuous progress, measured by his advance toward Aslan in Narnia. Interestingly, this process bears some similarity to the spiritual process of Augustine in *Confessions,* Dante the character in *Inferno,* and Lewis in *Surprised by Joy*—all "professors" in a sense, through professing their faith in writing and/or teaching.

The *eucatastrophe* in this chronicle is far-reaching. In England, Digory's mother is healed by the apple whose seed sprouts up into a tree that would bear apples "more beautiful than any others in England" (220). Joy comes in Digory's life because he learns that his father will come home from India, "so that Digory felt, just as sure as you that they were all going to live happily ever after" (219). In Narnia there is also a *eucatastrophe.* The Beasts, King Frank and Queen Helen and their children also lived happily, and the lamp-post, brought by Jadis from London, would forever give light. This *eucatastrophe* is not expanded into a full-fledged pageant as in the rest of the chronicles. Nevertheless, it adequately suggests Lewis's belief that "evil imprisons, good sets free" (*Spenser's Images* 95). Digory and others through him, the Narnians and his mother, experience the regenerative love of Aslan. Through highly charged metaphors of sowing and cultivating seeds and caring for fruit, not plucking them and eating them at the wrong time, Lewis illustrates the Christian *caritas* which Digory understands experientially and we, the readers, vicariously: to live for others and God in imitation of Christ, the doctrine of *thèōsis.*

In Narnia Aslan selects and summons his followers to collaborate with him in an on-going struggle against the onslaughts of evil beings who have lost the good of the intellect, besotted as they are, Augustine and Dante would say, with self-love. In *MN* Lewis concentrates his efforts on creating the Eternal Present of "holy moments" offered to characters and readers alike, often in a garden setting, by the Great Lion of Narnia. However, through the interaction of a boy, a lion, and a witch, Lewis's mythopoeic imagination transforms the Edenic garden with the apple tree—destroyed by Satan, Adam, and Eve in the Bible and *PL*—into a shining icon of Christian hope and regeneration as opposed to the dead, evil, heathen city of Charn.

III. Gardens of Restoration in *The Voyage of the* Dawn Treader [5]
A. Garden of Restoration (1)

Eustace's preference for materialism and comfort over any relationship with his companions metamorphoses him into a dragon and isolates him physically and spiritually from his group. His dragonization is a metamorphosis of appearance or shape while his identity stays human, like Apuleius who was changed into an ass's form and Io into a cow's, while maintaining their identities. Eustace's undragonization through Aslan can be perceived as Christian regeneration, repentance, and conversion. Marina Warner describes a "boss," an architectural term for a knob or protrusion of stone or wood, in the choir vaults of Iffley church, near Oxford, with a picture of a dragon "'scraping off its skin of evil'" (84). Lewis may have been familiar with this picture. The landscape of the first Garden of Restoration in *VDT* is first presented to us in Eustace's narrative. In an unusually splendid passage, Aslan makes his first appearance to the suffering Eustace in this haunting tableau:

> I looked up and saw the very last thing I expected: a huge lion coming slowly towards me. And one queer thing was that there was no moon last night, but there was a moonlight where the lion was. So it came nearer and nearer. I was terribly afraid of it. You may think that, being a dragon, I could have knocked any lion out easily enough. But it wasn't that kind of fear. I wasn't afraid of it eating me, I was just afraid of *it*—if you can understand. (113)

Aslan's purpose is to lead Eustace to a garden, on top of a green mountain, in order to transform him back into a human. Inspired by the Lion, whom he thought was just an ordinary lion—although suspiciously surrounded with light and possessing an awe-inspiring majesty and the gift of speech—Eustace follows him obediently. He had never seen Aslan before. Aslan's iconic role is obvious in Eustace's acceptance and recognition of him as his savior. This openness to Aslan propels Eustace toward regeneration.

As Eustace narrates, the Lion takes him to "the top of a mountain I'd never seen before and on the top of this mountain there was a garden—trees and fruit and everything. In the middle of it there was a well" (114). The traditional Edenic garden motifs are all here: the mountain, trees, fruit, and well. This place is of great significance to Eustace because he is immersed in that well by Aslan to enable him to regain his human shape. With careful ministration, the process of Eustace's regeneration, described through baptismal imagery, is completed: the undressing, the peeling off of Eustace's dragon skin, the throwing of Eustace into the water, and Aslan's dressing him in new clothes. As a result, in regaining his humanity through interaction with Aslan, Eustace loses his sloth and hostility to others—even to Reepicheep. He is accepted into the community of the other travelers as a committed member (of the church by analogy), since one of Lewis's strong beliefs about worship is that it must be done in fellowship with others.

The iconic image of Aslan as a persistent Christ figure who enters a human life and transforms a willing soul into participation in such a fellowship is obvious here, as it was in *MN*, in *LWW*, in *HHB*, and will be seen in *SC* and *LB*. For, as Alister McGrath states, "We [Christians] are not meant to travel alone" (27). So this garden where Eustace is restored is the Garden of Restoration (1) and Aslan is the gardener as he was described in *MN*, planting the apple tree and healing souls. Eustace will forever remember this garden as a place of regeneration through Aslan's love. However, he does not remember its specific location or the means of getting there. Like the Garden of Restoration (2) at the end of *VDT*, and like the Celestial Garden in *LB*, this garden, which mirrors both of them, does not conform to laws of space and time.

B. The Garden of Restoration (2)

The last tableau in *VDT* incorporates all the motifs of the garden that have been discussed in previous sections. It, however, is the most sublime so far. All laws of space and time are broken. At the end of their voyage,

> They [the three children and Reepicheep] saw a wonder ahead. It was as if a wall stood up between them and the sky, a greenish-gray, trembling, shimmering wall. Then up came the sun, and at its first rising they saw it through the wall and it turned into wonderful rainbow colors. Then they knew that the wall was really a long, tall wave—a wave endlessly fixed in one place as you may often see at the edge of a waterfall. (263-64)

The shimmering high wave, like a waterfall, that seems to be a boundary between the Narnian world and Aslan's, is surmounted only by Reepicheep, who goes over it in his coracle. He has already attained the state analogous to the state of sainthood in our world and does not need, like the children, to wade into the calm water (their final stage of regeneration). In the Judeo-Christian tradition, the terrestrial paradise is separated from the rest of the world by a body of water instead of a wall, based on Ezekiel 47 and Rev. 22.1: "And he shewed me a pure river of water of life, clear as crystal, proceeding out of the throne of God and the Lamb." For example, the island of earthly paradise in *Saynt Branden* is full of ripe fruits, clear light, and precious stones. Like Aslan's Country, it is at the farthest eastward edge of the world, from which it is separated by a body of water: "For on that other fyde of this water may no man come that is in this life" (sig. 10ʳ). In his vision the medieval *Pearl* poet describes a stream between him and paradise. In *Till We Have Faces* (1957) Lewis describes a stream separating the god-like Psyche from Orual (174). There is also a waterfall functioning as a boundary between the Created and Celestial Gardens and the rest of Nania in *MN* and *LB*, respectively.

Even the huge sun is not an obstacle to their vision. Beyond it the four travelers can see the high green mountains of Aslan's Country—beyond the borders of the world, which they will later climb in *LB* toward the Celestial Garden. As the sun rises, the sight of the mountains disappears, again suggesting that light (Christ) is the source of all meaning in the universe. This dynamic scene integrates all natural motifs of the Narnian landscape (light, green mountains, trees, and water) with Aslan to suggest that Narnia and Aslan's Country are actually linked, and Aslan is the Bridge Builder. This tableau invites readers to conceive that the loci of our experience are in a real sense spiritually meaningful. Lewis himself states in *Miracles* that the physical and spiritual are actually one: "That archaic sort of thinking will become simply the correct sort when Nature and Spirit are fully harmonized—when Spirit rides Nature so perfectly that the two together make rather a *Centaur* than a mounted knight" (164).

A short time later, the children wade into the calm water (the final stage of regeneration) to get to a flat, green meadow where, sure enough, sky and water meet. There is a blue wall of glass. "But between them and the foot of the sky there was something so white on the green grass that even with their eagles' eyes they could hardly look at it. They came on and saw that it was a Lamb (267-68). Aslan's light shines more and more intensely on the children as they approach the destination of their pilgrimage. This scene parallels St. Paul's description of the transformation of Jesus's followers when the light of the Gospel should shine on their faces (2 Cor. 4.6). As the British children approach Aslan's Country, his glory shines on them because they are entering into his country. Then, as they eat the fish offered by the Lamb, suggesting the Eucharist, the Lamb transforms into Aslan: "Then all in one moment there was a rending of the blue wall (like a curtain being torn) and a terrible white light from beyond the sky" (270). In this great scene of revelation, the children, as a group, are rewarded after their struggles with a direct experience of Aslan's presence. However, this is not the Celestial Garden, the final destination of the voyagers in the *Chronicles*. For after restoring their spirits, Aslan sends them back to earth. Being in this garden is a process of baptizing their imagination and heart, a rehearsal for the apocalypse in *LB*. Edmund Spenser also describes the Garden of Adonis in *FQ*, after which the travelers are sent forth "[i]nto the world, it to replenish more" (3.6. 36.1-2).

The iconography in these last two scenes, the richest yet in *VDT*, pulls together all the preceding motifs in a glorious finale, an intensely powerful *eucatastrophe*, a truly iconic scene. Aslan's country in *VDT* with all these iconic images—its rising sun, its spreading rainbow colors, and its fragrant smells and musical sounds—is clearly an analogue to an earthly paradise and so a part of a sacred cosmos. The Lamb and the white light (magnified so that it is all that the children see for one moment) are icons of Christ (the Lamb of God who takes away the sins of the world) and can also be perceived as "the fruitfulness of Christ's union with the church" (Stanley Stewart 168). The green meadow is one of the traditional motifs of the earthly and celestial gardens. The image of glass is right out of the description of the New Jerusalem in Revelation: "And before the throne *there was* a sea of glass like unto crystal" and "the city *was* pure gold, like unto clear glass" (Rev. 4.6 and 21.18, respectively). In a relevant remark, Aldous Huxley points out that glass was valued in the Middle Ages specifically for its vision-inducing features, which led to the installation of stained-glass windows in cathedrals (108-09). Also, "The Welsh had a blessed land called Yrisvitrin, the Isle of Glass" (101). The last island in *The Lyfe of Saynt Branden* bears similarities to Aslan's Country as mentioned earlier. All the natural icons in the East of Narnia are integrated in this collage with Aslan at the center. This scene is the perfect example of *theōsis*, with the characters in close communion with Aslan.

Lewis is deliberate in portraying the physical ambiguity of Aslan's Country. Children and readers are left with bewildering instructions on how to find Aslan's Country again. Aslan tells the children that he can be reached "from [their] own world" (268) or from all worlds (269), direction being of no importance. Earlier, as already shown, Eustace was mysteriously transported by Aslan to a green garden with a well on top of a mountain to be transformed back into a boy. But we were never told where the mountain was specifically located. Aslan's Country in the East, the Garden of Restoration, like the Celestial Garden, is not topos-centered. It is a Utopia (a No-Place), at the same time that it is a Pantopia (All-Places). As George Sayer maintains, "We are in Aslan's Country usually without knowing it" (317). The paradox of the East can be better understood if it is viewed more as a form of relationship with Christ than a physical place in Lewis's fictional cosmos. Maybe Reepicheep is our best guide after all: it is a place "where sky and water meet"—and land, one might add, the three main divisions of the cosmos. They form a composite vision of earthly images to mirror a more significant union of the two realms: the earth and the spirit, the human and God. Nancy-Lou Patterson remarks, "Christian writings must be always striving to include rather than exclude." She quotes the words of John Oxenham's hymn: "'In Christ there is no East or West, / In him no South or North'" ("Narnia and the North" 16).[6] These images of life transform the East from a physical geographical place to a Garden of Restoration in readers' hearts.

IV. The Celestial Garden in *The Last Battle*

In *LB* the old Narnia is destroyed, leveled with water and blighted by total darkness. All Narnians, including the Pevensie children, are actually dead in the human sense, and so are liberated from time and space, ready to enter Aslan's real country if they believe in him. The procession of Aslan and his followers up to the Celestial Garden includes a landscape, ambiguous in its geographical location, and with traditional garden motifs discussed earlier. A gentle daylight shines over the landscape. In proximity to the garden proper, there is the Great Waterfall mentioned earlier as one of the boundaries in *MN*, dividing Aslan's Edenic Garden from Narnia. Water is abundant. There are blue lakes and "tons of water every second, flashing like diamonds in some places and dark, glassy green in others" (215). As they go through the Great Waterfall they go "up and up, with all kinds of reflected lights flashing . . . from the water and all manner of colored stones flashing through it, till it seemed as if [they] were climbing up light itself" (217). This is the final metamorphosis from shadowlands to light, from dream to an everlasting morning. The motifs of transfiguration and regeneration are all present here in this powerful pageant, which expresses the motifeme of Resurrection. Jewels and glass pertain to the heavenly Jerusalem as has been discussed in the section on *VDT*. And as readers have been expecting all along, there, on top of "a smooth green hill" (219) lies the Celestial Garden, complete with a green wall enclosing trees with leaves like silver and fruits like gold.

Thus the final destination of Aslan's followers, the Celestial Garden, includes the most powerful and intense motifs of all gardens that hark back to the Miltonic/classical garden of *MN*, but with no evil being in it (Rev. 21.18-22). Furthermore, the garden has great golden gates that swing open only to Aslan's followers, and they enter "into the delicious smell that blew toward them out of that garden, into the cool mixture of sunlight and shadow under the trees, walking on springy turf that was all dotted with white flowers" (222). This passage is redolent with Christ's presence: the "sunlight" is an icon of Christ; the "shadow" takes us back to Song of Solomon 2.3 and *MN*, with the apple tree representing Christ and the beloved (the soul) sitting "under his shadow with great delight"; the white flowers with their heavenly fragrances allude to Christ (Rhodes and Davidson 88) and to the Edenic garden in *MN*. To round out the picture of this Celestial Garden, a phoenix perches on one of the trees. Used by Lactanius for his own Christian purposes in *Carmen de Ave Phoenice*, the phoenix is mentioned as an inhabitant of paradise (Pearsall and Salter 65; *The Discarded Image* 150). Generally, the phoenix is a symbol of Christ's resurrection. It is important to note that Lewis is careful to describe these pleasures of paradise as sensual experiences first that are later transmuted into a resounding experience of eternal Joy.

Finally, inside the garden, at the top of the green hill, which seems bigger on the inside than on the outside, the travelers are treated to an Olympian view of the real Narnia. To their amazement (and the readers') Aslan's garden is at the center of all real worlds. All mountains with the gardens on top of them discussed earlier are part of one great chain of mountains that circles all real worlds, including the "real" England: the Created Garden in *MN*, the Gardens of Restoration in *VDT*, Aslan's Country beyond the sea—are all "spurs jutting out from the great mountains of Aslan" (226). The voyagers, and we, have reached the center, the final destination of the *Chronicles,* the Christ at the center of our world. "Here, then the blessed will find themselves translated from the thorny world to a place where only the 'flow'rs of grace' and all good things grow—a place safe at last from the ravages of the anti-gardener Satan and from all earthly anxiety" (Rhodes and Davidson 95). Lucy and the Faun, who are the most philosophical of all humans and Talking Animals in Narnia, apprehend the ambiguous structure of this quest early on but can only explain it in paradoxes. It is like an onion, says Tumnus, where "each circle is larger than the last" (225), or like a stable, concludes Lucy, where "it is far bigger inside than it was outside" (224). The movement towards the garden is a physical and spiritual elevation like Jacob's vision (Gen 28.12) or the lifting up of St. Paul on the road to Damascus. In a Platonic sense, everything and everybody is absorbed into their antitypes.

LB, like the other chronicles, ends in a pageant, a truly communal experience, with everyone walking in a bright procession towards high green mountains, sweet orchards, and flashing waterfalls, one above the other (227). Finally, Aslan re-appears, "leaping down from cliff to cliff like a living cataract of power and beauty" (227), an image reminiscent of the beloved in Song Solomon 2.8: "[B]ehold, he cometh leaping upon the mountains, skipping upon the hills." No tame lion, Aslan, like Christ, pursues his followers unabashedly and finally reverses the catastrophes of Narnia to restore his elect to the Celestial Garden. The Celestial Garden is an analogue of the Christian Heaven, although it has no specific geometrical shape; nor is it symbolically oriented like the four-square biblical City of God with jeweled streets, or like the *Pearl* poet's vision of Heaven, for example. It is not an artificial garden like Guillaume de Lorris's *Roman de la Rose*, but more like the enclosed garden of de Meun's, where there is no deceit, misery, or death, and nature is whole and more beautiful than ever. It is the "real" garden, the spiritual center of Narnia. The Real Narnia is bigger than cities. It is a cosmos, the "center" of any universe, where all levels of life intersect without beginnings or end. Moreover, it is fluid, ever-changing, becuase Lewis's purpose is to present the journey to the Celestial Garden as a dynamic, mystical experience of infolding in Aslan beyond space and time, as Christians are "in-Godded" when they are transported into God and enter His garden to partake of His divine nature. Hence the lack of specificity in geography and location.

Moreover, the ending of *LB* is a *eucatastrophe* of gigantic proportions, with Aslan and his followers mounting "further up and further in" with unflagging energy—another example of what the good meant to Lewis. As he states in *Spenser's Images*, far more often "good is a matter of knightly quests, of dances, revels, and love-making, of 'skipping like wanton kids,' of romping" (94). All this energy abounds in this final pageant, a procession to Aslan's Country, the Celestial Garden. Aslan, while remote in some ways and not tame, has a warm and personal relationship with his followers. He inspires with his physical presence and Grace. As Michael Ward states, "Lewis's model of the universe has standing room for bleakness but no throne" (211). In receiving His grace, one becomes, "like a tree planted by the rivers of water, that bringeth forth his fruit in his season; his leaf also shall not wither; and whatsoever he doeth shall prosper" (Ps. 1.3)—an appropriate image to end the discussion on the Celestial Garden. So are we in our world directly connected to Heaven through Christ, the Bridge Builder.

V. Minor Gardens in Narnia

There are other minor gardens in Narnia that are used for specific literary purposes. In *HHB*, as if the intensity of the racial contrast between the Calormenes and the Narnians were too much, Lewis gives his readers a reprieve by describing a garden, albeit a minor one, to take readers' minds off of the social issues and distinctions he has been building up. When Shasta is captured by King Edmund, he is taken to "a courtyard which was also a garden. A marble basin of clear water in the center was kept continuously rippling by the fountain that fell into it. Orange trees grew round it out of smooth grass, and the four white walls which surrounded the lawn were covered with climbing roses" (63). This medieval-or Renaissance-like garden is refreshing after the miserable scenes in the streets of Tashbaan. It represents a type of an earthly, secular garden, a reprieve from the crowded urban center with all its social issues. However, the garden is an example of artifice and hardly sacramental like the three major gardens in Narnia.

There are two other evocative scenes of beautiful landscape in *HHB* that may suggest an Edenic garden. Running away from the Tisroc's palace, Aravis finds herself out "in midstream with a huge real moon overhead and a huge reflected moon down, deep down, in the river. The air was fresh and cool and as she drew near the farther bank she heard the hooting of an owl. 'Ah! That's better!' thought Aravis" (134). Later on, the moon reveals to Shasta and his companions a valley, a river with soft grass along its sides and flowery shrubs, a glimpse of an Edenic garden, reminiscent of Lewis's experiences with S*ehnsucht*. Further north, near Anvard, the capital city of Archenland, there is a partial archetype of an Edenic garden in the House of the Hermit. When Shasta and his group enter the gate of his house in the green wall,

> They were in a wide and perfectly circular enclosure, protected by a high wall of green turf. A pool of perfectly still water, so full that the water was almost exactly level with the ground, lay before him. At one end of the pool, completely overshadowing it with its branches, there grew the hugest and most beautiful tree that Shasta had ever seen. Beyond the pool was a little low house of stone roofed with deep and ancient thatch. There was a sound of bleating and over at the far end of the enclosure there were some goats. The level ground was covered with the finest grass . . . It was a very peaceful place, lonely and quiet. (154-55, 159)

The greenery suggests fertility and abundance. The body of water is calm and temperate, like the sea close to Aslan's Country later on in *VDT*. The house of stone suggests the stone table in *LWW*, ancient in its roots though not a place of sacrifice. The hermit's home may also be linked to Ramandu's cave, Ramandu being another hermit/wise *magia* figure in *VDT*. The hermit in *HHB* heals Aravis's wound and grooms the tired horses. He is a spiritual advisor, instructing Aravis about the fact that there is no such thing as luck, but "there is something about this that I do not understand," he says (158). His house and garden represent a type of the earthly garden in Narnia, but, although they lack grace, they are open to it since Aslan visits the garden to empower Aravis and the depressed Bree as he had empowered Shasta on his journey to Anvard from the Hermit's House.

Another enchanting garden exists in *SC*, Aslan's garden, a piece of Aslan's Country. From Experiment House (a progressive school) in England Jill Pole and Eustace Scrub arrive in this Secondary World where they are greeted with a "blaze of *sunshine*" and "smooth turf, smoother and brighter than Jill had ever seen before, and blue sky, and darting to and fro, things so bright that they might have been *jewels* or huge *butterflies*" (10-11, italics mine).

This passage reminds one of the strong light and intensity of colors that, according to J. R. R. Tolkien, a fairy tale provides (see

Fig. 12. The butterfly soul flies free of the mortal body on classical memorials of the dead, as on this Roman cameo portrait. (Warner fig. 21).

introduction). Lewis here focuses our attention on specific paradisiacal motifs which he associates with Aslan: of particular importance is the sun whose existence the Green Witch of the Underland will insistently deny. As mentioned earlier, the sun is the symbol of life and Christ; the jewels are scriptural imagery; and butterflies are symbols of the soul and resurrection (Mary Bernetta Quinn 229).[7] Marina Warner indicates that butterflies figured as the soul in ancient Egypt and Rome (see fig. 12). They occur in the early Christian imagery of the creation of Adam and Eve, for example in the mosaics of San Marco, Venice. *Psyche* is also Greek for "butterfly" and "moth" (Aristotle, *Historia Animalium* 551^a 14; see Warner 90). Warner also writes that the "angelic butterfly" in Dante's *Purgatorio* (10.121-26) is an image of the "etherealized self," the essence, the soul (84), a most appropriate image to suggest Aslan's Country (what our Heaven is supposed to be in Narnia). Birds also, in all their different types and colors, with "yellow, as dragonfly blue, or rainbow plumage" (*SC* 13) are also symbolic of the soul.

The Gardens of Narnia

The running water, "the stream, bright as glass" is a reminder of heaven, as the water of life. Jill drinks from it and finds it "the coldest, most refreshing water she had ever tasted" (21). It is antithetical to the dark waters of the sunless sea in Underland, the city of the Green Witch, to which they will travel to rescue Prince Rilian. The stream in Aslan's Country recalls the stream in *PC* of "liquid glass," the agent of King Caspian's resurrection. It also recalls the "drinkable light," Reepicheep's description of the sweet water near Aslan's Country in *VDT*. This section on Aslan's Country in *SC* is Lewis's rendition through his own imagery of Psalm 118.23: "This *is* the Lord's doing; it is marvelous in our eyes." It is as if Lewis is filling the imagination of Jill and his readers with intense colors and beautiful imagery of the wonders possible in Narnia, to be held in memory and used as shields against the later mental assault of the Green Witch on them and Prince Rilian. Thus prepared, with the water of life as one of her shields (John 4.14), Jill, is ready to learn from Aslan about her and Eustace's quest: i.e., to seek and find the lost Prince Rilian, die in the attempt, or else go back to their world. This shield of beauty, coupled with the shield of memory, does work eventually to help in the children's rescue of Prince Rilian.

This study of the Narnian gardens has been an attempt to reconstruct the classical and Christian traditions that Lewis resourced in describing the gardens in the *Chronicles* and shows him to be on a par with his great predecessors. Lewis used these garden motifs as settings to suggest the struggles in the depth of the Christian soul, the restoration of the soul through grace, and the union of the soul with Christ, i.e., *thèōsis*. The enclosed garden with its silver and golden fruit, heavenly scent, and golden gates, perched on top of a hill or mountain is the garden of the human soul, the church, and the real heavenly abode of all Christians who received salvation. Whether Lewis's gardens focus on cultivating and caring for fruits and trees, on the state of regeneration in the presence of the Lamb, or on the final state of being with Aslan, their iconography speaks to the Christian soul and inspires it with longing for the lost paradise.

As has been shown, the garden is a major image in Lewis's *Chronicles*, and his integration of classical/Christian motifs drawn from earlier authors endows it with an iconic role and thus credibility to suggest the story of the Gospel from Creation to Redemption. Furthermore, there is a clear movement in the chronological order of the gardens in *Chronicles*. As the story of the chronicles unfolds, the garden becomes more of a locus for unitive and communal experience than for individual transformation and purgation. Lewis suggests the significance of the community in the Christian experience, the belief that a true Christian does not worship in isolation, but develops in relationship with others. In a letter to his father dated March 27, 1948, Lewis turned to the garden as an image of hope in a turbulent world. He writes, "I have always believed that Voltaire, infidel that he was, thought aright in that admonition of his to cultivate your own garden" (*CL* 2: 844).

In 1961, he turned to the image of the garden again, but poignantly this time. In true Renaissance fashion, he compares his wife Joy, who had already preceded him in death, to "a garden. Like a nest of gardens, wall within wall, hedge within hedge, more secret, more full of fragrant and fertile life, the further you entered" (*A Grief Observed* 73). In this image he unites his sensual and spiritual love and indicates the strong links between the Good, the True, and the Beautiful.

Endnotes

1. Joe R. Christopher, in an article entitled "Mount Purgatory Arises Near Narnia" in *Mythlore: A Journal of J. R. R. Tolkien, C.S. Lewis, Charles Williams, and Mythopoeic Literature* 23.2 (Spring 2001) 65-90, discusses the garden imagery mostly in relationship to Dante's garden of Eden in *Purgatorio* and provides different details on Lewis's garden in *The Magician's Nephew* and John Milton's *Paradise Lost* from those in my paper.

2. Alain Corbin classifies gardens according to a Platonic order into 1) paradise, representing the divine order 2) the princely garden representing sovereign power, and 3) the productive garden representing the working man (286).

3. The underlying linguistic theory of Lewis, which is based upon the sacramental power of words, was discussed in chapter 3.

4. This action is the essence of fraud, heavily punished in Dante's *Inferno* (cantos 18-29) and *FQ*, as seen through, for example, the exposure of the false Duessa's filthy nature (1.8) and the capture of Archimago (1.12).

5. This section on *VDT* has already been published. See Salwa Khoddam, "Where Sky and Water Meet: Christian Iconography in C.S. Lewis's *The Voyage of the Dawn Treader*" in *Mythlore: A Journal of J. R. R. Tolkien, C.S. Lewis, Charles Williams, and Mythopoeic Literature* 23.2 (Spring 2001) 36-52.

6. In *The Pilgrim's Regress* also John's journey to the West actually takes him to the Eastern Mountains for the "only way to go is East" (Grand Rapids, MI: Eerdmans, 1992) 71.

7. The story of how Venus turned one of her nymphs, Astery, into a butterfly is treated in Spenser's *Muiopotmos* based on Ovid and *Apuleius* (Hulse 256). The butterfly links the realms of gods and humans. For an ironic view of the butterfly see Chaucer's "The Nun's Priest Tale."

CHAPTER EIGHT

The Ship, the Bifurcated Sea, and the Sea Serpent in The Voyage of the Dawn Treader

Where Sky and Water meet:
Where Waves grow sweet,
Doubt not, Reepicheep
There is the utter East.
    VDT (248)

Who fares on sea may not command his way.
    Edmund Spenser *FQ* (2)

The sea voyage, as a motifeme, accrues philosophical and religious meanings, if its travelers have heroic aspirations rather than commercial ones. For example, rather than wandering aimlessly on the sea like Spenser's Phaedria floating on the Idle Lake in her little gondelay, heroes must sail towards a specific place, searching for a missing person, or escaping to a microcosm where they can question moral and social conventions. The sea can provide a context for these purposes, which can transform humans into better people. Also, sea travelers were brought face to face with harsh realities and dangers, most obviously shipwrecks. One can interpret these hardships as metamorphic experiences, for shipwrecks can result in redirection in one's life. Loss and suffering can be evangelic and turn people hopeful. A deep immersion in the sea's depth can lead to a "sea change," a realization producing valuable insights (Muscogiuri 209). It can also serve as a test for the helmsmen, because "[t]he success of the navigator depends on his ability to master or collaborate with the power of the sea," writes Philip Edwards in his analysis of the symbolism of the sea in books 3 and 4 of *FQ* (32). Voyaging, for Francis Bacon, was also symbolic of the process of amassing knowledge. The image of the ship sailing beyond the Columns of Hercules, thought by classical thinkers an infraction since these columns represented the limits of the known world (see ch. 1), is to Bacon a positive image of intellectual adventure and discovery: "Why should a few received authors stand up like Hercules' Columns, beyond which there should be no sailing, or discovering?" (*Advancement of Learning* 2.75). Also, a sea journey usually involves contact with cities, courts, countries, and islands, "symbols of all man's subconscious longing for happiness, love, freedom from responsibility and the chance of a fresh start" (La Croix 8). In his long adventure on the island, Robinson Crusoe concludes that it has "delivered" him (Seidel 70).

In its picaresque form as a sea journey to the East, *VDT* is filled with cities and islands as points of departure and destination that function as places of sin or redemption. This long journey provides Lewis with ample opportunities to create moments of intersection between the voyagers and Aslan (the true pilot of the ship). Lewis makes it clear at the very beginning that the sea voyage has heroic, noble aspirations, not mercantile or commercial ones. On the frame narrative or diachronic level, its purpose is to search for the seven missing Narnian lords, sent away earlier by the usurping King Miraz in *PC* on an ostensibly mercantile mission to explore the sea beyond the Lone Islands in the East, but actually to rid himself of them. The noble mission of this sea voyage is repeatedly impressed upon the reader by using the sea journey and the direction of the East as metaphors. This chapter will focus on interpreting the sea voyage to the East as a metaphor or motifeme of life's journey between profane and sacred places, ending in restoration with Aslan as the true navigator who integrates the sea journey with the spiritual transformation of his characters and, indirectly, of Lewis's readers. According to Robert de la Croix, islands are symbols of human longing for happiness, love, freedom from responsibility. Most importantly for this study, islands open a "door of escape into the unknown" (8). Lewis's voyage in *VDT* touches on all these types of voyages. It involves heroes, a shipwreck and certainly a "sea change" in the characters. But the basic image of the bifurcated sea and sea-serpent form the core of the story, give it shape, and exemplify the theme of metamorphosis.

I. The Bifurcated Sea

Sea adventure stories, which flourished in the age of exploration in Europe, belong to a genre with a long history. They are built on a rich, pre-Christian iconographic tradition of the sea as remote and terrifying, involving such motifs as storms and storm-tossed ships, islands, savages, and, especially before the age of oceanography, sea-monsters. The non-seafaring Hebrews and the seafaring Greeks and Romans equally condemned the sea. Early Christians joined forces with these people but differed in their own belief that the sea is paradoxically the source of death and life (see ch. 1). This bifurcated view of the sea is clear in St. Augustine's *De beata vita* (*The Happy Life*) as both a symbol of death (and thus diabolic) and a source of life (and thus salvific). In this work, St. Augustine compares the journey of life towards philosophy, which grants happiness, to a journey over the sea with human beings as sailors. Along this journey, he writes, there might be a tempest "that to fools would appear adverse [but which might] cast us, without our being aware, from our erroneous course to some most welcome haven" (Schopp 41).[1]

The bifurcated view of the sea as both diabolic and baptismal, a metaphor of fallen human nature as well as its redemption, is reconciled in the Christian view (see ch. 1). A medieval riddle (# 81) suggests that water brings blessing, yet it is the most devouring of all things (qtd. in Black 31). Philip Edwards writes, "The sea which indicates calamity and affliction also indicates baptism" (77). It is the storm-tossed sea as well as the waters stilled by Christ. While one's own navigation contributes to smooth sailing, "God is the owner of the ship and Christ is the pilot" (Clement's letter to James, qtd. in Daniélou 58).[2] The sea, with all its conflicting meanings, is an instrument to carry out God's plan for all history. This bifurcated view of the sea inspired the plot structure and the metamorphic imagery of Lewis's *VDT*. Lewis, like other Christians, embraces the classic and Hebraic view of the monster-torn, storm-tossed sea of adversity and evil and conflates it with the Christian view of the sea as baptismal, its waters stilled by Christ.

II. The Voyage to the East

Throughout their harrowing experience in the storm, in the black cloud and with the sea serpent, the travelers in *VDT* become aware of the demonic aspect of the sea early on. However, this view in this story will eventually be subsumed by the affirmative view of the sea as an instrument of salvation that facilitates the travelers' journey to the East and thus to a state of redemption. This bifurcated view of the sea is at the foundation of any symbolic interpretation of it in *VDT*. To develop his thematic strands, Lewis adopts this Augustinian view and synchronizes it with other motifs from classical, Judeo-Christian stories, as well as early adventure sea voyages, some recorded in Richard Haklyut's *The Principall Navigations Voyages Traffiques and Discoveries of the English Nation* (1589). Lewis enjoyed reading Haklyut (*CL* 1: 243) and allots a brief section to him in *English Literature* (1954), although he writes, "Haklyut deserves a chapter" (437). He had perused Haklyut's work in preparation for writing *English Literature* and praises him for "his scientific zeal, his patriotism, and his 'huge toile'" as a collector and editor of travel stories (437). Lewis states that some of these travel stories might have come out of Rider Haggard (437), an author whose novels he greatly admired and drew upon in *MN*.[3] The common motifs of sea travel literature that appear in *VDT* are the islands, tempest, ship, sea serpent, dark cloud, and underwater garden city. The metaphoric sea voyage in *VDT* is thus the diachronic frame upon which he builds his major theme of metamorphosis through Aslan, which runs throughout the *Chronicles*.

In the first part of *VDT*, King Caspian and his retinue set sail from Cair Paravel, his capital, a modified type of the City of God, as discussed in chapter 6, and, after being joined by the English children, continue to sail eastward to the Lone Islands, Dragon Island, Burnt Island, Deathwater Island, The Island of Voices, the Dark Island, and Ramandu's Island, in that order. None of the travelers has experiential knowledge of the East, their destination, because no one had been there before. In Lewis's sea voyage, sin is spread across all the islands on the itinerary. After Prince Caspian had sailed from the Island of Brenn, the British children come on board from England (the Primary World) through the painting of a Narnian ship in the back bedroom of Aunt Alberta's house, where they are staying. It is Lucy who first notices that the ship seems to be moving, and, moments later, the children are swept into the waters and onto the *Dawn Treader*. The transformation of the painting from inanimate to animate makes possible the plot, of course, and the pilgrimage that leads to the children's regeneration. It also sets up the series of incidents of metamorphosis, the quickening of souls and natural objects in a dynamic universe, a major theme in all the *Chronicles*, this time in *VDT* over and through the waters of the sea.

A. Island of Slavery

The next stop for the children is the island of Felilimath, one of the Lone Islands. At first glance it seems like a Spenserian Isle of Delight. Lucy enjoys the "downy turf," "the sand pleasant to her feet," and the "lark singing" (*VDT* 41). However, this island turns out to be the island of the slave trader Peg. Caspian and the British children, except Eustace, are captured to be sold as slaves, but the man who bought Caspian turns out to be the Lord Bern, one of the missing Narnian knights. They are taken to the port city of governor Gumpas in the Lone Islands, a city of slave trade, living on "broken hearts" (85) where Talking Animals, like Reepicheep, are considered "beasts" to be sold as slaves (43). Any blight that happens to these animals in the *Chronicles* occurs under a tyrannous regime: the petrified animals under Jadis in *LWW*, the enslaved Hwin and Bree in the city of Tashbaan in *HHB*, and the captive animals under King Miraz in *PC* and the Telmarines in *LB*. The governor's quarters portray the lazy bureaucracy of the island, which is considered "progress" by Gumpas. His city is, on a small scale, a type of Babylon that had become a city of merchants trading with all kinds of merchandise, including "slaves and souls of men" (Rev. 18. 11-17). The governor himself is "a bilious-looking man with hair that had once been red and now mostly gray" (58), an allusion to the color of Judas's hair as conceived in religious tradition. When Gumpas is confronted by King Caspian, he defends himself with bureaucratic buzz words, "Nothing in the minutes. We have not been notified of any such thing. All irregular. Happy to consider any applications—" (59).

The port city is soon overturned by the bravery and courage of the Narnian travelers and Lord Bern, who is installed as the new governor of the Lone Islands. The adventure terminates in a feast on the island of Avra, Lord Bern's estate. This experience on the Lone Islands suggests the Odysseus-like cunning strategy of the Narnians and the heroic actions of Caspian in confronting the evil Gumpas and abolishing the slave trade. In this vignette, Lewis underscores the noble cause of the voyage as opposed to the commercial and colonizing motives of many of the voyages of exploration that began in the Renaissance, like the voyages of Sir Francis Drake and others recorded in Haklyut. Like Spenser and Milton before him, Lewis condemns slavery which is associated with colonization and the use of the sea for self-serving mercantile interests (see ch. 1).

B. The Storm

A sea voyage could not be complete without a storm, so Lewis offers us one in *VDT*. The storm portrays the violent aspect of the sea as part of its tradition. Horror follows brief, delightful experiences at sea after the confrontation with Gumpas, the slave trader, on the Lone Islands.

Lucy spends her time looking at the reflection of sunlit waters on the ceiling each morning and watching the sea getting brighter blue and the weather warmer each day. Suddenly, one evening the storm strikes. Lucy sees

> a great rack of clouds building itself up in the west with amazing speed. Then a gap was torn in it and a yellow sunset poured through the gap. All the waves behind them seemed to take on unusual shapes and the sea was a drab or yellowish color like dirty canvas. . . . In a moment everyone became frantically busy. The hatches were battened down, the galley fire was put out, men went aloft to reef the sail. Before they had finished the storm struck them. It seemed to Lucy that a great valley in the sea opened just before their bows, and they rushed down into it, a deeper down than she would have believed possible. A great gray hill of water, far higher than the mast, rushed to meet them; it looked certain death but they were tossed to the top of it. Then the ship seemed to spin around. A cataract of water poured over the deck; the poop and forecastle were like two islands with a fierce sea between them. (71-72)

For a time, the sea looks like the abyss of Chaos that Milton describes before the creation of the world (*PL* 2.898-1044). It is like Spenser's "watry wildernesse" (*FQ* 2.12.29.9) and "raging seas" (*FQ* 1.11.21.1). W. H. Auden's remark about the ship being "a metaphor for society in danger" (8) applies here since the storm reflects the violation in the kingdom, i.e., Miraz's earlier usurpation of the throne of Narnia and the missing seven knights.

Aside from reflecting the demonic aspect of the sea, the tempest functions also as a moral test of courage. It recalls St. Paul's shipwreck narrative (Acts 27), thus adding a Christian dimension. Lewis's powerful description of this storm is in the tradition of early English voyagers' graphic tales like those recorded by Haklyut and Maunderville. For example, one storm from the voyage of the Earl of Cumberland in 1509, described by Edward Wright and recorded in Haklyut, bears some similarities to the storm in *VDT*: "The raging waves and foaming surges of the sea came rowling like mountains one after another, and overraked the waste of the shippe like a mightie river running over it" (7: 25). Lewis's "hill of water" and a "cataract of water" are close to Haklyut's "mountains" of water. Here is a similar image of the storm, this time from Sir Francis Drake's three terrifying encounters with the sea recorded in the *The World Encompassed* (1638): "The seas, which by nature and of themselues are heauie, and of weightie substance, were rowled up from the depths, even from the roots of the rockes, as if it had beene a scroll of parchment, which by the extremity of heate runneth together" (qtd. in Terneer 165). Some of these overwhelming tempests caused shipwrecks that could be viewed as metaphors of defeat, suffering, and loss. But Drake and his voyagers were delivered "by the mercy of God" and went on to new discoveries about the geography of the Pacific (Haklyut 12: 160). In the case of *VDT*, the storm functions as a test of survival and skill in resisting evil forces. The storm is soon over and one can attribute the survival of the travelers (only one fell overboard) to the skill of the pilots, at least on the frame level, for Aslan has not appeared yet. Both these incidents recall the Augustinian bifurcated view of the sea as ostensibly diabolic but salvific as well.

In *VDT*, the storm also exposes the perversion inherent in Eustace's soul. His derogatory remarks, whinings, and grumblings are recorded in a journal during the storm (he describes himself as "kidnapped"), as well as his "Dream City of Technology," which includes all comforts and physical stuff like saloons and radios, motorboats (not sailboats), aeroplanes, and submarines (30-31). By putting these dreams in the mind of the least favorite child in the *Chronicles*, the unregenerate Edmund in *LWW* coming in close second, Lewis makes his negative views on modern technological "progress" clear. Eustace will, on the next island, be changed into a dragon temporarily, for his material greed and chronological snobbery. Eustace's Dream City represents in the *Chronicles* a city of material consumption estranged from the self and nature, prone to the onslaughts of scientism, which is the *bête noire* in Lewis's philosophy. (See ch. 7).

C. The Sea Serpent

After the travelers recover from the storm and the dramatic incident of metamorphosis on Dragon Island, which brings relief to the travelers, the plot continues to unfold, leading to the encounter with the sea serpent, another traditional component of the sea adventure story, perhaps the most powerful. Aside from sea storms and shipwrecks, responsible for the horror of the sea aroused in the imagination of the classic, medieval, and Renaissance writers, there are also the monsters of the deep. These denizens of the sea are diverse. There are the mermen and mermaids that appear in fine weather. But there are also the fierce sea monsters of classical mythology, the most horrific being Scylla, who sat on nearby cliffs along the shores of the Strait of Sicily, with its three rows of teeth and barking like a dog, waiting to pounce and snatch her victims (*Odyssey* 12. 109-110; there is also Charybdis, the whirlpool that swallows and vomits sailors). Then there are the underwater monsters that Beowulf had to kill, notably Grendel's mother. There are also the whale and an octopus-looking monster called the Kraken, which were often mistaken for islands by sailors and gave rise to the myth of the floating islands (Pontoppidan 212; Frederic Moorman 44). But according to Erich Pontoppidan, a member of the Royal Academy of Sciences at Cophenhagen, the sea-snake, s*erpens marinus magnus*, is the most horrific infernal creature. Sometimes called a dragon, it is 600 English feet in length and can sink ships by coiling around them (195-203).

This serpent may be the biblical Leviathan, Behemoth, or the Dragon of the Ocean (Pontoppidan 204), equivalent to the ghoulish Scylla of classical mythology. This Hebraic monster has a long history. It is mentioned in Psalm 104 as evidence of God's glory and might: "O Lord how manifold are thy works! / . . . *So is* this great and wide sea, wherein *are* things creeping innumerable, both small and great beasts. / There go the ships: *there is* that Leviathan, *whom* thou hast made to play therein" (24-26). Job also attests to the power of God who "formed the crooked serpent" (26.13). God describes the Leviathan's extreme power, which only He can dominate (Job 41). In Job 40. 15-24 he is called Behemoth. God's punishment of the Leviathan is described also in Isaiah 27.1: "In that day the Lord with his sore and great and strong sword shall punish leviathan the piercing serpent . . . . and he shall slay the dragon that *is* in the sea." In the Book of Revelation, the Leviathan/dragon/Satan is cast out into the earth (12.9). It was a common belief that the dragon slain by the archangel St. Michael rose out of the sea (Corbin 6). The imagination of many poets and writers has been haunted by these horrible sea monsters. "No one who has read 'Les Travailles de la Mer' [by Hugo] can ever forget the octopus with its snaky twining arms," writes Treneer (189).

In *VDT*, Lewis introduces the snake very subtly and slowly in a manner already used by his predecessors. First, the attention of the travelers is focused on objects in the sea that looked like "smooth rounded rocks," a whole line of them with intervals of about forty feet in between (*VDT* 122-23). Soon, the voyagers begin to realize that these "rocks" are moving and suddenly,

> an appalling head reared itself out of the sea. It was all greens and vermilions with purple blotches—except where shellfish clung to it—and shaped rather like a horse's, though without ears. It had enormous eyes, eyes made for staring through the dark depths of the ocean, and a gaping mouth filled with double rows of sharp fish-like teeth. It came up on what they first took to be a huge neck, but as more and more of it emerged everyone knew that this was not its neck but its body and that at last they were seeing what so many people have foolishly wanted to see—the great Sea Serpent. The folds of its gigantic tail could be seen far away, rising at intervals from the surface. And now its head was towering up higher than the mast. (123-24)

Eventually, at Reepicheep's advice, they pushed the looping snake backward over the broken stern, and the sea serpent disappeared into the waters.

This sea serpent adventure attains more heroic and religious dimensions through linking the serpent to the classical, biblical, medieval, and Renaissance traditions mentioned above. Lewis associates it with classical tradition by giving it "double rows of sharp fish-like teeth" (124) similar to the mythical Scylla with three rows of teeth set thick and close in each of her six mouths. There are similarities between Lewis's sea serpent and the biblical Behemoth. The Behemoth has a huge tail that he moves like a cedar (Job 40.17). Also, Lewis's sea serpent has skin like that of the Behemoth that cannot be penetrated by arrow or sword: "The sword of him that layeth at him cannot hold" (Job 41.26). There is also a reference to the terrible teeth of the Leviathan (Job 41.14). In Europe, there was a strong belief that this sea monster actually existed. In *The Lyfe of Saynt Branden* there are three references to a huge fish that suggest its deceptive and horrifying nature. The first fish is so huge that the pilgrims thought it an island and so alighted and built a fire on it. When it began moving, the travelers discovered it was actually a fish and ran back to the ship (Sig. A3^r). Another huge fish followed them, casting so much water out of its mouth into the ship that they almost drowned (Sig. A6^r). A third one, larger than the last one, fought them and was finally caught (Sig. A10^r). The Renaissance historian Haklyut recounts a similar incident in the 1589 voyage of the Earl of Cumberland to the Azores regarding the deceptive sea serpent that appears as a fish:

> This day, as we sayled neere Saint Georges Island, a huge

fish lying still a little under water, or rather even therewith, appeared hard by a head of us, the sea breaking upon his backe, which was blacke coloured, in such sort as deeming at the first it had been a rocke, and the ship stemming directly with him, we were put in a sudden feare for the time: till soone after we saw him move out of the way. (7: 10)

In book 1 of *Paradise Lost*, Milton compares the hugeness of Satan to that of "*Leviathan,* which God of all his works / Created hugest that swim th' Ocean stream" (1.201-02)—considered a symbol of the anti-Christ by Protestants (Engetsu 3). In a Homeric simile, the poet then tells the story of a mariner who mistakes Leviathan for an actual island:

> Him haply slumb'ring on the *Norway* foam
> The Pilot of some small night-founder'd Skiff,
> Dreaming some Island, oft, as Seamen tell,
> With fixed Anchor in his scaly rind
> Moors by his side under the Lee, while Night
> Invests the Sea, and wished Morn delays:
> So stretcht out huge in length the Arch-fiend lay. (1.203-09) [5]

As late as 1755, Erich Pontoppidan records that a large sea-snake was seen in Norway with scales and firey eyes that could raise itself like a mast to snap men from the ship (208) (see fig.13). This horrifying snake bears similarities to Lewis's equally horrifying one with its "enormous eyes" (*VDT* 123) and head "towering up higher than the mast" (124). The common qualities of the sea serpent in all these versions, which Lewis is drawing upon in *VDT*, are deceit, horror, and evil.

Fig. 13. Pontoppidan, Erich. *The Natural History of Norway* (212).

E. Further Transformations: Deathwater Island, The Island of Voices, and The Magician's House

The next island is the setting of another metamorphosis by Aslan. In a tableau that depicts Edmund and Caspian fighting on Deathwater Island over ownership of a pool that transforms everything into gold, suddenly Aslan appears to them: .

> cross the gray hillside above them—gray, for the heather was not yet in bloom—without noise, and without looking at them, and shining as if he were in bright sunlight though the sun had in fact gone in, passed with slow pace the hugest lion that human eyes have ever seen. (136-37)

Stunned by Aslan's appearance, Edmund and Caspian forget the reason for their quarrel and scramble to the ship, purified of their greed. As Captain Drinian notes, "Their Majesties all seemed a bit bewitched when they came aboard" (138). Aslan, shining brightly in the darkness, directs them back to the right destination—the East—and Deathwater Island becomes a landscape of regeneration, not death, as Aslan's iconic image illuminates it and the characters.

In the Island of Voices, the Magician's House is a place of some degree of holiness because it is temporarily sanctified by the presence of Aslan. It is a place of learning virtue and ethics to live by. Lucy is asked to go into the Magician's House to consult the book of magic for a spell to make hidden things visible to help the Monopods.[5] (See fig. 14). In this incident she learns the consequences of vanity and eavesdropping (spying). She gets sidetracked by an eavesdropping spell to make her beautiful and succumbs to vanity. But when she intends to utter the spell,

> there in the middle of the writing, where she felt quite sure that there had been no picture before, she found the great face of a Lion, of the Lion, Aslan himself, staring into hers. It was painted such a bright gold that it seemed to be coming toward her out of the page . . . He was growling and you could see his teeth. (*VDT* 165)

Aslan comes alive in this Christ-like image as in a medieval illumination to warn Lucy of her vanity, and she turns the page in a hurry.

What is also significant about this scene is its use of traditional convention, built upon the Scriptures, of associating the sacred with gold. As has been discussed earlier in chapter 6, the New Jerusalem is described as "pure gold" (Rev. 21.18). In this tableau Lewis uses Aslan as a Christological medieval icon. In discussing scriptural imagery of Heaven, Lewis writes that gold is used to "suggest the timelessness of heaven (gold does not rust) and the preciousness of it" (*Mere Christianity* 137).

FIG. 14. THESE MONSTERS BELONG TO A LONG TRADITION GOING BACK TO HERODOTUS AND PLINY. FOL. 29V ILLUSTRATING THE *TRAVELS OF MARCO POLO*, ONE OF THE TEXTS IN MANUSCRIPT FR. 2810 OF THE BIBLIOTHÈQUE NATIONALE (LATE FOURTEENTH OR EARLY FIFTEENTH CENTURY), KNOWN AS THE *LIVRE DES MERVEILLES*. (BYNUM FIG. 9).

Aslan becomes physically visible to Lucy again, ostensibly because she has uttered the spell to make things visible: "[W]hat stood in the doorway was Aslan himself, The Lion, the highest of all High Kings. And he was solid and real and warm, and he let her kiss him and bury herself in his shining mane" (*VDT* 169). Again, this tableau associates Aslan with light (his "shining mane"). He is also a real live lion, solid and warm, as he was experienced earlier by Lucy and Susan in *LWW* and will again be experienced by his followers in *LB*. He assures her that he has been here all the time. The simple yet powerful tableau suggests Lewis's belief that Christ, like Aslan, is real in his humanity and close to our desires and thoughts. Through right conduct and thinking we can make visible the Christ to us as the story of Lucy shows. Also, like Christ, Aslan is on an active crusade to redeem those who are open to him, as in Eustace's metamorphosis earlier and all the other metamorphoses in the *Chronicles*.

The dark rooms of the Magician's House and Lucy's heart are illuminated by the iconic Aslan, and Lucy is purged of the sins of vanity and the coveting of forbidden knowledge. The tableau that materializes in a dark, secret room far away from the hustle and bustle of action outside the Magician's House suggests the Christian mystery at the center of the story. Aslan, like Christ in the human world, has been/is present the whole time without being visible. The frame narrative recedes and is forgotten for a while as the mystery of Aslan becomes known to Lucy (and the readers) in this poignant tableau, as analogously, God's grace in our world is offered to us. This metamorphosis of Aslan from inanimate to animate in the presence of Lucy (and the witnessing reader's imagination) suggests the Incarnation. The focus of this image is on Aslan as a transforming and transformative force. The Magician's House becomes an *axis mundi* in Narnia, a sacred center because it invokes a theophany, a personal revelation of Aslan to one of his followers (Eliade, *Patterns of Comparative Religion* 371-73).

D. The Black Cloud

Later on in the voyage, a more suspenseful incident occurs. The travelers battle with a mysterious black cloud that covers the ship twelve days after they set sail from the Island of Voices. In Psalm 105.28 the psalmist tells of the darkness sent by God to punish his enemies. Here, the biblical event suggests trial more than punishment, a trial of courage and faith. Edmund sights what seemed to be a "dark mountain" on their left side (189). They discover it is a tunnel of darkness, "as if they had come to the edge of moonless and starless night" (190). They were turning back from this mass of darkness when Sir Reepicheep, the noble mouse, reminds them of their heroic mission to "seek honor and adventure" and not fill their bellies or their purses (192). Again it is through Lucy's point of view that the event of entering the darkness is described:

> At one minute the gilded stern, the blue sea, and the sky were all in broad daylight: next minute the sea and sky had vanished, the stern lantern—which had been hardly noticeable before—was the only thing to show where the ship ended. In front of the lantern she could see the black shape of Drinian crouching at the tiller. . . . And the lights . . . when you have to have them at the wrong time of day, looked lurid and unnatural. (*VDT* 194)

After rescuing the missing Lord Rhoop, they try rowing backward, but still the darkness surrounds them. The contest of light and dark—ending in the defeat of the latter—is described dramatically on the Dark Island in a stark monochromatic scene. Aslan, taking on different forms, appears in order to rid the ship of darkness as soon as Lucy prays for his aid. Appearing as a speck of light at first, then a beam of light, then a cross, an airplane, and an albatross, he floods the ship—but not the surrounding water—with light. In the form of an albatross, a Coleridgean symbol of a Christian soul ("The Rime of the Ancient Mariner" 65), a bird of good omen (notes on 11.63-66), and a traditional angel of God (Ramos 184), Aslan guides Captain Brinian, who "steered after it not doubting that it offered good guidance" (201). But the iconic figure speaks literally and imaginatively only to Lucy, for she is the only one to hear Aslan's words of comfort: "'Courage, dear heart'" (201).

The same motif of the dark cloud is described in *The Lyfe of saynt Branden* where Abbot Beryn relates the journey of his son Mervoke to the East. The travelers sailed through a "derke cloude" before God removed the darkness so that they arrived at an island shining with light "as bryght as the sonne," with herbs and trees and "full of grene pasture whein were y whyteft ā gretest shepe that euer they sawe" (Sig. A2^v-A2^r), all motifs of the terrestrial garden as discussed in chapter 7. Interestingly, there is a similar event described in Haklyut's *The Principall Navigations* regarding a cloud hanging over the ship. Haklyut writes, quoting from Master John Locke's voyage to Jerusalem in 1553, "The same day in the afternoone we sawe in the element, a cloud with a long tayle, like unto the tayle of a serpent, which cloud is called in Italian Cion, the tayle of the cloud did hang as it were into the sea: and we did see the water under the sayde cloude ascend, as it were like a smoke or myste the which this Cion drew up to it" (5: 90). It vanished only because the mariners stuck a "black hafted" knife in it using some type of conjuration. Haklyut wonders whether this incident is to be attributed to the bravery of the mariners or to their enchantment. In *VDT*, however, the Darkness can only disappear with the help of Aslan, since as the voyagers get closer to the East, to Aslan's Country, Aslan plays a stronger role in neutralizing the demonic and chaotic forces of the sea. [6]

E. Ramandu's Temple and the "Perilous Table"

As a whole, all the travelers in *VDT* acquire more control over their environment intellectually and imaginatively as they draw closer to Aslan and his home in the East. Their degree of regeneration i.e., their ability to see clearly, is measured by their physical (and thus spiritual) distance from the East. Lewis is preparing readers for the second view of the sea, this time calm, harmonious, and baptismal. This view begins to appear onward from the Island of Ramandu, one of the voyagers' most regenerating stops—Ramandu and his daughter being types of Jungian/Druidic/biblical prophet and virgin. Although Aslan does not appear on this Island, the last stop before Aslan's Country at the eastern rim of the world, there is an abundance of significant imagery related to the East and to him. Lewis prepares his readers for the upcoming scene with Ramandu and his daughter by describing dramatic changes in nature: the winds have grown so gentle that the ship seems to be gliding as if on a lake, and light has intensified because of an increase in the number of constellations that no one had ever seen in Narnia before (205).

Ramandu's temple on the island is "a wide oblong space flagged with smooth stones and surrounded by gray pillars but unroofed" (207). Inside this Stonehenge-like structure is a long table, laid out with food like a banquet, covered by a rich crimson cloth, surrounded by richly carved stone chairs with silk cushions. Caspian, the three children, and Reepicheep take their seats at the "perilous table" laden with unconsumed food beside the three sleepers, who are actually the last three of the missing lords who have come under an enchanted spell because of their divisiveness regarding whether or not to proceed forward to the East. In anger one of the lords takes the Knife of Stone that lay on the table (which is not right for him to do, because it was the same knife that the White Witch used to sacrifice Aslan in *LWW*); so they all fall asleep under the magic spell, never to wake up until Ramandu's oracle is fulfilled. The regenerative power of the East is clear in this prophecy, which will be fulfilled at the end. Ramandu's Island signals "the beginning of the end" for the voyagers, the last step before restoration. In a liturgical pageant (see ch. 2), Ramandu issues a prophecy that will release the sleeping knights from their spell if one remains behind (Prince Caspian) and marries his daughter.

F. The Underwater Garden City

There is one more intriguing experience that the travelers go through before they get to Aslan's country. As they travel eastwards, closer to Aslan, their needs for sustenance and sleep diminish, and their eyesight grows keener. Meanwhile, Lucy is presented again with a most unusual scene. As she is looking in the water, she is able to see a "submarine forest" (239) at the bottom of the sea: "The sunlight was falling across Lucy's shoulder, so the shadow of the thing lay stretched out on the sand behind it. And by its shape she saw clearly that it was a shadow of towers and pinnacles, minarets, and domes" (241). Later on, she sees the underwater Sea People, colorful with their coronets and purple hair, riding on sea-horses, surrounded by a "park-like country, dotted with little groves of brightly colored vegetation" (242). It is no wonder that captain Drinian worries that the sailors may see and fall in love with a sea-woman or with the under-sea country and therefore dive into the sea (245). This Underwater Garden City parallels Earthly Cities, except that, as Edmund and Lucy explain later on, it is built on top of a mountain, rather than in a valley where humans usually build their cities.[7] In this intriguing tableau, Lewis's inclusiveness is evident in the metonymic "towers," "pinnacles," "minarets," and "domes," which allude to Christian as well as non-Christian civilizations. It suggests that to Lewis, Christianity embraces non-Christian religions.[8]

It is possible that since Lewis's submarine Garden City in *VDT* is close to Aslan's Country, it is open to Aslan's redemptive powers, as humans are infused by the grace of Christ in different degrees. In some respects, Lewis's underwater Garden City harks back to the underwater paradise of Greek mythology, a favorable view of the sea, albeit that Edmund and Lucy believe that the Underwater City might house in its deep layers "the squid and the Sea Serpent and the Kraken" (241). Again the bifurcated view of the sea. As Alain Corbin has written, some scholars believed "that the present seas and oceans were similar in form and size to those that existed before the coming of the flood" and that

> [b]eneath the sea are gardens, orchards, forests, and meadows. The authority of the Fathers of the Church and the accounts of sailors strengthened the belief in an underwater nature full of magnificence, forming a moving replica of earthly paradise. Far from being a dark, merciless abode of cruel monsters, the bottom of the ocean was perceived as the invisible receptacle for the perfection of Creation and a repository for innocence. It was the flip side of the exposed earth, and, paradoxically, it was more luminous and more colourful. (30)

These ideas led to the concept of a submarine earthly paradise (Corbin 30). After all, classical mythology had the palace of Neptune on the ocean floor. Spenser carries on with this submarine paradise tradition by placing the bower of Cymoent, one of the Nereids, on the ocean floor (*FQ* 3.4.43). The belief in the submarine paradise also has a biblical source in Psalm 107.23-24. Interestingly, it is these same biblical verses, to which Richard Haklyut was directed by his cousin, a gentleman of the Middle Temple in London with his namesake, that inspired him to study geography and publish *The Principall Navigations* (The Epistle Dedicatorie in the First Edition, *The Principall Navigations* 1: xvii). Lewis refers to this passage as one "that warms the heart" (*English Literature* 438).[9]

This inclusive Christian view suggested by the Underwater Garden City can be perceived by the soul only when the light of Christ has infused and purified it. Again, the human and the godly powers merge in these visions en route to the East, in our world when the soul is close to Christ. There is one scene in *VDT* that is a clear analogue to Christ's Transfiguration. Again, light is the operating force in this iconic scene. After the children taste the sweet water, light increases: "They could see more light than they had ever seen before. And the deck and the sail and their own faces and bodies became brighter and brighter and every rope shone" (249-50). Aslan's light shines more intensely on the children as they are approaching the destination of their pilgrimage. As the British children approach Aslan, his glory shines on them because they are entering into his country. The symbolic baptism in the waters of the Silver Sea that follows is equivalent to the metamorphosis of the human heart by art or natural beauty, which radiate godly light, an example in our world of *thèōsis*. Metaphor and metamorphosis again work together in Lewis's mythopoeia. Lewis may also be following Plato here in the notion that sight and hearing are the only two senses that reveal the harmony of the world (*Timaeus 45 ^{b}*).

III. The Ship as Symbol

Above all, sea voyaging can be seen as a restorative process, a baptismal rite with the ship functioning as a person's religious faith. Christians saw the ship as the church "with the Holy Spirit at the helm guiding it to the eternal haven, which was the object of Christian longing" (Corbin 9). Although Tertullian, one of the Roman Church Fathers, rejected the baptismal interpretation of the sea, he believed that "[t]he ship prefigured the Church, which on the sea of this world is buffeted by the waves of persecution and temptation" (Daniélou 68). In a more general view, Noah's ark was seen in terms of an eschatological deliverance (Daniélou 67). Philo of Alexandria "saw the ark as an image of the soul moving towards the life of blessedness" (67). Another related meaning is that the voyage is purgatorial suffering leading to the hands of God (Corbin 9).

In *VDT*, the name of the ship, *Dawn Treader*, underscores the moral and theological significance of the direction of the East in this story for the travelers, since the word "Dawn" suggests rebirth or regeneration, a significant theme in the chronicles. On the frame narrative or the diachronic, this theme is explained thus by Caspian: Sailing on the *Dawn Treader* is a "privilege." "Every man that comes with us shall bequeath the title of *Dawn Treader* to all his descendants," he says (232). However, the name *Dawn Treader* opens up another whole field of Judeo-Christian associations regarding the demonic aspect of the sea as the home of the Leviathan or Sea Serpent (Berkeley 114-30) and the ability of humans to tame it. The word "Treader" suggests the act of "treading on" in the sense of "stepping on" as a means of power and control (as in God's curse that the offspring of Eve shall "bruise" the serpent's head (Gen. 3.15); so the name *Dawn Treader* suggests that the ship will traverse and control the dark, chaotic and (presumably) demonic waters of the sea as the ship travels to the dawn, an action that is reminiscent of the Hebrews' crossing of the Red Sea and the River Jordan in the Old Testament and Christ's walking on the sea and calming the sea storms in the New Testament. This interpretation is in line with Lewis's typological thinking.

Christian tradition also translates the ship into a symbol of the church which can be threatened by sin. According to David Berkeley, the ship symbolism occurs in patristic literature from about AD 200 (135). Also, in patristic thought the church as a ship sailed East to paradise (91) like the *Dawn Treader*. In *VDT* the characters sail on their mission in various means of navigation that include ship, boat, and Reepicheep's coracle. The scenes involving these diverse means of sailing can be interpreted by way of the Christian tradition as other diverse means of attaining grace: the church, intimate fellowship with the Christian community, and individual actions, respectively. Although the church is essential to draw mankind to Christ, grace can be offered through extraordinary means that affirm God's freedom. For God can reveal himself to those who are "individually good."[10] Such is the case of Reepicheep. In his little coracle, he will later glide up one side of the wave and down the other into Aslan's Country. Like the British children,

Reepicheep is a traveler on the ship (the church) and later one of the small select group that embarks on a boat (the Christian community) after the ship is grounded. As mentioned earlier, unlike the children, he is in no need of regeneration. Nor, as narrated in the final chapters, does he have to, like the children, wade through baptismal waters or partake of the fish (the Eucharist) in order to get a glimpse of Aslan's Country. Reepicheep sails up and over the wave directly into Aslan's Country, his everlasting home, in his little coracle, an icon of individual salvation. He is all goodness, as "a mirror is filled with light" (*Mere* 130), but unconscious of this goodness because he and people like him are "too busy looking at the source from which it comes" (131). Reepicheep is the ideal pilgrim who has arrived at his destination, the exemplary state of sainthood. He is both volunteer and elect like Dante's saints in the uppermost spheres of Heaven, where souls fly up to God faster the closer they are to Him, on the wings of their desire and pulled by the strings of His love. Navigating the sea to Aslan's Country in a ship, boat, and coracle points to the different means of Christian salvation, whether taken individually or collectively, through extraordinary or ordinary grace, thus enriching the meaning of the heroic rescue mission in *VDT.*

IV. Other Views of the Sea in Narnia

The positive view of the sea, in a general sense, is found in many of Lewis's other works. To relieve the reader from the oppressive atmosphere of Calormen, Lewis inserts one of his refreshing natural scenes, this one of the sea. The sea, like the green pools in *MN*, has a positive meaning in *HHB*. On his journey to Anvard, Shasta wakes up one morning only to see that behind where they (he, Aravis, and the two horses) were "lay a little copse. Before them the turf, dotted with white flowers, sloped down to the brow of a cliff. Far below them, so that the sound of the breaking waves was very faint, lay the sea." (20) He had not seen the sea so varied in color or from such a height: "On either hand the coast stretched away, headland after headland, and at the points you could see the white foam running up the rocks but making no noise because it was far off. There were gulls flying overhead and the heat shivered on the ground; it was a blazing day" (20). The air was "new," so "delicious," with no smell of fish in it (20, 21). This idyllic scene of the calm sea, tamed from a distance, energizes him and he asks for breakfast.

The affirmative view of the sea, as an instrument of salvation that facilitates the travelers' journey to the East and thus to a state of redemption, subsumes the earlier one of the sea as demonic. This bifurcated view of the sea is at the foundation of any symbolic interpretation of *VDT*. To develop his thematic strands, Lewis adopts the Augustinian view and synchronizes it with motifs from classical, Judeo-Christian, and early voyage literature. The travelers' courage and skill in surviving the sea storm and defeating the terrifying, deceptive sea serpent, as well as their experience of beauty and plenitude in the Underwater City—all prepare them for the final experience with Aslan. Although Aslan has appeared to several characters along the way (to Eustace in Dragon Island, to Edmund and Caspian in Deathwater Island, to Lucy in the Magician's House, and to Caspian in his cabin), his full role as the real pilot of the ship is not comprehended until the end of the story. The sea voyage to the East in *VDT* is a process of regeneration through struggle and transformation by the divine light of Aslan/Christ. Without this light, the artist cannot create nor the beholder perceive. For to Lewis there is no art without Beauty, no Beauty without the ultimate Good. According to Robert Houston Smith, to Lewis, "all earthly beauty is but an imperfect mirror of the absolute beauty of the creator" (58). In *Weight* Lewis writes, "The scriptural picture of heaven is therefore just as symbolical as the picture which our desire, unaided, invents for itself; heaven is not really full of jewelry anymore than it is really the beauty of Nature or a fine piece of music" (6). Sailing to the East suggests the process of learning to appreciate the Platonic triad here on earth. As the old Narnia dissolves into the Real one, Lord Digory says in *LB*, "It's all in Plato, all in Plato: bless me, what *do* they teach them at these schools!" (212).

The sea voyage, ostensibly to find the missing Narnian lords, is thus simply the diachronic frame to convey Lewis's theme of metamorphosis of the self through fellowship with Aslan (Christ in our world). The Narnian ship, the boat, and Reepicheep's coracle become iconic images of the church or a community of faith in our own pilgrimage of the sea of life, the means of overcoming evil in the form of serpents, black clouds, storms, and *goeteia* one might add, pointing the way to Christian salvation. Through Lewis's "scholarship of imagination," a mere sea adventure story becomes a journey of finding meaning, hope, and Joy.

Endnotes

1. I am indebted to Alain Corbin's *The Lure of the Sea* for information on St. Augustine's *De beata vita* and the traditional motifs of the sea, in general.

2. Of course there are too many biblical examples to include here. For further information on water as a Christian symbol, see Jean Daniélou, *Les Symboles chretiens primitifs* (Paris: Editions du Semil, 1961), trans. Donald A. H. Water. *Primitive Christian Symbols*. (Baltimore: Helicon Press, 1964) 42-57.

3. Lewis had the works of Haklyut in his personal library, which he annotated. For further discussion on Haggard's influence on Lewis, see chapter 4, n. 5.

4. Katsuhiro Engetsu's research (in an unpublished paper read at the International Milton Forum in London, July 2008), shows that Milton and Cromwell were interested in the Baltic Sea and the supremacy of English ships there. Thus, the association between the biblical sea monster and the non-biblical place, Norway (2).

5. One may wonder what the source of the Monopods is. In his *Book of the Infante, D. Pedro of Portugal, who walked through the four corners of the Earth*, by Gomez de Santisteban (Seville: Jacobo Cromberger, 1515), the author mentions "giants, pygmies, and the men with a single round foot, who 'are not good for battle but are farmers'" (99); see Maundeville (118). Kath Filmer (140 n2) refers to an editorial note in Maundeville that explains that the monopods are derived from Pliny's *Natural History* (book 2, ch. 2).

6. Walter Hooper believes that Lewis may have taken the image of the black cloud from Rider Haggard and Andrew Lang's *The World's Desire* (*Past Watchful Dragons* 107).

7. In *The Four Loves*, Lewis refers to the "valley of sorrows" as a place for humans (191).

8. Though earlier, in *HHB*, his Narniacentric attitude shows in his negative descriptions of the non-Narnian Calormenes, a type of Middle Eastern people, as has been discussed in chapter 5.

9. Lewis wrote above Haklyut's line in his personal copy of the "Epistle Dedicatorie in the first edition, 1589" "How I first fell in love with geography." Marion E. Wade Center, by permission of The Lewis Company Pts. Ltd.

10. This belief is stated or implied in many of Lewis's works, specifically in *God in the Dock* (262), *The Weight of Glory* (13-14), and *Mere Christianity* (63, 149).

CHAPTER NINE

The Narnian Apocalypse in *The Last Battle*:
Rágnarök, *The Book of Revelation*, and the Narnian Apocalypse

The LORD loveth the gates of Zion more than all the dwellings of Jacob.
Psalm 87

Great is my knowledge, I can see / the doom that awaits almighty gods.
Völuspá (st. 31)

"The term is over: the holidays have begun. The dream is ended: this is the morning."
LB (228)

The Last Battle is another unique chronicle like *HHB* (where Narnians make a brief appearance), *PC* (where there is no witch or supernatural, evil force to contend with directly), and *SC* (where Aslan makes an unusually early appearance). *LB* is an intensely dark story, with evil forces spread all over Narnia, turning it into a truly "enemy-occupied territory" (*Mere* 46). Enemy forces like the Calormene invaders and the insurgent Telmarines with their followers are surging and resurging, and, in spite of all this danger, Aslan still makes his usual late appearance. King Tirian, the last King of Narnia, alone except for his Narnian friends in the first half of the story, is overwhelmed by the situation, and even when the British children arrive, Narnia's fate is sealed. There is no way out but "further up and further in." The evil that infiltrates Narnia brings it to its doom. *LB* contains few man-made structures since its locus is the Western Wilds, the terrain of Shift the Ape, which he and the Calormenes have laid to waste. Tirian in his hunting lodge with his animals are pitted against the malicious Shift in his stable with his followers. The major plot hinges upon the enmity between the good pair, Tirian/Jewel, and the evil one, Shift/Tarkaan (Calormene captain). On a bigger scale, the enmity is between Aslan and the god of the Calormenes, Tash, who makes two cameo appearances in this story. On a metaphorical level, Shift's stable, his new headquarters, is one of those lurid structures built on top of a hill, a travesty of Cair Paravel in Narnia, which represents the city of Jerusalem in the Christian dispensation. It also houses the false Aslan (Puzzle in a lion skin); the Ape, a devil figure; and Tash, the demonic type of Aslan. The plot moves away from Shift's stable to the Celestial Garden, the third major garden in the *Chronicles*— the Real Narnia (see ch. 7). The movement away from these false creatures leads to restoration, as in all chronicles, and involves a huge metamorphosis of all Narnia, the final metamorphosis, the destruction of the Old Narnia followed by the transition to the Real Narnia. This is the Narnian apocalypse.

The idea of the world's destruction appears in many cultures. According to Eliade, "The end of the world was made an integral part of the [German] cosmology, and, as in India, Iran, and Israel, the scenarios and the principal actors in the apocalypse were known" (*A History of Religious Ideas* 2: 168-69). The Book of Revelation is obviously older than the period of crystallization of the Nordic myths. Sturluson Snorri's *Prose Edda* (or the *Younger Edda*) and the later anonymous *Poetic Edda* are two of the most reliable sources of Norse mythology, though they are fragmentary narratives laced with vivid images of a hazy but powerful world-picture: "Certainly the myths give no impression of a neat, circumscribed universe," H. R. Ellis Davidson states (*Myths and Symbols of Pagan Europe* 171). This Nordic world, and especially the Rágnarök myth, or what is commonly called "The Twilight of the Gods," or more accurately, the doom of the gods (*rágna*, of the gods; *rök*, destiny) (Munch 100), was popularized by Richard Wagner in *The Ring of the Nibelung*, with which Lewis became enamoured early in life (*Surprised* 74-75 and ch. 10). Arthur Rackham's illustrations for *Siegfried and the Twilight of the Gods*, which romanticized the Valkyries as beautiful women, while in reality they were "hideous creatures, akin to vampires" (Grant 98), also had much to do with Lewis's early enchantment with Norse mythology. He writes in *Surprised* describing his feelings as a young man, "The Valkyries seemed to me more important than anything else in my experience" (76) (see fig. 7). He later passed on from Wagner to everything he could read about Norse mythology (78).[1] The major account of the myth of Rágnarök is in the "Völuspá" of the *Poetic Edda*, a Sybil's vision of the creation, Rágnarök, and the emergence of a new earth. Similar accounts of this myth are found in the "Lay of Vafðruðnir" also in the *Poetic Edda*, as well as in the first part of "Gylfaginning" in Snorri's *Prose Edda*.[2]

A study of the Narnian apocalypse in *LB* reveals that it contains analogous correspondences to both St. John's Book of Revelation and the Norse myth of Rágnarök. According to Charles A. Huttar, "The vivid sensory images of Revelation have entered into Lewis's mind and are coming out at other places in the story" (133). So are the Nordic myths. All three texts are apocalyptic, yet different in form. Pursuing the analogues in all these three texts will provide some significant clues about Lewis's views on Christianity with respect to the biblical story and pagan mythology. The analogues I will discuss in this chapter are 1) the characters involved; 2) the prequel to the last battle; 3) the last battle between the gods and evil forces; 4) the sequel to the last battle: the creation of a new earth, New Jerusalem, and new Narnia. The last section is a discussion of the links between the three versions.

I. Characters of the Apocalypse:
Allegorical Figures, Nordic Gods, and Talking Animals

The Book of Revelation is a poetic vision of an allegorical struggle between Christ and his types against the Antichrist and his types. Like "Völuspá," it lacks linearity and is a vision of what is, was, and will become, an uncovering of hidden spiritual realities. In his study of the book, Austin Farrer, Lewis's long-time friend, claims that St. John's mind was controlled by the Spirit of Christ as he was writing it: "The Spirit passes through the divinatory technique like sunlight through clear glass, and falls straight upon the scriptural images behind, which are the natural types of Christian fact" (262). This line uncannily brings to mind the definition of the icon (see ch. 2). He refers to the Book as an "inexhaustible mine of truth" (22). Although it is full of "riddles" and "mysteries," which seem to render it a "mere pile of visions and oracles" (36), Farrer was able to discover a "schematic architecture" at its basis.[3] Revelation presents evil as "that old Serpent, which is the Devil, and Satan" (20.2), crystallized in the red dragon, his army of beasts (generic symbols of the false prophets and earthly tyrants), false gods like Belial and Baal, giants Gog and Magog, and the great whore of Babylon, the ultimate symbol of the doom of Babylon and all such Earthly Cities; the dragon fights against the woman crowned with stars, and the demons and their human instruments fight against the warrior on a white horse, called Faithful and True (an apparent symbol of Christ) as well as against the saints.

In Rágnarök, the "everlasting" battle occurs between the gods (e.g. the Sky Father Odin/Wodan; his sons Tyr, the war god; Thor, the god of thunder; and the white-god Heimdall) against Loki, the trickster figure, who sides with the giants, beasts, and demons in the battle.

On the other hand, *LB* is a relatively long narrative, with an extended plot and vividly described and developed characters, which allows Lewis to elaborate on his Christian views. On the plot level, Tirian's antagonist is a most cunning beast, a Talking Ape named Shift, an appropriate name for him because he is a shape changer. His appearance in front of his stable, acting as the mouth-piece of Aslan, belies his dissembling nature:

> He [Shift] was wearing a scarlet jacket which did not fit him very well, having been made for a dwarf. He had jewelled slippers on his hind paws *which would not stay on properly* because, as you know, the hind paws of an Ape are really like hands. He wore what seemed to be a *paper crown* on his head. There was a great pile of nuts beside him and he kept cracking nuts with his jaws and spitting out the shells. And he also kept on pulling up the scarlet jacket to *scratch himself*. (*LB* 34; italics mine)

He adds on to this attire King Tirian's sword, the symbol of honor and royalty, which he hung "round his own neck: and it made him look sillier than ever" (34). Shift's jacket is that of a dwarf, his jewelled slippers are those of a Calormene, his paper crown is a mock-crown of Tirian's, and his sword is also that of Tirian. In this ridiculous, incongruous attire, the Ape, "Lord" Shift to the Calormenes, goes around masquerading as a man: "I'm a Man. If I look like an Ape, that's because I'm so very old" (37). He says to the Bear: "I'm a Man: you're only a fat, stupid, stupid old Bear" (39). He asserts these false statements while walking in these unfitting clothes, clothes made for other species, and demanding his favorite food, "nuts and fruits."

Leland Ryken remarks, "Ill-fitting garments [are] (often symbolic of a position that is usurped)" (*Triumphs of the Imagination* 86). As we have seen in chapter 1 and throughout this study, dissonance, hybridity, and incongruity are characteristics of the denizens of hell. Shift brings to mind the White Witch riding on a chariot with her incongruous, ridiculous entourage (see ch. 4). Furthermore, Shift dreams Edmund-and-Eustace-like dreams, of comfort and self-pleasures. From the money the Narnian animals will earn as slaves in the Calormene King's mines, he says, "We'll be able . . . to make Narnia a country worth living in.

There'll be oranges and bananas pouring in—and roads and big cities and schools and offices"—as well as "whips and muzzles and saddles and cages and kennels and prisons" (38), the latter recalling Jadis's cruel City of Charn in *MN*. Lewis successfully links Shift with the archetype of evil in his first two chronicles.

Lewis also dips into ape lore from medieval and Renaissance literature and art to depict the Ape as a dehumanized "human." H. W. Janson states that the ape is seen in tradition as a "debased replica of ourselves" (13). As was discussed in chapter 1, the sliding boundaries between humans and animals posed for some people a "postlapsarian trajectory of decay" (Knowles 139). "For Protestant writers, in particular, animal-human cross-dressing reveals the dangerous 'animality of humanity'" (139). Inversely, Shift could also be seen as a falsely elevated "beast," in contrast to the Talking Animals that Aslan elevated by giving them the power of speech in the Creation of Narnia in *MN*. One may also see in Shift a parody of evolution, since the ape, in his "human" consciousness degrades humans and thus questions the supremacy of man (Perry 33). Rather than being an object of natural, positive metamorphosis, Shift is a "negative" and false one, since he is not a product of true change, not to mention his false claim to royalty. He is like a a malevolent Renaissance actor masquerading as an ape, masquerading as a man, propagating illusions—which makes him an impostor. In the art world of appearances and reality, he is like a fictional object perceived as a real object, a skillful *trompe l'oeil* (Allen 82). His malicious intentions to deceive, however, gain him power among some of the Narnians, but at the same time make this "cleverest, ugliest, most wrinkled ape" not only a parody of a human, but also of Aslan, the Lord of all Narnia.

Aside from representing "heathen depravity" (Janson 17), the ape in literature and art was associated with many of the seven deadly sins in one way or another, with pride, avarice, sloth, lust, despair (e.g. Breughel's apes; see Janson, chs. 2 and 4). As a representative of a degenerated man, the ape is a trickster, a sycophant, hypocrite, a coward, and a seeker after voluptuousness (Janson 33). According to Augustine, the ape is the devil, a mimic, a deceiver who would create the illusion of such feats (Stuart Clark 82). In a word, the ape is a *figura diaboli*, not simply a false copy of a man. This negative term was used for all enemies of Christ (Janson 16). There is a miniature of Christ standing on the head of an ape in a scene that replicates the Temptation of Christ (21). As Paul Ford remarks, "The ape as a figure of great evil has at least one antecedent: the Antichrist ['The Antichrist, the Ape,' from John Daus, tr., Bullinger's *Hundred Sermons Upon the Apocalypse*, 1573"] (398). The term "ape" was also applied to bad rulers who bribe their way into power: "Those who strive after earthly riches are fundamentally as infra-human as the apes, no matter how much they may resemble man externally" (Janson 93). It follows logically that the Ape's natural allies in *LB* are the Calormenes, whose rulers are tyrants as shown earlier in *HHB*, abusers and exploiters of nature and animals, and very cunning, long thought by Lewis to represent an inferior Middle Eastern race (see ch. 5). As in *HHB* the Calormenes are conceived, here in the mind of Tirian, as "dark, bearded men from Calormen, that great and cruel country that lies beyond Archenland" (*LB* 26), their "white eyes flashing dreadfully in their brown faces" (33). As in *HHB* they smell "something of garlic and onions" (33). Most of the dwarfs also in *LB* are "apish" in their materialism.

However, the major abused Talking Animal in *LB* is a donkey, a victim of Shift's cunning, named Puzzle. The relationship of Shift and Puzzle is a classic example of predator and prey. In literary tradition, the donkey represents weak aspects of humanity like curiosity, stubbornness, and a lack of culture. Plato compares the ass unfavorably to the noble horse, a higher creature (*Phaedrus* 260 ^{d}). In his tirade against his enemies the Persians, Herodotus calls King Cyrus a mule (Frangoulidis 161). Lewis has something to say about a donkey in *The Four Loves* (1960). In comparing the ass to the body, he writes, "No one in his senses can either revere or hate a donkey. It is a useful, sturdy, lazy, obstinate, patient, lovable and infuriating beast; deserving now the stick and now a carrot; both pathetically and absurdly beautiful. So the body" (143). Puzzle, however, is more foolish than stubborn, foolishness being another trait an ass received from antiquity (Frangoulidis 161), a contrast to the "lordly beast," Jewel the Unicorn, Tirian's dearest friend (*LB* 16).

II. Prequel to the Last Battle: "Brothers against Brothers"

In all three texts—the Book of Revelation, the Nordic myth, and *LB*—a prequel to the last battle between the god/gods and the evil forces of demons/giants/humans is a period of intense evil that precipitates the battle. In the Book of Revelation, the struggle is mainly allegorical as mentioned earlier. Aside from the major struggle between Christ and the Antichrist, there are struggles between the two constituents of pagan power themselves: the Beast and Babylon, symbols of military kingship and urban wealth (Farrer 297-98). Another such symbol is the red dragon with seven heads, ten horns, and seven crowns, symbolizing the ten kings and seven crowns, i.e. the power of the earthly kings. There is a prevalence of corruption in the City of Babylon and other Earthly Cities, a theme that is dear to Lewis's heart as discussed earlier in chapters 1 and 2. In Revelation, there are other strange beastly forms and hybrids like the horses with lion heads and serpent tails. Such extreme physical hybridity is missing in Rágnarök and limited in *LB* to certain creatures. As in Rágnarök, there are cosmic/apocalyptic images: "The first angel sounded, and there followed hail and fire mingled with blood, and they were cast upon the earth: and the third part of trees was burnt up" (8.7). "And the third angel sounded, and there fell a great star from heaven, burning as it were a lamp" (8.10). The sun turns black, and the moon turns to blood. There is also an earthquake that moves mountains and islands out of their places, and a flood (12.15). Most of these images, however, are not precursors of the last battle as in *Rágnarök* or of the Celestial Garden in *LB*, but images of judgment and punishment of rebellious humans and demons.

The first stage of the great battle in Rágnarök is composed of geological/climatic changes that bring on moral decay. Before the onset of the last battle, there are three years of winter (*Fimbulvetr*) with snow, frost, and wind, without summer. Then after three more years of winter, there is an age of harlotry, an "axe-age" of moral corruption where "brothers slay brothers." As the Sybil chants,

> woe to the world then, wedded to whoredom,
> battle-axe and sword rule, split shields asunder,
> storm-cleft age of wolves until the world goes down,
> only hatred in the hearts of men. ("Völuspá" st. 32)

Darkness ensues as a wolf devours the sun, and another wolf takes the moon. Stars are hurled from heaven, trees are torn up by the roots, and mountains tremble and crack. Different types of roosters (the light-red, the gold-combed in Odin's hall, and the soot-red in Hel) crow to awaken the heroes. The Ship of the Dead (Naglfar) sails in preparation, steered by Loki; the sea rushes over the earth, the monsters are loosened from captivity: Fenrir (the giant) advances and opens his mouth wide, fire flashing from his eyes and nostrils. The Midgard Serpent vomits poison, and the eagle screams. Heaven is cleft into twain. The sons of Muspell (fiery region outside the realm of the gods) ride through. Surt, a giant and one of the sons of Muspell, comes from the south bringing fire, like one of the angels in the Book of Revelation:

> Surt moves northward, lord of the fire giants,
> his sword of flame gleams like the sun;
> crashing rocks drag demons to their doom,
> men find the way to Hel, the sky splits open.
> ("Völuspá" st. 39)

The widely spread moral decay in Narnia is the first stage of the apocalypse. It is manifested in two areas: 1) relationships based on perpetrated fraud and 2) destruction of trees and enslavement of animals. No other relationship manifests evil more than the master/slave relationship between the ugly Ape and Puzzle, the donkey. A devil figure, a false prophet (Matt. 23-24), Shift uses the language of dissembling like Jadis in tempting Digory in the Created Garden in *MN*, the White Witch in tempting Edmund in *LWW*, and the Green Witch in tempting Prince Rilian and his rescuers in *SC*—and, one might add, Lewis's Screwtape and Wormwood in tempting humans. In the language of deception there is no conventional link between words and things, the signifier and signified. Shift constantly and maliciously misrepresents and misconstrues facts. First, he deceives Puzzle into becoming his servant, using fear and guilt tactics. He succeeds in making Puzzle feel intellectually inferior to him so that he would do the work like bringing him fruits and nuts from the towns. His fraudulence is obvious from the very beginning, though not to Puzzle. When they see a yellow thing floating in the pool, Shift's first instinct is that it may be "something useful" (3), and so the Ape complains of a "weak chest" (5) in order to coax Puzzle to go into the cold water, despite the latter's lack of paws, to retrieve it. When they discover it is a lion's skin, Shift wonders how he can profit from it, while Puzzle asks whether they should not give it a "decent burial" (7). Later, in attempting to persuade the reluctant Puzzle to wear the lion skin to impersonate Aslan, the Ape asks in a hurt voice, "Why don't you treat me as I treat you?" and "What does an ass like you know about things of this sort?" (8). There is an interesting analogue in classical mythology and a story by Edmund Spenser which, if juxtaposed to the Ape/Puzzle story in *LB*, are sure to arouse derision for the Ape. In classical mythology Hercules, the great strong hero, and Cadmus, the founder of Thebes (before being transformed to a serpent) wear a lion skin as emblems of their heroism, as opposed to the pitiful donkey, enslaved by Shift, who is forced to wear one for despicable reasons. Also, Spenser's satirical "Prosopopoia; or Mother Hubberds Tale" tells the story of a cowardly, yet power hungry ape, who is duped by a fox. He asks the fox to steal a lion's skin and his crown, and after putting them on and ruling as a lion over animals, the ape becomes a tyrant and is finally captured by the lion. An ass also appears as one of the ape's victims (420-31). In this tale, the ape as a mock-king closely approximates the conniving, ambitious Ape in *LB*.

Second, Shift's art of illusion (i.e. putting the lion's skin on Puzzle so as to impersonate Aslan) deceives most of the Narnians, especially the dwarfs, who had become skeptical about Aslan, more isolated ("the dwarfs are for the dwarfs"), obstinate and materialistic as seen in their alliance with the exploiters of Narnia, the Calormenes. They represent people who are especially open to self-deception because they see with their eyes and not with their hearts. To deluded people, "'believing is seeing'" (Gombrich 210), which recalls the Scriptures: They lack the convictions of things unseen (Heb. 11.1; 2 Cor. 4.18). Consequently, most of the dwarfs end up "not seeing at all," huddled in the dark stable, although light is available to them (*LB* 181), misconstruing everything around them, including Aslan. These misguided creatures wallow in their illusions. "They have chosen cunning instead of belief. Their prison is only in their own minds, yet they are in that prison," says Aslan (*LB* 185-86). By analogy, they are people of our world who are shut out from Grace by their own willfulness. As the scholar Theodor Thumm wrote in 1621, such creatures are deluded by the devil to "'believe that that which is not, is, and imagine that which is, to be something else'" (*Tractatus theologicus* 28, qtd. in Stuart Clark 166). Saul Smilansky notes that illusions aid in avoiding social norms and personal distress, and, in general, cause and reflect self-delusions and a detachment from reality (149). The dwarfs are happy in their denial; the diabolical Ape is thrilled to "ape" a human; but the innocent Puzzle is miserable at his enforced role of aping Aslan.

In this decaying landscape, light (the image of Aslan as the substitute in Narnia of the transcendent Platonic/Christian Reality) and darkness (the image of evil) both have a role in this game of illusion versus reality as they do in all the chronicles. Light will accompany Aslan and the good characters and withdraw from the evil ones, and it will eventually dispel all illusion, as it also does in all the other chronicles. About light, the wise Centaur apothegmizes, "The Stars never lie, but men and Beasts do" (*LB* 19), referring to the horrible Shift's evil machinations. King

Tirian has his own apothegm: "*The light is dawning, the lie broken*" (87) which he utters as he gets ready to fight with the Calormene soldiers after exposing the Ape's trick. While the false and true are agonizingly conflated for some time, light will eventually break all lies because, as Lewis writes, "In any fair comparison with the genuine the false is instantly unmasked and discredited, as illusion is dispelled" (*Spenser's Images* 82). On a practical level, light functions as a guide for Jill, who relies on the North Star for direction. Light also functions as an attribute of the beauty of the landscape, irradiated by sunlight, a rare scene in this story contrasts with the darkness that has spread all over Narnia: "The sunlight slanted through the trees, birds sang, and always (though usually out of sight) there was the noise of running water. It was hard to think of horrible things like Tash" (108).

Yet the major antagonist of light and all that it symbolizes is inescapable. The savage Tash, god of the Calormenes, has made the whole of Narnia his home. Tash moves in the heavy darkness, covered by smoke, or hides in the "dark" stable, in contrast to the shining, golden Aslan. Tash appears for the first time in Narnia in this chronicle, although Tirian had seen its statue as a child when he visited the temple of Tash in Tashbaan, "carved in stone and over laid with gold and [with] solid diamonds for eyes" (*LB* 103). But Tash is alive and well now, going northward, to the land of the evil giants. Like Hell's creatures he is a hybrid:

> It was roughly the shape of a man but it had the head of a bird; some bird of prey with a cruel, curved beak. It had four arms which it held high above its head, stretching them out Northward as if it wanted to snatch all Narnia in its grip; and its fingers—all twenty of them—were curved like its beak and had long, pointed, bird-like claws instead of nails. It floated on the grass instead of walking, and the grass seemed to wither beneath it. (101)

When it disappears into the woods, darkness disappears with it and the sun comes up (102). Unlike the Ape, who as an impostor seems to have a double nature, Tash is actually a hybrid of man and bird, like some ominous creature from classical mythology or Dante's *Inferno*, perhaps the harpies, half women and half birds, who symbolize terror and pestilence. Tash will later appear in Shift's stable to take away the Tarkaan with him into oblivion.

Yet another type of evil is perpetrated in Narnia, the destruction of trees and enslavement of animals. In cahoots with Shift, the Telmarines and Calormenes are cutting down all the holy trees to acquire timber for their business enterprises and enslaving the free Talking Animals. Dryads' shrieks fill the air. When Tirian goes with Jewel to the woods to investigate, he describes the destruction in this poignant passage:

> Right through the middle of that ancient forest—that forest where the trees of gold and of silver had once grown and where a child of our world had once planted the tree of protection [a reference to Digory in *MN*]—a broad lane had already been opened. It was a hideous lane like a raw gash in the land, full of muddy ruts where felled trees had been dragged down to the river. (26)

These destructive actions are far more severe than the abuse of the trees in *PC*. The image of the "raw gash in the land" suggests murder, since the trees and the whole landscape to the Narnians are alive and holy as the creation of Aslan. Shift and his cohorts are thus not only murderers but also tyrants since they are usurpers. Consequently, all of Narnia is victimized by these evil forces. Slavery, exploitation, deception, and violence are rampant in Narnia. What is interesting to note here is that the evil is so pervasive that the Narnians and their rightful leader, for the first time in the chronicles, are themselves not exempt from evil. In the first half of the story, Tirian and Jewel themselves are guilty of shedding Calormene blood in secret attacks, a horrifying experience to them. The King, like a Greek tragic figure, laments, "If we had died before today we should have been happy" (25).

Lewis makes his farewell to Narnia with long flashbacks through the Unicorn's reminiscences about Narnia's glorious history under the previous Kings and Queens in the earlier chronicles, in an attempt to tie up all the plot strands and prepare readers for the last battle on Stable Hill (109-10). (Lewis gives the battle a name like one of the major battles between the Swedes and the Geats in *Beowulf,* called Raven Hill). These stories of Narnia's past glory make Jill want to go back to live in "those good, ordinary times" (110) only to be reminded by Jewel that "all worlds draw to an end, except Aslan's own country" (111). There is another moment of relief in this depressing atmosphere when Tirian and his followers have a final experience of the beauty of Narnia:

> It was a little after two in the afternoon when they set out, and it was the first really warm day of that spring. The young leaves seemed to be much further out than yesterday: the snow-drops were over, but they saw several primroses. The

sunlight slanted through the trees, birds sang, and always (though usually out of sight) there was the noise of running water. It was hard to think of horrible things like Tash. The children felt, "This is really Narnia at last." Even Tirian's heart grew lighter as he walked ahead of them, humming an Old Narnia marching song which had the refrain:

> *Ho, rumble, rumble, rumble,*
> *Rumble drum belabored.* (*LB* 108)

For a short time, they forget about evil and endings. Poggin, the dwarf, is telling Eustace the names of trees, birds, and plants (possibly like J. R. R. Tolkien in his hikes with Lewis). However, pretty soon, dark reality sets in. Farsight, the eagle, brings them devastating news that Cair Paravel has been taken from the sea, Roonwit the good Centaur is dead, and "all worlds draw to an end and that noble death is a treasure which no one is too poor to buy." "So," replies the King, after a long silence, "Narnia is no more" (113).

III. The Final Battle between the Forces of Good and Evil

In the vision of St. John there is a reference to war in heaven with Michael and the good angels against the dragon and to their finally capturing him (12. 7-9; 20.2). There are increasing images of judgment and punishment like the throne and chariot descending for judgment. Borrowing from the prophet Ezekiel, St. John uses the sickle as a symbol of judgment. There is a vision of Jesus crowned with gold and riding the sky armed with a sickle (14.19). As Austin Farrer states, "The Son of Man himself gathers the righteous, the angel gathers the wicked. . . . We do not see the *reward* of the righteous at all" (153). One of the vials that falls from angelic hands drives the wicked to Armageddon. The blasphemers of God are beaten to earth, in accompaniment to lightnings, voices, thunder, earthquake, and hail, which destroy the cities of the world. Babylon is overthrown to make way for Jerusalem (Rev. 17-18).

There is some agreement in the various mythological accounts of Rágnarök about its motifemes. When the Norse demons are loosed, Heimdall, the father of humans, sounds the giallar-horn (the trumpet) ("Völuspá" st. 33) and the battle begins in Vigriðr, the plain where all giants, demons, and heroes meet. Yggdrasill (the World Tree, or "Odin's Horse"), starts to shake ("Völuspá" st.34). After Odin rides to Mimir's well for advice (Mimir being a giant associated with wisdom), he combats

Fenfir the giant and both die. Other gods fight their enemies and they die on both sides: Thor fights with the World Serpent (dragon); the dog Garm, who breaks loose, attacks Tyr; and Loki fights with Heimdall. The Norse call this period "axel-tide," "sword-tide," "wind-tide," and "wolf-tide." The whole universe is consumed and the earth sinks:

> the sun turns black, the earth sinks below the sea,
> no bright star now shines from the heavens;
> flame leap the length of the World Tree,
> fire strikes against the very sky. ("Völuspá"st. 44)

In *LB*, Tirian and his followers prepare for battle against Shift, the Telmarines, and Calormenes in a tower that, according to Tirian, was built in his grandsire's time to guard against outlaws. (Incidentally, the tower resembles the Carfax Tower in Oxford, a squat tower with very few and narrow windows). It is also like the Tower of Virtue in *PC*, where Caspian learns about his ancestry and with this knowledge provided to him by the dwarf/man Cornelius, he is prepared to fight against the usurper King Miraz. The tower is also like Aslan's How in *PC*, a place for war council, except that the latter is underground, where Aslan's party holds a war council with the dwarf Nikabrik and his followers. This tower represents the military culture of the Narnians, their courage, and resourcefulness. It also serves to advance the plot in that it provides Tirian and his followers with a bottle filled with juice which, when rubbed on their hands and faces, can make them brown, a useful disguise to spy on the enemy, but which they remove, honorably, when they are in actual combat. Tirian and the children also find Calormene clothes there, which they put on, a successful counter disguise to Shift's.

In the meantime, Shift's camp (consisting of Shift, Rishda Tarkaan—the Calormene Captain—Ginger the Cat, and a group of assorted Beasts) assembles behind a bonfire, in front of the stable, the final setting in Narnia. To underscore the element of disguise in that camp, Lewis describes this assembly as if it is theater:

> For really, as it happened, the whole thing was rather like a theater. The crowd of Narnians were like the people in the seats; the little grassy place just in front of the stable, where the bonfire burned and the Ape and the Captain stood to talk to the crowd, was like the stage and the stable itself was like the scenery at the back of the stage; and Tirian and his friends were like people peering round from behind the scene. It was

a splendid position. If any of them stepped forward into the full firelight, all eyes would be fixed on him at once: on the other hand, so long as they stood still in the shadow of the end-wall of the stable, it was a hundred to one against their being noticed. (125-26)

The layers of deception are prevalent: Tirian and his friends in legitimate disguise are spying on Shift and his friends, who are also in disguise, only fraudulent disguise, in the sense that they are conspirators or impostors. The scene is like a Jacobean tragedy or Restoration play in its layers of spying and disguise. The bonfire associates this scene and its characters with hellish fire.

Before the final battle there is only silence, fear, and gloom. No "good night" from a hedgehog, no cry of an owl, no fauns dancing, no hammering noises from the dwarfs underground. The pace quickens and soon the two camps engage in a brief last battle: Tirian, the children, the unicorn, Puzzle, the dog, horses, Bear, Boar, and mice pitted against Shift and the Tarkaan with fifteen Calormenes, a Talking Bull, a satyr, and Slinkey the Fox. With the secession of the dwarfs ("Dwarfs are for the Dwarfs" [152, 153, 158]), Tirian and his followers are defeated, and he and the children, one by one, end up inside the stable, where "a terrible figure was coming toward them . . . it had a vulture's head and four arms. Its beak was open and its eyes blazed" (164). The terrible Tash reappears one more time, only to vanish into thin air at the sight of the Seven Kings and Queens of Narnia, who stand in the stable in their glittering clothes, with crowns on their heads and swords drawn in their hands. Light again ends all illusions. In our world, the oracles were silenced at the coming of Christ. John Milton writes that when Christ was born, "The Oracles are dumb / No voice or hideous hum / Runs through the arched roof in words deceiving" ("On the Morning of Christ's Nativity" 19. 1-3).

IV. The Sequel: New Earth, New Jerusalem, and New Narnia

In the Book of Revelation, an open door is set up before the saved: "I know thy works: 'behold, I have set before thee an open door, and no man can shut it: for thou hast a little strength, and hast kept my word, and hast not denied my name'" (3.8). "'This is the Door of the Father by which enter in Abraham, Isaac, and the Prophets, and the Apostles, and the Church'" (St. Ignatius qtd. in Ouspensky and Lossky 14). There is also a focus on the living waters, which signify baptism:

"The Lamb shall rule them and shall lead them to the fountains of the waters of life" (Rev. 7.17; 22.1). Out of the cryptic images comes a familiar image of hope. The New Jerusalem comes down out of heaven (21.2). The Rebellious Woman (19.2) is overthrown to make place for the pure Bride, the spiritual Zion, and the Rider on the White Horse (Easter Christ) appears (19.11). The heavens open and a white horse descends to preach the word of God. The saved souls reign a thousand years with Christ (20.4), but the others are condemned to a lake of fire and brimstone (20.10). The City of God is like a garden—but also a city on a mountain with a fountain of water, 12 gates, angels; and it is filled with light (21.10-13), like the New Earth at the end of Rágnarök, and it is free of evil (21.27). It has the Book of Life (20.12) and the tree of life in it (22.2). (See ch. 6 for a discussion of Cair Paravel as partaking of the attributes of the City of God). (See fig. 15).

In the myth of Rágnarök, after the whole universe is consumed and the fires have done their worst, the earth sinks into the ocean, but a new

FIG. 15. *POLYPTICH OF THE APOCALYPSE* (CENTRAL PANEL) BY JACOBELLO ALBEREGNIO, (1360-1390).

earth rises up with green grass and morning sun. It is a place of rebirth but not resurrection: "She [the sybil] sees the earth rising again / out of the waters, green once more" ("Völuspá" st. 45). With it come Thor's sons, Modi and Magni, as well as Odin's sons, Vidar and Vali. These new sons of gods will take up the ruling of the world. The god Balder and his brother Hodur will also return. A man and a woman, Lif and Lifthrasir, analogues of Adam and Eve, who survived the dissolution of the earth, will appear as Vafðruðnir tells Odin:

> Lif and Lifdrasir will both be left—
> they'll hide in Hoddmimir's forest.
> the morning dew will be their meat;
> they will beget more men. ("Vafðruðnismal" st. 44)

Fimbultyr, god from everlasting to everlasting, gathers all the virtuous into Gimlé—a structure whose hall is brighter than the sun, roofed with gold, filled with light and song—and the bad into Nastrand to be torn by Nidhug (the Serpent of the Underworld) until they are purged (Anderson 9). There will be other places for giants and dwarves also. In this manner, evil is restrained after Rágnarök (249). The "Vafðruðnismal" states that this is a new age. Life begins afresh. In one manuscript version of the "Völuspá" there is a two-line stanza of controversial authenticity at the end: "The mighty one comes down on the day of doom, / that powerful lord who rules over all" (Terry 10). Terry notes that a literal translation of these two lines may carry inappropriate Christian connotations (10).

On the other hand, *LB* offers a stronger note of hope than its predecessors. The stable door pre-empts the Day of Judgment, and the plot ends in a powerful pageant of the saved. At first glance Tirian refers to the doors of the stable as "more like a mouth," an allusion to the medieval Hell's Mouth in early religious drama, the entrance to hell. But the noble Jewel says, prophetically, "It may be for us the door to Aslan's country and we shall sup at his table tonight" (161). Jewel is right. Since Narnia is the land of redemption under Aslan, the dark stable door will function for his followers as the gate of redemption rather than judgment. Like the door frame in *PC*, which is the gateway from Narnia to earth, the stable door here is the gateway from Narnia to the Celestial Garden. Those who do not cross it are Aslan's enemies who chose "cunning instead of belief" (*LB* 185). They will remain in the world of darkness and bonfires, symbols of a pagan culture in our world. One Christological interpretation of Emeth the Calormene, who is embraced by Aslan as one of his sons, is that Christ also works on many who do not know him. In one of his letters, Lewis writes, "I think that every prayer which is sincerely made even to a false god . . . is accepted by the true God and that Christ saves many who do not think they know Him" (*CL* 3: 245). In *Problem*, Lewis explains the relationship of free will and getting out of hell: "The doors of hell are locked on the *inside*" (127). Presumably, the door to Heaven is open for everyone wishing to open it.

Inside the stable, Tirian finds himself, as in the Nordic myth, actually standing on green grass under a deep blue sky as if in a day in early summer (171). Around him there is also a grove of fruit trees, whose fruit taste is indescribable because, as Lewis writes, "You can't find out what it is like unless you can get to that country and taste it for yourself" (172). It is only for those who choose the way to the Celestial Garden. As a garden motif the fruits appear in *MN* and are found also in section 3 of *Pearl*, the Middle English poem, where their scent is deemed refreshing. They signify in both *Pearl* and *LB* the Eucharist, but bear no association to the forbidden fruit of *MN*. In this pristine elemental nature, there is no room for structures of any kind. Tirian observes, "It seems, then . . . that the stable seen from within and the stable seen from without are two different places." Lord Digory replies, "Its inside is bigger than its outside" (177). To which Lucy responds, "In our world too, a stable once had something inside it that was bigger than our whole world" (177). The followers of Aslan ascend "further up and further in" to the Celestial Garden, the Real Narnia, the closest Narnian analogue to the Christian Heaven.

V. Links between the Book of Revelation, Rágnarök, and *The Last Battle*

Old themes about the end of time, destruction, and renewal grow and develop under the hands of gifted poets and narrators. According to Mircea Eliade, "The religion of the Germans was one of the most complex and original in Europe . . . [and] their religious creativity was not paralyzed by the conversion to Christianity . . . [rather] flowering as a result of symbiosis with Christianity" (*A History* 2: 170). Because certain beliefs and motifs from the Book of Revelation appear in Germanic religion, one may conclude that there are Christian influences on the Norse myth. As John Lindow points out, "Thor and his fellow gods thus exited history at about the time Christ entered it in the North, that is, in the tenth and eleventh centuries" (45). Preben M. Sørensen's view is that "in the Viking Age in particular, Christianity was a source of inspiration to the poets who were the custodians of the Nordic myths" (213). Rágnarök may have been given new significance by the Christian Judgment Day. The Norse "Völuspá," compiled in the thirteenth-century, may have borrowed Christian ideas.

However, scholars have different views on this matter of influence. Some believe that the prophecy of "the mighty one" in the controversial last stanza of the "Völuspá" quoted above may constitute a parallel between heathen and Christian elements, if taken as a reference to Christ (Lönnroth 21). Gabriel Turville-Petre is more confident than other scholars that "Völuspá" "is coloured by Christian symbols, and particularly the description of the Rágnarök" (9). Indeed, the following similarities tie the myth of Rágnarök with Judeo-Christian motifs: 1) the World Serpent that fought with Thor resembles in symbolic terms the biblical Leviathan and the Old Dragon that was captured by Michael and the good angels in Rev. 12.7-9, 20.2 (Turville-Petre 76) and possibly the sea-serpent in *VDT* and the Green Serpent in *SC*; 2) Thor in the last battle resembles Christ fishing to catch the devil, the hook being seen as the cross (Sørensen 119; Turville-Petre 76); 3) the Norse Loki is the analogue of the Anti-Christ bound in Hell, who breaks loose before the Day of Judgment (Turville-Petre 145); 4) Surt, the giant of fire scorches men like the good angel in Revelation; 5) the trumpet sound in "Völuspá" is like the trumpet sounds of the seven angels in Revelation, but used for a different purpose; 6) Gimlé (the hall of the surviving gods) in Rágnarök is similar to the New Jerusalem in Revelation in that it is a constructed building and also well lighted, while Nastrand, the place for purgation, resembles the place for punishments dealt the blasphemers in Revelation.

This division of the two cities is close to St. Augustine's two cities in Heaven. As he states in "Enchiridion," after the resurrection, once the general judgment has been brought to a conclusion, "the boundaries will be laid out of two cities: one of Christ, the other of the devil; one of the good, the other of the bad; yet both made up of angels and of men" (4.463). Besides these motifemes, "Völuspá," as a prophecy about the end of the world is not only like the Book of Revelation, but also like Matthew 24 and Mark 13.8, 24-25. According to H. R. Ellis Davidson, "biblical prophecies like that in Matthew 24 may have been a favourite theme of preachers in the tenth or eleventh centuries. Once Christian learning reached the North, all kinds of eschatological ideas and images are likely to find a way in the literary sources" (*Myths and Symbols* 193).

Some scholars offer a different view about the relationship of Nordic mythology to Christianity. Ralph Metzner and historian Jan de Vries believe that the "Völuspà" is a revelation of a soul between two world epochs (246); H. R. Ellis Davidson believes that Rágnarök is a "requiem" for the old gods and their replacement with Christ and his angels (*Myth and Symbols* 192; c.f. Anderson 236), which Lewis hints at in the Stable Scene at the end of *LB*, when the Calormene Tash vanishes in the radiance of Aslan and his crowned Kings and Queens of Narnia; on the back free endpaper of his copy of M. Mallet's *Northern Antiquities*, Lewis summarizes Mallet's views: "Mallet (p. 104) wd. Be tempted to see Christian influence in the prose Edda but is deterred by Voluspo [sic] which he deems ancient and uncorrupted to admit this. In his notes on the prose Edda he points out the similarity between R. [ágnarök] and the Stoic conflagration (pp. 514 et seq) and suggests that Zeno and the Germanic races both get it from the 'Eastern philosophers and more particularly the Persians.'" [4]

Looking at these similarities between the Book of Revelation and Rágnarök, with respect to *LB*, one finds in *LB* some of the same motifemes: 1) there are plenty of evil creatures, even dragons and serpents, that wasted the vegetation and died; 2) Tash and Shift are diabolic figures like Loki and Satan in Revelation; 3) the sun and moon are darkened, the stars fall down, and Narnia is in total darkness as in Revelation; 4) there is also the trumpet sound in all three texts, but the one sounded by Old Man Time in *LB* does not signal judgment as in Revelation or battle as in Rágnarök, only the start of the procession to the Celestial Garden; 5) the stable door in *LB* is similar to the "open door" in Rev. 3.8, but is open to everyone who chooses Aslan, recalling John 6.37: "All that the Father giveth me shall come to me; and him that cometh to me I will in no wise cast out"; 6) the Celestial Garden is also filled with light like the New Jerusalem or New Earth in Rágnarök, but is not essentially a structure; and 7), *LB* also shares with Rágnarök, to a limited extent, the Germanic sense of loss, of the passing of an era of heroism and *magia*, when humans and divine beings interacted directly, as described in Lucy's mourning for Narnia. As Charles W. Dunn writes, for the Norse poets, "the gods are viewed as awesome, remote, and mysterious beings. Man's life is essentially tragic; an inexorable fate constantly threatens to snatch him away to a cold and cheerless afterworld" (introduction to *Poems of the Elder Edda* xxv). This is a predominant worldview in *Beowulf* and Anglo-Saxon literature in general.

However, although *LB* shares with Revelation and Rágnarök the intensity and ubiquity of evil, both the pagan Nordic/Germanic tendency to pessimism and the foreboding atmosphere of Revelation are subsumed in *LB* by one of clear hope and promise within reach of every follower of Aslan. The most important difference between *LB*'s version and the other versions of the apocalypse is that Lewis's version pre-empts Judgment and Aslan leads his followers right away up to the high mountain to the Celestial Garden, depending upon their acceptance of him. There are no more prophecies; the Narnian Heaven is actually at hand; and the gate is large enough to accommodate all believers in Aslan. There are no more purifications or trials; the end is here.

What with the ensuing confusion about what is real or unreal and the paradoxical statements of "further up and further in," "the interior is bigger than the exterior," and Emeth, a Calormene, being admitted into Aslan's presence, one finds that Lewis in *LB* is proffering a view of a reality that is more mysterious and philosophically more complex than in his earlier chronicles, without losing narrative appeal. Consequently, in the last chronicle, light and dark imagery intertwine in the final tableau to signal the end of the Old Narnia. Darkness reigns for a while over the Old Narnia and then there is an apocalyptic white light as the scene changes to the New Narnia. The roles of light as an image of Grace and as a component of *Sehnsucht* (the sense of longing) are all intensified in *LB* to describe the New Narnia. After all, transcendent Reality, Platonic or Christian, is numinous and deeper than anyone can imagine it. Lewis's story, however, assures us of this Celestial Garden in a powerful way. No dissembling Ape or cruel Calormene, not even a despairing Dwarf or cunning cat, can stand in the way of anyone going through that stable door. No one can close it unless he chooses to. Lewis's Christianity in this work subsumes other myths that prefigure it—a fundamental typological belief in consonance with Lewis's thinking (see introduction and *passim*). The New Law subsumes the Old Law, and the Celestial Garden subsumes the New Jerusalem of St. John and the Norse New Earth in Lewis's imagination. Through his own mythopoeic fiction Lewis assures Christians, as St. Mark does, that after all the cataclysmic events, the sun and moon darkening, the earthquakes, the wars, and the stars falling down, "then shall they see the Son of man coming in the clouds with great power and glory" (13.26).

Lewis affirms the hope that there is "divine presence in human loneliness" (Ward 203). As he wrote to Dom Bede Griffiths on December 20, 1946, even if the future is very dark, "there's usually light enough for the next step or so" (*CL* 2: 748). And so Aslan appears physically to lead his followers to the Celestial Garden, to create the final metamorphosis of Narnia into the Real Narnia, the final *eucatastrophe* in the series. His actual appearance is more powerful compared to one prophetic two-line stanza of dubious authenticity in "Völuspá" and more heartwarming than the cryptic vision of St. John. Joy and redemption are available to everyone who chooses Aslan, even to those like Emeth the Calormene, who do not choose Him consciously, but are seeking Him without knowing. Lewis found it useful to draw on these two sources, one mythical and one scriptural, and to juxtapose them with his own elaborate story about an apocalypse, in an endeavor to define Christianity as being inclusive, personal, and full of hope and redemption—and to woo his readers to such a belief.

Endnotes

1. In his diary, Lewis records on February 8, 1927, the following: "...Spent the morning partly on the *Edda* .... an exciting experience, when I remember my first passion for things Norse under the initiation of Longfellow ... at about the age of nine : and its return, much stronger, when I was about 13, when the high priests were M. Arnold, Wagner's music, and the Arthur Rackham Ring. It seemed impossible then that I should ever come to read these things in the original. The old authentic thrill came back to me at once or twice this morning: the mere names of god and giant catching my eye as I turned the pages of Zoega's dictionary was enough" (*All My Road Before Me* 448). The three books that Lewis went on to read about Norse mythology are *Myths of the Norsemen*, *Myths and Legends of the Teutonic Race*, and Mallet's *Northern Antiquities*, "which he found the most stimulating discovery so far" (Green and Hooper 22). The last one, in the same edition that Lewis read, is among the works I consulted. See n. 2 below.

2. Primary sources for Rágnarök are Sturluson Snorre, *The Younger Edda*, trans. Rasmus B. Anderson (Chicago: S. C. Griggs and Company, 1880) 139-45 and *passim*; *Poems of the Elder Edda*, trans. Patricia Terry, rev. ed. (Philadelphia: U of Pennsylvania P, 1990); Information on Rágnarök is gathered from M. Mallet, *Northern Antiquities*, trans. Bishop Percy (1770. London, UK: Bell and Daldy, 1873) 451-58; H. A. Guerber, *Myths of Northern Lands* (NY: American Book Company, 1895) passim; valuable discussions of this myth can be found in H. R. Ellis Davidson's two books: *Gods and Myths of Northern Europe* (1964; Hamondsworth, UK: Penguin, 1976) 202-23; and *Myths and Symbols in Pagan Europe* (Syracuse, NY: Syracuse U P, 1988) *passim*.

3. Farrer believes that the book is divided into six equal parts, the four sevens (messages, seals, trumpets, vials) and the two blanks (sections comparable with the others) (45); also it includes six visions (the Woman and the Dragon, the Beast, the Second Beast [with a false Lamb], the True Lamb, three flying angels with proclamations, and the Son of Man on clouds with three angelic harvesters) (49). He also uncovers diagrams, cyclic patterns, and numerological symbolism in the work.

4. By permission of the Marion E. Wade Center, Wheaton College, Wheaton, Illinois, and The C.S. Lewis Company Pte. Ltd.

CHAPTER TEN

OVIDE MORALISÉE IN NARNIA: METAMORPHOSIS AND *THÈŌSIS*

> ARIEL's Song: *Full fathom five thy father lies;*
> *Of his bones coral made;*
> *Those are pearls that were his eyes.*
> *Nothing of him doth fade*
> *But both suffer a sea-change*
> *Into something rich and strange.*
> Shakespeare *The Tempest* (1.2.398-04)

> *I change, but I cannot die.*
> Shelley "The Cloud" (line76)

I. Ovid's *Metamorphoses* in Narnia

It is the universal theme of Metamorphoses, then, represented through a series of transformations from one form, substance, or psychological position to another, that intersects Lewis's, Ovid's works, and to a limited extent, Norse myths. A student of the classics and Norse myths, Lewis was thoroughly immersed in both. He thought highly of Ovid's *Metamorphoses*, quoted from it, and recommended it for reading.[1] (See fig.16). However, I am not suggesting that this popular work was a major influence on the *Chronicles*, but there is an overall thematic similarity between them. Like the Ovidian world, Narnia is a world-in-progress, dynamic, always threatened by the forces of evil, sometimes on the brink of destruction. In both works there is a cycle of miraculous changes on which the myths are based.

As mentioned above, each chronicle is based on the concept of change, but Aslan is dominant in his cosmos, while the demi-urge of Ovid, who created the world, disappeared, allowing these wild gods and goddesses to run rampant in the universe. While *Metamorphoses* is half cynical, lacking a religious/moral purpose, there is always in

FIG. 16. BOOK III OF GEORGE SANDYS (ED.), *OVID'S METAMORPHOSES ENGLISHED, MYTHOLOGIZ'D AND REPRESENTED IN FIGURES*.

Narnia a *eucatastrophe* (see introduction) when order is restored by the miraculous intervention of Aslan—in each individual story and at the ending of the Big Story, or the Christian monomyth, if we follow a chronological reading of the *Chronicles*. There are appearances of some general Ovidan mythical figures in Narnia like centaurs, minotaurs, and specific ones like Bacchus, Silenus, and Pomona (invented by Ovid) in *PC*, but certainly no modeling of characters on any of Ovid's. The Big

Story of Narnia begins with Creation, as in *Metamorphoses*, but ends with a somewhat Nordic apocalypse to end all change like that of the Christian apocalypse, while Ovid remains concerned with Roman history and metempsychoses, or transmigration of souls, until the very end. There are no Ovidian verbal echoes in the *Chronicles*, and Ovid's brilliant, artificial language, addressed to the adult reader, is missing. So is his stress on feminine psychology, love, and domestic relationships. Here are Lewis's own comments on Ovid's *Metamorphoses*:

> When I open Ovid, or Grimm, I find the sort of miracles which really would be arbitrary. Trees talk, houses turn into trees, magic rings raise tables richly spread with food in lonely places, ships become goddesses, and men are changed into snakes or birds or bears. It is fun to read about: the least suspicion that it had really happened would turn that fun into nightmare. ("Miracles," *God in the Dock* 32)

Lewis goes on to explain that the true miracles (the miracles in the Gospels) express God, not simply a god, but the Creator. They are not arbitrary, theatrical, or meaningless interruptions of Nature, but divine events working with Nature, i.e. *magia*.

B. Norse Mythology

Norse mythology, on the other hand, was a more powerful direct influence on Lewis. Its myths contain many incidents of metamorphoses. It was common for Norse gods to assume the shapes of animals, even plants, for the purpose of revenge or deception. Odin was a shape changer; for instance, he appeared as an old man in battle against the enemy; so was Freya, the goddess of fertility, transformed into a bird. According to Snorri Sturluson, Odin was skilled in magic lore and was able to embody animal forms. "Odin could change himself. His body then lay as if sleeping or dead, but he became a bird or a wild beast, a fish or a dragon" ("Yngling Saga" qtd. in Davidson, *Gods and the Myths of Northern Europe* 145). Werewolves abound in the Norse imagination as well as a basic belief in totemism. Sigmund and Snfioti, his son, metamorphosed into wolves by donning wolf skins. Gefion the goddess changed her children into oxen to plough the land. Poisons and spells are also common fare of Nordic myths. In *The Ring of the Nibelung* Gudrun uses her magic potion to make Sigurd fall in love with her—a psychological change caused by magic. In these fragments of narratives, such rapid, destructive metamorphoses reflect the violent culture of the warring Norse people. In the *Chronicles*, similar quick, violent transformations were used by Lewis mostly in battle scenes—especially the Battle of Beruna in *LWW*, where the White Witch would avail herself of her magic wand to petrify her enemies, while Aslan responded by de-petrifying them. However, one major metamorphosis, the apocalyptic end, Rágnarök, or "The Doom of the Gods" in Nordic mythology, is a major source for Lewis's own Narnian apocalypse in *LB* (see ch. 9). The concept of "Northerness" and the remote, cold Nordic vistas appear mostly in the settings of *LWW* and the land of the giants in *SC* (see ch. 3).

C. *Thèōsis* as a Type of Metamorphosis in Narnia

Lewis created his own "new" mythology out of his readings and imagination to support his mythopoeic analogies of Christian transformation. In Lewis's Christianity, the final state of conversion, of becoming fully Christian, is *thèōsis*, a basic doctrine in Eastern Orthodox theology, which suggests Lewis's openness to the doctrines of the Eastern Orthodox Church. This process of transformation culminates in a union with God which, according to Lewis is the whole purpose of life (*Mere Christianity* 161). Another way to look at the process is to see it as a participation in the Body of Christ and the Holy Trinity—to become "little Christs" (*Mere* 177, 192). (See chs. 1 and 2 for a detailed discussion). The process of *thèōsis* per se in the *Chronicles* is represented by the metamorphoses of characters in Narnia in two forms: 1) in individual characters as they become like Aslan, and bring harmony and regeneration to themselves and Narnia, and rid all of evil until the final apocalypse, and 2) in a collective metamorphosis as in a pageant.

1. Individual Metamorphoses

All the British children, except Susan, grow in Christian and classical virtues as their stories unfold. There are many examples of Aslan's direct interventions in individuals' lives for this purpose. In *HHB*, he punishes the evil Radabash by downgrading him to a donkey à la Apuleius, and perhaps succeeds in making him a better person; in *PC*, he regenerates the Talking Animals and Trees, which make Miraz's defeat possible; in *VDT*, he "un-dragonizes" Eustace and metamorphoses into an albatross to save the children from the Black Cloud and a lamb (ch. 8); in *SC*, he restores Prince Rilian to the throne by possibly initiating the destructive metamorphosis of the Green Witch from human to serpent (the latter's transformation from serpent to lady and back again is one of the most powerful incidents of destructive metamorphosis in literature that parallel Dante's metamorphosis of the thieves into serpents in circle 7 of the *Inferno),* while Shift's poor attempt at "metamorphosing" Puzzle into Aslan in *LB,* by putting over him a dead lion's skin, is a parody of this process of change (see ch. 9); also, whenever Aslan appears to his followers, he breathes "lion strength" into them to regenerate them as Jesus breathed on his disciples in John 20.22. There are other processes of metamorphosis that are indirectly caused by Aslan like giving life to inanimate objects like the paintings in Aunt Alberta's house and in the Magician's House in *VDT* (see ch. 8). These are strong notes of hope and redemption that Lewis wants to leave his readers with. He uses all the sources that he has amassed in memory and his readings to construct these powerful scenes, which form the core of the stories.

Another individual metamorphosis occurs toward the end of *SC* when the dead King Caspian, while in a stream, is resurrected through a drop of Aslan's blood that splashes over him. Like the stream that Jill drank from in Aslan's Country, the stream here represents in Christian iconography resurrection or baptism. As he has done in the scene of the statues' liberation in *LWW,* and in all scenes of coming to life, Lewis describes the change in the dead king in slow motion: "His white beard turned to gray, and from gray to yellow, and got shorter and vanished altogether; and his sunken cheeks grew round and fresh, and the wrinkles were smoothed, and his eyes opened, and his eyes and lips both laughed, and suddenly he leaped up and stood before them—a very young man" (252). Also, before the story ends there is a scene with the children standing in "great brightness of mid-summer sunshine" (251) on green grass, with a stream of "liquid glass" (251) flowing by—another glimpse of the Christian heaven by analogy, which creates in the children and us the ubiquitous longing for it. It is the ascent of the soul up to God (the sun).

In *HHB,* during a most frightful time in his life, Shasta, separated from his friends, is riding on a lackadaisical horse towards Anvard, surrounded by fog and literally blinded as to his location, when he soon discovers that someone is walking with him. He could hear the Lion breathing "on a very large scale" (173) and thinks it is a ghost from the dead. When the Lion breathes upon his hand and face and assures him of his aid, Shasta begins to feel awe in the presence of this creature, "a new and different sort of trembling" (176) and then

> [t]he whiteness around him became a shining whiteness; his eyes began to blink . . . He knew the night was over at last. He could see the mane and ears and head of his horse quite easily now. A golden light fell on them from the left. He thought it was the sun.
>
> He turned and saw, pacing beside him, taller than the horse, a lion. It was from the lion that the light came. No one saw anything more terrible or beautiful. . . .
>
> The High King above all Kings stooped toward him. Its mane, and some strange and solemn perfume that hung about the mane, was all around him. It touched his forehead with its tongue. He lifted his face and their eyes met. Then instantly the pale brightness of the mist and the fiery brightness of the Lion rolled themselves together into a swirling glory and gathered themselves up and disappeared. (177-78)

Aslan comes to Shasta in this splendid passage and brings with him light, an image of safety, protection, and grace as he anoints Shasta to be the protector of Narnia, an analogue to Christ's call to his followers on earth.

The last example of individual metamorphosis has to do with Caspian in *VDT*. It is the marvel of an object come to life. After Caspian retires to his cabin in a temper because he is not allowed to go along with Reepicheep and the British children farther eastward to the World's End, he witnesses a miracle. As he later reports to the sailors, "Aslan has spoken to me. No—I don't mean he was actually here. He wouldn't fit into the cabin, for one thing. But that gold lion's head on the wall came to life and spoke to me. It was terrible—his eyes" (262). Aslan appears to purge Caspian of his sin of pride. After this metamorphic experience, Caspian accepts that his duties as a King and a future husband to Ramandu's daughter must take priority over his private adventurous desires, so he returns to Ramandu's Island to pick up the sleeping lords, awakened from their sleep by the fulfillment of Ramandu's command, marry Ramandu's daughter, and sail westward back to Cair Paravel. Memory is also at work, for he has to remember Aslan's words to make decisions about his life. So also any author, according to Lewis, has to remember God's words in his creative imagination as a source of inspiration.

2. Pageants of Metamorphosis

One of the most exquisite pageants takes place in *LWW*. After the melting of the snow at the coming of Aslan, his martyrdom and resurrection, the forces of liberation composed of Aslan and his followers descend upon the Witch's Castle of Ice. The whole pageant is suggestive of Christ's descent to Hell in some Christian traditions to raise the saints of the Old Testament (Ford 90). Aslan's action is somewhat chronologically appropriate since he goes to the Witch's Castle after his own resurrection. Also, the walls of the Witch's Castle and the towers are broken in the process as the medieval tradition has us believe about the gates of Hell. Aslan leaps over the wall of the Castle to begin the process of metamorphosis: regeneration from death. He breathes on the stone lion, the dwarf, the two centaurs, and a rabbit, and they all come alive. The stone lion's regeneration is described in slow motion, as if to engrave it in our memories: "A tiny streak of gold began to run along his white marble back—then it spread—then the color seemed to lick all over him as the flame licks all over a bit of paper—then while his hindquarters were still obviously stone, the lion shook his mane and all the heavy, stone folds rippled into living hair" (184). This is a Dantean image of metamorphosis, of the sinners in the slow process of changing into serpents, their bodies mixing together:

> so neither seemed what he had been before;
> Just as, when paper's kindled, where it still
> has not caught flame in full, its color's dark
> though not yet black, while white is dying off.
> (*Inferno* 25. 63-66)

In both passages the operating symbol is fire, which here represents energy and life in Lewis's passage, as opposed to the "evil-looking torches" of the demons at the Stone Table, and punishment in Dante's. In one, the creatures regain their natural form, in the other they lose it; one is a positive metamorphosis, the other is a negative one. The good stone giant comes alive in slow motion. Soon, a blaze of colors erupts all around, dazzling plumage of birds, red-brown furs of foxes, yellow stockings and crimson hoods of dwarfs, and the long silence is broken by the sounds of animals, songs, and laughter (185).

This is a striking scene of metamorphosis similar to the Creation scenes in Genesis and *MN*. This scene is also reminiscent of spiritual rebirth in the Old and New Testaments. For example, in Ezekiel 11.19: "And I will give them [exiles of Israel] one heart, and I will put a new spirit within you; and I will take the stony heart out of their flesh, and will give them a heart of flesh." Also, "A new heart will I give you, and a new spirit will I put within you: and I will take away the stony heart out of your flesh, and I will give you an heart of flesh" (36.26). Similarly, rebirth means achieving full identities and glory in Christ. Aslan's liberation of these petrified creatures annuls the power of the Witch. The appearance of Jesus to the apostles in John 20.2 comes to mind here: "And when he had said this, he breathed on them and saith unto them 'Receive ye the Holy Ghost.'" It is analogous to the Miracle of Reversals that Lewis discusses in *Miracles*, the miracle of raising the dead (146). The liberation of the statues and Nature itself from the chains of Death and of Aslan from the Stone Table forcefully bring home to the reader the Death and Resurrection of Christ, the greatest metamorphosis in Christian history. Lewis presents a typological view on this matter in the following passage from *Miracles*: "We get Law before Gospel, animal sacrifices foreshadowing the great sacrifice of God to God, the Baptist before the Messiah, and those 'miracles of the New Creation' which come before the Resurrection" (154). If Narnia is considered analogous to our world, then Aslan's resurrection and the liberation of the stone animals point to the Resurrection in our world and in our stony hearts. Transformation or metamorphosis through Christ is the *magia* that annuls sin. After this miraculous event Aslan's forces leave the Castle to prepare for the First Battle of Beruna, the strong ones helping the weak, the tall carrying the small. Already a sense of fellowship is developing among Aslan's followers that is analogous to Christ's disciples and the Christian community in our life.

Another most powerful pageant scene of metamorphosis that has not been discussed yet is the one that ends *PC*. With Miraz and his followers defeated, Nature in Narnia is regenerated, like the humans, and reclaims itself. The complete regeneration of Narnia is described as a powerful, if sanitized, Bacchanalia that sweeps through the community and gathers the diverse groups of Old Narnians in a ceremony of joy and dancing.[2] We are treated to an overwhelming, spectacular pageant complete with classical gods, as the final metamorphosis of Narnians occurs with "Aslan leading, Bacchus and his Maenads leaping, rushing . . . and Silenus and his donkey bringing up the rear" (211). The river-god's chains are loosened by Bacchus at the order of Aslan and the Telmarine bridge collapses into the swirling waters and changes back to the Ford of Beruna. All of Narnia is renewed in every field and wood. Trees are changed back into Dryads and Hama Dryads, sad donkeys become joyful and young, and chained dogs and bridled horses break free to join the procession. A tired headmistress and a healed old woman join the procession, the latter being Caspian's old nurse. The headmistress's desk becomes a rosebush, and the stick with which a man was beating a boy bursts into flowers in the man's hand. This last metamorphosis is of special significance because it has two sources that reflect Lewis's scholarly interests: the first is the story of Aaron's rod in Numbers 17.8, which blossoms into flowers to confirm the exclusive right of the Tribe of Levi. This incident has been typologically interpreted in the Christian tradition as the Incarnation of Christ and his Virgin Birth. Linking this biblical miracle with this incident in *PC* enriches the theme of positive transformation in the story and adds credibility to the dynamic quality of the Narnian universe, potentially open to the metamorphosing presence of Aslan. The second source of this incident is a sixteenth-century story in *The Voiage and Travayle of Sir Maundeville, Knight*, a story among many other marvels, about some "men [who] cast in anger a firebrand or burning stick after our lord, but the same burning sticke did fall on the earth, and incontinent grew out of the same sticke a tree, and is waxen a bigge tree, and growth yet, and the scales of the tree be all blacke" (86). Here, it is used as a form of punishment rather than prophecy. Similarly, the man who was beating the boy in *PC* is transformed into a tree as punishment, an allusion to the myth of Daphne (see fig. 17), who metamorphosed into a laurel tree (to escape Apollo's lust), and to Dante's suicides who are transformed into trees and bushes in circle seven (*Inferno* 13) as punishment. Also, evil boys are turned to pigs à la Circe, which, as in classical myths, reflects their inner natures (*PC* 24). The whole scene of regeneration is a powerful tableau of classicism merged with Christianity, a tableau of syncretism as in much of Dante's *Inferno* and Milton's *Paradise Lost*. It is one of the four most powerful scenes of *eucatastrophe* in the *Chronicles*, the rest being those in *LWW*, *VDT*, and *LB*.

Lewis uses the pageant of human and animal, male and female Bacchantes, to illustrate the metamorphoses in Narnia. But it is noteworthy to observe that Lewis's own conversion to Christianity was facilitated by his reading about the myth of Dionysus and other pagan gods. His own primal belief that had earlier set him on the path to Christianity was that the dying and rising god of pagan myths—of which Bacchus (or Dionysus, in Greek) is certainly a type—became a

FIG. 17. *APOLLO AND DAPHNE* BY ANTONIO DEL POLLAIUOLO (1470-80). (THE NATIONAL GALLERY)

fact in Christ; this is the Great Miracle (*Dock* 80-88). There are numerous parallels drawn between Dionysus and Christ which place them in the motifemic pattern of "the suffering hero, posthumously deified" (Harris 285).[3] However, this pattern is modified in *PC*. Aslan, Bacchus, and Christ, return to Narnia/Earth, respectively, not as sacrificial lambs but as ferocious lions. Dionysus also appears as a lion in the Homeric "Hymn to Dionysus," to punish those who did not accept his divinity (Harris 133). Stripping Bacchus of his ambivalences, antisocial, and orgiastic behavior, Lewis brings out his positive attributes as the dying and rising vegetation god, liberator from death in its many spiritual and physical forms, a Christ figure, leading his followers under the leadership of Aslan, another Christ figure. Bacchus is an appropriate agent here because he is the "quintessentially metamorphic divinity" (Barkan 38) in addition to being the god of non-rationality and ecstasy. He is the deity of transformation, a potential source of salvation (Hardie 8), who obscures the divisions between man and god.

The authentic pagan chants "Euan, euan, eu-oi-oi" (*PC* 167) seem to me an aspect of *thèōsis* as discussed earlier. They also obliterate the separation between gods and their followers, adding to the unification of the two. The vine branches that crawl all through Narnia are emblematic of Dionysus, since he rescued himself and his followers from the ship he was kidnapped in with vines that crawled on the ship and entangled his enemies. The vines in *PC* are also derived from biblical passages, namely John 15. 5: "I am the vine, ye *are* the branches / : He that abideth in me, and I in him, the same bringeth forth much fruit: for without me ye are nothing." This passage hints at the doctrine of *thèōsis*, which Lewis may also be doing with the crawling vine branches all over the city. Thus the scene of regeneration can be interpreted as a transformation of the self, "a kind of mystic union by which heaven and earth are present in a single individual" (Barkan 44), another close description of the doctrine of *thèōsis*. These symbols from classical mythology unify the Narnian people under Aslan, the Narnian god. Later on, after Caspian is crowned King, the festivity climaxes in a truly Bacchic scene including a bonfire, a magic dance, banqueting, and drinking all kinds of wines, and Lewis's favorite image of the dance, symbolizing fellowship with Aslan.

Beginning with the regeneration of ruins in memory, then in humans, Talking Animals, and now trees, all Narnia is regenerated in different ways by Aslan and his followers, the protector of justice and conqueror of evil as he is in all the *Chronicles*. Later on, in a moving passage, Aslan, like Lucy earlier, is in a deep communion with the moon, one of his images, like the sun. While all his followers are asleep, after being sumptuously feasted by him, the Golden Lion stays awake, his work done: "All night Aslan and the moon gazed upon each other with joyful and unblinking eyes" (*PC* 228). Aslan has fulfilled Narnian divine law and conquered the evil Telmarines. This is a huge "synchronic moment" in which the divine intersects with the linear plot to create the expected final *eucatastrophe* that is to follow soon. The next day, light swaddles him in the field at Beruna and "[t]he living and strokable gold of Aslan's mane outshone them all" (230), as opposed to the darkness that depicts the children's early confusion in the woods and Nikabrik, the evil dwarf, in his council, against the king and his evil watch guards (who turn out to be a werewolf and none other than the White Witch disguised as a hag). Eventually, after the experience of transformation, Aslan builds an imaginary (yet real) doorway, three beams put together, through which the Telmarines, as well as the children, leave Narnia back to earth: the imaginary/real doorway is one other miracle of Aslan.

The door is a foreshadowing image of the final door in Narnia in *LB*—the door to the Celestial Garden.

The pageant of regeneration on the Island of Ramandu in *VDT* is yet another example of a powerful collective and ritualistic metamorphosis, which deserves explication. Ramandu and his daughter enter from a cave on the hillside to complete this most apocalyptic vignette. The old man and his daughter, holding up their arms, turn to the East. In this position they begin to sing:

> And as they sang, the gray clouds lifted from the eastern sky and the white patches grew bigger and bigger till it was all white, and the sea began to shine like silver. And long afterward (but those two sang all the time) the east began to turn red and at last, unclouded, the sun came up out of the sea and its long level ray shot down the length of the table on the gold and silver and the Stone Knife. (222)

The iconographic images in this tableau are pulled together and enhanced in significance by the beam of light that comes from the East. This seemingly Celtic instance of sun-worship has strong Christian associations. We later learn that the crimson table with food laid on it is a symbol of Aslan's sacrifice since it is the same table on which Aslan was slain by the Witch earlier in *LWW*. In our world all these are symbols of Christ's passion and Resurrection: the color red, a reminder of the crucifixion; the food, also the feast of life for the redeemed. The pageant of Aslan's table represents the act of communion, the food and the wine being the body and blood of Christ. The turning of Ramandu and his daughter to the East to pray links them to the long classical and Judaeo-Christian traditions of the East discussed in chapters 6 and 7. The central character, Ramandu, actually a "retired" star, who is allegedly getting younger due to consuming a fire-berry fetched daily by a bird from the valleys of the sun, foreshadows both in his prophetic character and the orientation of his prayer, the resurrection and redemption scene that occurs further east in Aslan's Country, the Garden of Restoration (see ch. 7). He is a *magus* figure.

The apocalyptic imagery continues to set the baptismal motif as the scene slowly changes and the narrative moves forward. As Ramandu and his daughter continue with their early morning song, the rising sun looks bigger: "And the brightness of its ray on the dew and on the table was far beyond any morning brightness they had ever seen" (222). Again, the sun ray coming from the East links the table of sacrifice and the dew on the grass, both symbols of rebirth: one sacred and one natural. Another rich tableau is then presented. After a while a large flock of white birds appears and joins in the singing. One bird flies to the old man "with something in its beak that looked like a little fruit, unless it was a little live coal, which it might have been, for it was too bright to look at. And the bird laid it in the Old Man's mouth" (223). The image of the live coal comes from Isaiah 6 .6-7 and symbolizes his call for prophecy. Ramandu, in his own pagan/biblical setting is also a prophet. He issues his own prophecy: the travelers must sail to the World's End, earth's eastern rim, but must leave one behind there. Pilgrimage to the East is required to break the spell cast on the three sleeping lords. The children must meet Aslan to grow in faith and be restored by him, although on the diachronic level the quest for the missing knights is over.

Finally, the Cosmic Dance is Lewis's ultimate image for *thèōsis*, which I am arguing is a type of metamorphosis bringing about harmony, love, and order in the world. The most powerful illustration of this image, outside the *Chronicles*, occurs in *Perelandra*, where the dance begins with voices blessing Maledil, God in our world, who is at the center of the Perelandran universe: "All things are by Him and for Him. He utters Himself also for His own delight and sees that He is good. He is His own begotten and what proceeds from Him is Himself. Blessed be He" (344). Then Ransom, the human protagonist, "thought he saw the Great Dance. It seemed to him woven out of the intertwining undulation of many bands or cords of light" (344). Suddenly, "the movement grew yet swifter, the interweaving yet more ecstatic the relevance of all to all" (345). These images recall the Dantean images in *Paradiso*, of the angels in interwoven circles around the Tenth Heaven, the empyrean, the source of Light and Life (28.94-139). (See fig. 18). The closer to the Empyrean, the faster the souls move. Lewis's image of the Dance appears also in *Mere Christianity* (175-76) to describe the pattern of the three-Person God for each Christian. In *Problem*, Lewis discusses the Incarnation as God's self-giving, an act of God's Love, and an

> eternal dance [which] 'makes heaven drowsy with the harmony.' All pains and pleasures we have known on earth are early initiations in the movements of that dance; but the dance itself is strictly incomparable with the sufferings of this   present time .... There is joy in the dance: but it does not exist for the sake of joy .... It is Love Himself, and Good Himself. (153)

On the other hand, the Witches also play the transformation game. As agents of negative or destructive metamorphoses, they, like the jealous Hera in classical mythology or Loki in Norse mythology, transform others and seemingly themselves (in the case of the Green Witch) through instruments of Dark Magic, *goeteia*: Jadis's bell and hammer in *MN* bring her back to life as a tyrant to wreak havoc on Narnia, the White Witch's wand in *LWW* petrifies the Narnians and her Turkish Delight stupefies Edmund, and the Green Witch's green powder in *SC* casts a spell on Aslan's followers—albeit temporary changes to be reversed by Aslan.

Fig. 18. Ezekiel's fiery wheel with its four creatures as illustrated in the Geneva Bible (1576).

Navigating to and from these places in Narnia under the illumination of the sun (and its satellites, the moon and the stars), constitutes the metamorphic journey in each chronicle. The topic of metamorphoses seems to organize most of the Aslan-centered plots in these novels. The Old Law must be superseded by the New Law, the Dark Magic of the Witches by the White Magic of Aslan. Aslan works his miracles, as the

Ovide Moralistée in Narnia

gods in Greco-Roman and Norse mythologies, and the Judaeo-Christian God, either through interventions in individuals, through their actions in Narnia, or in pageant-like events with much romping and dancing. Either way he is the healer in Narnia as Christ is the healer in our world.

Endnotes

1. See *CL* 2: 880, 1541; 3: 1375.

2. Unfortunately, this powerful scene was omitted from the 2008 movie production of *Prince Caspian*.

3. For more information on the Dionysus/Christ analogy, see Stephen L. Harris and Gloria Platner, *Classical Mythology: Images and Insight*, 5th ed. (Boston, MA: McGraw-Hill, 2008), 282-86.

CONCLUSION

> *If God chooses to be mythopoeic—and is not the sky itself a myth—shall we refuse to be* mythopathic? *For this is the marriage of heaven and earth: Perfect Myth and Perfect Fact.*
>
> Lewis "Myth Became Fact," *God in the Dock* (67)

In *Spenser's Images,* Lewis claims that Spenser's *FQ* is "a simple fairy-tale pleasure sophisticated by polyphonic technique, a simple 'moral' sophisticated by a learned iconography" (17). It has been my effort in this study to uncover some of the "learned" sources and traditions of the major images (iconographical at times) in the *Chronicles* that Lewis stored in memory to show how they enriched the theme of metamorphosis/*thèōsis* in each of the seven chronicles, what in mythical terms is termed metamorphosis and in Christian terms *thèōsis*. I attempted to achieve this goal by first discussing his mythopoeic aesthetics, which involves his emphasis on myth as a means to express our relationship to God, his belief in a sacramental universe, his preference for the fairy tale as a genre to express his Christian beliefs, and his use of sources that are stored in his memory and give rise to images as vehicles for the theme of metamorphosis. This study has shown that memory, as a faculty for storing the materials for an author to draw upon as well as for inspiring him/her to initiate the creative process, is of prime importance in Lewis's mythopoeic aesthetics. It is part of the process that makes art "esemplastic." It is a major theme in the *Chronicles* also. What becomes obvious from this exploration is that classical and Christian images are at the foundation of Lewis's memory and "scholarship of imagination," and are tied very closely to the major theme of metamorphosis. They intersect and interweave to support Lewis's claim founded on the belief that "all myths and hieroglyphs hide a profound meaning, in agreement with Christianity" (*Spenser's Images* 9). Luci Shaw summarizes her view about poetry: "Art is in the impulse that gathers materials from our disparate but rich and compellingly diverse environment and assembles them in a way that brings a kind of order out of their chaos, an order with elements of conflict and resolution" (19).

In Lewis's *Chronicles*, cities, gardens, and the sea in Narnia, illuminated by the sun or moon, are Lewis's staple images of life, turned into metaphors, sometimes endowed with iconic grandeur, sometimes working to bestow iconic grandeur on settings and characters, specifically on Aslan. They succeed in offering readers a world of order out of chaos, a rich representation of a mythopoeic and transformative universe which facilitates reading the *Chronicles* analogously and linking it to our Primary World, and thus linking Aslan to Christ. "Art and religion are truly married" (Shaw 20). The brilliant iconic images stay in the mind as remembrances from a land visited long ago, which has neither boundaries nor directions, similar to the remembered myths and ideas in Lewis's own creative mind. Like Lucy, who has all but forgotten the story from the Magician's Book and remembers it only as a "good" story, in fact "the loveliest she has ever read" with "pictures that were real" about "a cup and a sword and a tree and a green hill" (*VDT* 167-68), the readers carry in their memories from the *Chronicles* pictures that are "real," icons of the Christian faith, particularly the view of redemption through Aslan's positive transformations, that all evil forces will be defeated in the here and now. The basic binary oppositions underlying the structure of each chronicle are dramatically presented in the form of metamorphic tableaux of such polarities as good subsuming evil; life, death; spring, winter; New Law Old Law; Joy, Despair—all forever pointing to the truth which is Christianity in our world. Lewis continually demonstrates his providential view that God needs and seeks humans to work with him to redeem this world. Aslan "isn't safe. But he's good" (*LWW* 86).

In constructing cities in Narnia, Lewis relied on Judeo-Christian, Augustinian, Platonic, and Dantean concepts and motifs drawn and stored in his memory. All Narnian cities, except Cair Paravel and Anvard, are like biblical dens of iniquity. They are evil because their alleged rulers are self-deceived themselves, and, consequently, attempt to drive others by manipulating the truth in favor of illusion. They and their followers represent corrupt humanity in differing degrees. Like most modern cities in literature, where nature is inverted and transformed by greed and capitalism (Crawford 273), the Narnian cities, again except for Cair Paravel and Anvard, cut off their inhabitants from their spiritual roots. Without a spiritual center, the residents are isolated from each other and from Aslan. They are tyrants, usurpers, slave traders, and materialists. They and their followers are "besotted" with their own desires, "self love reaching the point of contempt for God" as Augustine would say (*City of God* 14.28, 593). In this respect, as Wendy Hambnet suggests, "The *Chronicles* clearly expose the dangers of blind allegiance and the folly of trusting corrupt leaders" (151). Presumably, these evil cities, like Babylon, provide for their citizens more opportunities to sin than rural settings do.

As Jacques Ellul reflects on modern cities, "The cities of our time are most certainly that place where man can with impunity declare himself master of nature. It is only in an urban civilization that man has the metaphysical possibility of saying, 'I killed God'" (16). I believe Lewis would have agreed. His cities represent the brute forces of chaotic, and potentially evil civilization—the ruined city of Charn, the Castle of Ice of the White Witch, the City of the Giants, the Underworld City of the Green Witch, and Shift's Stable, all harboring rebellion against Aslan, deceit, illusions, and spiritual death either in the past or in the present. As Charles A. Moorman incisively remarks, it is unique for the Oxford Christian authors that in all these cities there is a need to evoke aid from another city (138). That City in Narnia is Cair Paravel, a modified type of the New Jerusalem in our world.

However, we all must live in some form of a city whether we like it or not. "Man cannot regard neutrally his most manifold artifact, the city" (Doughtery 53). As Hawkins remarks, "It would, in fact, be worse for man on earth if he were not a citizen; indeed, he might cease to be human altogether" (80). Cities represent man's complex social and inner realities. The city of Cair Paravel is the model for the Narnians as the heavenly Jerusalem is the model for Christians. With its grassy courtyards, its lighted great hall, where exquisite suppers are served and epic stories are told, Cair Paravel represents Narnia's last stand against the enemies of Aslan, as the city of New Jerusalem with one voice stands against its enemy the Antichrist, as a Judeo-Christian civilization, for Lewis, stands against pagan religions and cultures. Only in Cair

Paravel does Lewis reconcile the dialectic between country and city, the beauty and spirituality of the Narnian countryside through which the British children wandered and struggled. The British children and Aslan's followers become citizens of Cair Paravel and later members of the Celestial Garden, as Christians are reminded of the church as a the City of God on earth but that their own citizenship is in heaven and that God has prepared for them a city (Heb.11.13-16).

Though Lewis generally presents an anti-city outlook in the Narnian stories, he offers us hope in that Aslan in the end is victorious over his enemies and their constructed cities. As we have seen, Aslan intervenes, directly or indirectly, to redeem the worst cities, even the Cities of the White Witch and the Green Witch. The petrified Narnians in *LWW* and the gnomes in *LB* are good, even though cruelly imprisoned by witches. Only Tashbaan of Calormen is left unredeemed, unsanctified by the tread of Aslan's footstep. Perhaps Lewis wants to express his belief that Grace is given on earth to those who are willing to receive it. As Lewis points out in *Problem*, "I willingly believe that the damned are, in one sense, successful rebels to the end; that the doors of hell are locked on the *inside*" (127) and "They will not be forgiven. To leave them alone? Alas, I am afraid that is what He [God] does" (128). Like Babylon, Tashbaan is not healed, and its Prince Radabash is heavily punished by a negative, degrading, metamorphosis. As the prophet Jeremiah says about Babylon, "We would have healed Babylon, but she is not healed: forsake her, and let us everyone into his own country" (51.9). Yet Tashbaan appears in the Celestial Garden, indicating the ultimate focus on inclusiveness and redemption in Lewis's Christianity.

Lewis pulls all the garden motifs from his memory and from mythical, literary, and scriptural traditions, to present the mysteries of Christianity. The Created Garden in *MN* with its healing silver apples, the flowery, colorful forest of Narnia that sprouts when the snow melts, and the Restorative Garden in Aslan's Country after a long and perilous sea journey—all prefigure the Celestial Garden in *LB*, the end of all travel. Lewis uses these garden motifs as settings to suggest the restoration of the soul through Grace and the union of the soul with Christ, *thèōsis*. The divine purpose is clearly expressed through Aslan, his gift of love, and the beauty of the gardens. Besides, the gardens as communal settings convey the belief to readers that no Christian needs to undertake the pilgrimage of faith alone (McGrath 23). Thus all of Aslan's followers unite as a group and march up with him to the

Celestial Garden, the Real Narnia.

Lewis's view of redemption is also implied in the metaphor of the sea. It is a powerful metaphor of life's journey from city to garden and vice versa, with struggles and perils that any journey would offer. It harbors terrifying sea serpents, tempests, and threatening black clouds. But it also provides voyagers with tests of courage and faith in a semi-invisible pilot of the ship. The voyagers on the *Dawn Treader* are like the Christian members of a church, navigating the sea of life towards salvation. They need courage, but they also need to trust the pilot.

Aslan informs the Narnian landscape with his Deeper Magic, his *magia*, out of time and place as Christ informs ours. He continually makes it known that he is behind every effort of those who believe in him and want to know him. This relationship is at the center of Lewis's Christian beliefs: human desire intertwined with Grace. In his confident, calming style Lewis wrote to Miss Bodle on June 22nd, 1948, "It is not really you who are holding fast to Him but He to you and it will bring you to wherever He wants" (*CL* 2: 857). By offering us Narnia, Lewis offers us, by analogy, possibilities of goodness in our world. In Lewis's hands, "[c]osmology became a work of art and a metaphysical delight" (Houston Smith 78). In a general sense, this "lifting" or "transfiguration" of space (and time) has eternal significance because as loci of our experience they are in a real sense meaningful—which says something powerful about the Incarnation. These scenes of metamorphoses suggest the transformative power of Christianity, which provides the answer to human longing, the eternal Joy which Lewis experienced in his conversion. "Nothing is more central to the Christian life, or even to the gropings after spiritual truth antecedent to Christ. Metamorphosis is another term to express St. Paul's admonition that man should put on the new man, Christ" (Quint 143). Another scholar offers his views on the relationship of metamorphosis and *thèōsis*: "The mythical dream of the love of the gods for human beings will come to an awakening in the self-giving love of God at the cross (*agape*), and metamorphosis becomes real in the raising of humanity to share in the fellowship of the divine life (*thèōsis*)" (Fiddes 152). As has been explained in this study, this link between metamorphosis and *thèōsis* is at the basis of Lewis's *Chronicles*.

The fairy tale, disregarded by some as a mere children's story, violent and pornographic at that, or a secular tale of psychological and therapeutic value, succeeds in the hands of Lewis in engaging the readers to experience their Christianity more fully. In each chronicle there is a continuous progress in the main characters, assisted by dramatic shifts in geographical settings, "in which one's state of soul is measured by what has gone before and by one's advance toward, or retreat from, a spiritual absolute" (Doughtery 37). Lewis's chronicles are Christian fairy tales built on a metamorphosis from darkness to light, from blindness to vision, from Despair to Joy, from city to garden. They show that evil can be finally conquered in the Real Narnia as in our Heaven, and art can be produced along the way also. For God also works through our memory to inspire us to become sub-creators.

Lewis's scholarship provided him with his ideas to write his chronicles as the starting point of his mythopoeic aesthetics. "Stories do offer a way of imaginary alternatives, mapping possibilities, exciting hope, warding off danger by forestalling it, casting spells of order on the unknown ahead" (Warner 212). As Mark Smith states, "Where knowledge fails, belief can triumph; when belief falters, make-believe can sometimes take its place" (10). *The Chronicles of Narnia*, I believe, is one of the most appropriate mythopoeic works for inspiring our faltering Christian beliefs. The stories unite Lewis's beliefs and art to present the powerful theme of metamorphosis through a Christ figure, always pointing across cities, gardens, and the sea the way to a Celestial Garden beyond. *Eucatastrophe* and *Evangelium* unite with Mnemosynë and her muses. Lewis writes about Edmund Spenser, "His poetry is born out of his deep brooding on his own experience and on the wisdom of the philosophers and poets and iconographers. It depends for its success on the obedience to the images that rise out of that brooding; and in that obedience he is a master" (*Spenser's Images* 139). Lewis also has his baptized memory to obey as well as his "scholarship of imagination," and, through his skill in using metaphors for his Christological purpose, he has succeeded in becoming, like Spenser, and other great writers in the Western Christian Imagination, a master of mythopoeia.

WORKS CITED

Aeschylus. *The Persians*. *The Complete Greek Tragedies*. Vol. 1. Ed. David Greene and Richard Lattimore. Chicago: U of Chicago P, 1959.

Acker, Paul, and Carolyne Larrington, ed. *The Poetic Edda: Essays on Old Norse Mythology*. NY: Routledge, 2002

Albertus Magnus. *De bona in Opera omnia*. Ed. H. Kuhle et al. Vol. 28 Monasterii: West falorum in aedibus Aschendorff, 1951. 82ff.

Allen, Richard. *Projecting Illusion: Film Spectatorship and the Impression of Reality*. Cambridge UP, 1995.

Ambrosini, Richard. "Self-Remembrance and the Memory of God: Chaucer's *House of Fame* and Augustinian Psychology." *Textus II*, (1989): 95-112.

Anderson, Rasmus B. Preface. Trans. *The Younger Edda* by Snorre Sturluson. Chicago: S.C. Criggs, 1880.

Annas, Julia. *An Introduction to Plato's Republic*. Oxford: Clarendon P, 1981.

The Apocryphal New Testament. Trans. M. R. James. Oxford, 1926.

Aptekar, Jane. *Icons of Justice: Iconography and Thematic Imagery in Book V of The Fairie Queene*. NY: Columbia UP, 1969.

Arendt, Hannah. "What is Existential Philosophy?" *Essays in Understanding: 1430-1945*. Ed. J. Khon. NY: Harcourt Brace, 1994.

---. *The Life of the Mind*. Ed. M. McCarthy. Vol. 1 NY: Harvest, 1978.

Aristophanes. *Clouds, Wasps, Birds*. Trans. Peter Meineck. Indianapolis: Hackett, 1998.

Aristotle. *De memoria et reminiscentia. On Memory and Recollection*. Trans. David Block. Lieden: Brill, 2007.

---. *Politics*. Trans. Carnes Lord. Chicago: U of Chicago P, 1984.

Arnold, Matthew. "The Forsaken Merman." *The Oxford Book of English Verse:1250-1900*. Ed. Sir Arthur Quiller-Couch. Oxford: Clarendon, 1919.

Asker, D. B. D. *Aspects of Metamorphosis: Fictional Representations of the Becoming Human*. Amsterdam: Rodopi BV. 2001. Studies in Comparative Literature 36.

Athanasius. *The Incarnation of the Word of God: The Treatise De Incarnatione Verbi Dei*. Trans. A Religious C.S.M.V. 1944. Crestwood, NY: St. Vladimir Seminary Press, 1993.

Augustine. *Confessions*. Trans. F. S. Sheed. Indianapolis: Hackett, 1993.

---. *The City of God*. Trans. Henry Bettenson. London: Penguin, 1984.

---. *De beata vita (The Happy Life)*. Trans. Ludwig Schopp. St. Louis, MO: Bo Herder, 1939.

---. "Enchiridion." *The Fathers of the Church*. Trans. Bernard M. Peebles. Vol. 4. NY: Cima, 1947. 458-59.

Auden, W. H. *The Enchafed Flood or the Romantic Iconography of the Sea*. NY: Random House, 1950.

Bacon, Francis. "The Advancement of Learning." *The Philosophical Works of Francis Bacon*. Ed. John M. Robertson. London: George Routledge, 1905.

Barasch, Moshe. *Icon: Studies in the History of an Idea*. NY: NY UP, 1978.

Barkan, Leonard. *The Gods Made Flesh: Metamorphosis and the Pursuit of Paganism*. New Haven, MA: Yale UP, 1986.

Bassham, Gregory, and Jerry L. Walls, eds. *The Chronicles of Narnia and Philosophy: The Lion, the Witch, and the Worldview*. Chicago: Open Court, 2005.

Bergvall, Åke. "The Theology of the Sign: St. Augustine and Spenser's Legend of Holiness." *SEL* 33 (1993): 21-42.

Berkeley, David S. *Inwrought with Figures Dim: A Reading of Milton's 'Lycidas.'* The Hague: Mouton, 1974.

Bettelheim, Bruno. *The Uses of Enchantment: The Meaning and Importance of Fairy Tales*. NY: Knopf, 1976.

Besson, Françoise. "Invisible and Broken Cities: The Image of a Quest in Nineteenth-Century European Travel Books on Mountaineering Accounts and Modern Native American Fiction." *Babylon or New Jerusalem? Perceptions of the City in Literature*. Ed. Valeria Tinkler-Villani. Amsterdam: Rodopi, 1990. 271-85.

Bible. Authorized King James Vers.

Black, Joseph. *The Broadview Anthology of British Literature*. Vol. 1. The Medieval Period. Toronto: Broadview Press, 2006.

Blake, William. "Jerusalem: The Emanation of the Giant Albion." *The Illuminated Books of William Blake*. Ed. Morton D. Paley. Vol. 1. Princeton, NJ: Princeton UP, 1997.

Bloch, David. *Aristotle on memory and recollection text, translation, interpretation, and reception in western scholasticism*. Boston: Brill, 2007.

Briant, Pierre. *From Cyrus to Alexander: A History of the Persian Empire. Histoire de L'empire Pers*. Paris: Librairie Arthene Fayard, 1996. Trans. Peter T. Daniels. Winona Lake, IND: Eisenbraums, 2002.

Brown, Devin. "A Dark Queen, Mixed-Race Kings, and Girls Whose Heads Have Something in Them: Lewis's Contemporary Stance on Race and Gender in *The Chronicles of Narnia*." The 12th Annual CSLIS Conference. Calvin College, Grand Rapids, MI. 26-28 March 2009 Address.

Bynum, Caroline Walker. *Metamorphosis and Identity*. NY: Zone Books, 2001.

Carruthers, Mary, and Jan M. Ziolkowski, eds. *The Medieval Craft of Memory: An Anthology of Texts and Pictures*. Philadelphia, PA: U of Pennylvania P, 2002.

Charbit, Yves. "The Platonic City: History and Utopia." *Population* 2. 57 (2002) 1-31. http://cairn.info. 9 / 25 / 2007.

Chaucer, Geoffrey. *The Complete Poetry and Prose of Geoffrey Chaucer*. Ed. John H. Fisher. 2nd ed. NY: Harcourt Brace, 1989.

Chesterton, G. K. *The Everlasting Man*. NY: Dodd, 1925.

Christensen, Michael J. *C. S. Lewis on Scripture*. Waco, TX: Word Books, 1979.

Christopher, Joe R. "An Introduction to Narnia: Part II, the Geography of the Chronicles." *Mythlore* 2.3 (1971): 12-4, 277.

---. "Mount Purgatory Arises near Narnia." *Mythlore: A Journal of J. R. R. Tolkien, C. S. Lewis, Charles Williams, and Mythopoeic Literature* 23.2 (Spring 2001): 65-90.

Cirlot, J. E. *A Dictionary of Symbols*. 2nd ed. Trans. Jack Sage. NY:

Philosophical Library, 1962.

Clark, Stuart. *Thinking with Demons: The Idea of Witchcraft in Early Modern Europe*. Oxford: Clarendon P, 1997.

Coleridge, Samuel. *Poetical Works*. Ed. Ernest Hartley Coleridge. Oxford UP, 1969.

Colonna, Guido de. *The Gest Hystoriale of the Destruction of Troy: An Alliterative Romance*. Trans. Geo. A. Panton and David Donaldson. EETS. Vol. 56. London: N. Trübner, 1874. Trans. of *Hystoria Troiana, 1350-1400*.

Corbin, Alain. *The Lure of the Sea: the discovery of the seaside in the western world, 1750-1840*. Trans. Jocelyn Phel Psalm Berkeley, U of California P, 1994.

Crago, Hugh. "Faintly from Elfland. Such was Charn, that Great City." *Children's Literature Association Quarterly* 19.1 (Sept. 1994): 41-45.

Cranz, F. Edward. "De Civitate Dei, XV, 2 and Augstine's Idea of the Christian Society." *Speculum* 25.2 (April 1950): 219-25.

Crawford, Robert. *The Savage and the City in the Work of T.S. Eliot*. Oxford: Clarendon, 1987.

Curtius, Ernest Robert. *Essays on European Literature*. Trans. Michael Kowar. Princeton, NJ: Princeton UP, 1973.

Daigle, Marsha Ann. "Dante's *Divine Comedy* and C.S. Lewis's Narnia Chronicles." *Christianity and Literature* 34 (Fall 1984/Summer 1985): 41-45.

Daniélou, Jean. *Primitive Christian Symbols*. Trans. Donald A. H. Water. Baltimore, MD: Helicon Press, 1964.

Dante. *Inferno, Purgatorio, Paradisio*. Trans. Allen Mandelbaum. NY: Bantam, 1982.

Davidson, H. R. Ellis. *Gods and Myths of Europe*. Baltimore, MD: Penguin, 1964.

---. *Myths and Symbols in Pagan Europe*: Early Scandinavian and Celtic Religions. Syracuse, NY: Syracuse UP, 1988.

Dente, Carla et al., eds. *Proteus: The Language of Metamorphosis*. Burlington, VT: Ashgate, 2005. Studies in European Cultural Tradition 26.

Dewald, Carolyn. "Form and Content: The Question of Tyranny in Herodotus." Morgan 25-58.

Doebler, John. *Shakespeare's Speaking Pictures: Studies in Iconic Imagery.* Albuquerque, NM: U New Mexico P, 1974.

Donne, John. "The Storm" and "Song: Go Catch a Falling Star." *The Norton Anthology of English Literature.* Ed. M. H. Abrams. 7th ed. Vol. 1. NY: Norton, 2000. 1260, 1237-38.

Dougherty, James. *The Fivesquare City: The City in the Religious Imagination.* Notre Dame, LA: U of Notre Dame P, 1980.

Downing, David C. *Into the Wardrobe: A Reader's Guide.* Downers Grove, IL: InterVarsity, 2005.

---. *Into the Region of Awe: Mysticism in C.S. Lewis.* Downers Grove, IL: InterVarsity P, 2005.

---. *Planets in Peril: A Critical Study of C.S. Lewis's Ransom Trilogy.* Amherst: U of Massachusetts P, 1992.

---. "'The Dungeon of his Soul': Lewis's Unfinished 'Quest of Bleheris.'" *Seven: An Anglo-American Literary Review* 15 (1998): 37-54.

Dundes, Alan. "From Etic to Emic Units in the Structural Study of Folktales." *American Folklore Society* 75. 296 (Apr.-June 1966): 95-105. http://www.jstor.org/stable/538171
Dulaney-Browne Library, Oklahoma City University. 28 Aug. 2010.

Dunn, Charles W. Introduction. Terry xv-xxvi.

Dürer, Albrecht. *The Complete, Etchings & Drypoints.* Ed. Walter L. Strauss. NY: Dover, 1973

Duriez, Colin. *The C.S. Lewis Encyclopedia: A Complete Guide to His Life, Thought, and His Writings.* Wheaton, IL: Crossway Books, 2000.

Edwards, Philip. *Sea Mark: The Metaphorical Voyage, Spenser to Milton.* UK: Liverpool UP, 1997.

Eliade, Mircea. *A History of Religious Ideas.* Trans. Willard R. Trask. Vol. 2. Chicago : U of Chicago P, 1978-1985.

---. *Images and Symbols: Studies in Religious Symbolism.* Trans. Philip Mairet. 1952. Rpt. Princeton, NJ: Princeton UP, 1991.

---. *The Myth of Eternal Return*. Trans. Williard R. Trask. NY: Pantheon, 1954. Bollingen Series XLVI.

---. *Patterns of Comparative Religion*. Trans. Rosemary Sheed. NY: World Publishing, 1972.

Eliot, T. S. *The Complete Poems and Plays. 1909–1950*. NY: Harcourt, 1971.

---. *Selected Prose of T.S. Eliot*. 1932. Ed. Frank Kermode. NY: Harcourt Brace Jovanovich, 1975.

Ellul, Jaques. *The Meaning of the City*. Trans. Dennis Pardee. Grand Rapids, MI: Eerdmans, 1970.

Engetsu, Katsuhito. "The Norwegian Leviathan in *Paradise Lost*: Milton behind Marvell, Meadows, and Morlan." International Milton Forum. The University of London. 6-11 July 2008 Address.

Eschholz, Paul, Alfred Rosa, and Virginia Clark, eds. *Language Awareness: Readings for College Writers*. 8th ed. Boston, MA: Bedford / St. Martin's, 2000.

Euripides. "Orestes." *The Complete Greek Tragedies*. Ed. David Grene and Richard Lattimore. Vol. 4. Chicago: U of Chicago P, 1959.

Eusebius. St. *Commentaria in Psalmos. Patrologiae Cursus Completus*. Ed. J. P. Migne. Turnholti [Belgium], n.d. (Series Graeca 23).

Farrer, Austin. *A Rebirth of Images: The Making of St. John's Apocalypse*. 1949. Albany, NY: State U of New York P, 1986.

Ferguson, A.S. "The Platonic Choice of Lives," *Philosophical Quarterly* 1.1 (Oct. 1950): 5-34. http://www.jstor.org Dulaney-Browne Library, Oklahoma City University. 18 Sept. 2007.

Ferzoco, George, and Miriam Gill. "Introduction: Dehereditate Protei: Ways of Metamorphoses." Dente 1-12.

Fiddes, Paul. "C. S. Lewis the Myth-Maker." Walker and Patrick 132-55.

Filmer, Kath. *The Fiction of C. S. Lewis: Mask and Mirror*. NY: St. Martins, 1993.

Finch, Jeffrey. "Irenaeus on the Christological Basis of Human Divinization." Finlan and Kharlamov 86-103.

Finlan, Stephen, and Vladimir Kharlamov, eds. *Theōsis: Deification in Christian Theology*. Eugene, OR: Pickwick Publications, 2006.

Princeton Theological Monograph Series.

Ford, Paul. *Companion to Narnia: The Complete Guide to the Magical World of C. S. Lewis's* The Chronicles of Narnia. 1985. Rev. ed. NY: HarperSanFrancisco, 2005.

Fowler, Alastair. *Spenser and the Numbers of Time.* NY: Barnes, 1964.

Frangouldis, Stavros. *Witches, Isis and Narrative: Approaches to Magic in Apuleius' Metamorphosis.* Berlin: Walter de Gruyler, 2008.

Frost, Robert. *Robert Frost's Poems.* Ed. Louis Untermeyer. NY: Washington Square P, 1960.

Fudge, Erica, ed. *Renaissance beasts: of animals, humans, and other wonderful creatures.* Urbana, IL: U of Illinois P, 2004.

Goffar, Janine. *The C.S. Lewis Index: A Comprehensive Guide to Lewis's Writings and Ideas.* Wheaton, IL: Crossway Books, 1995.

Gombrich, Ernst Hans. *Art and Illusion: A Study in the Psychology of Pictorial Representation.* NY: Pantheon, 1960. Bollingen Ser. 35. 5.

GoodKnight, Glen. "Lilith in Narnia." *Mythopoeic Society Conference.* 1969: 15-19.

---. "A Comparison of Cosmological Geography in the Worlds of J. R. R. Tolkien, C.S. Lewis, and Charles Williams." *Mythlore* 1.3 (1969): 18-22.

Gopnik, Adam. "Prisoner of Narnia: How C.S. Lewis Escaped." *New Yorker* 81. 37 (2005): 88-93.

Grant, John. *An Introduction to Viking Mythology.* NY: Shooting Star, 1996.

Green, Roger L. and Walter Hooper. *C. S. Lewis: A Biography.* 1974. Rev. ed. HarperCollins, 2002.

Griffiths, Dom Bede. "The Adventures of Faith." *C.S. Lewis at the Breakfast Table and Other Reminiscences.* Ed. James T. Como. NY: Macmillan, 1979. 11-30.

Guerber, H.A. *Myths of Northern Lands.* NY: American Book Company, 1985.

Guroian, Vigen. "Faith and Journey to Aslan's Kingdom." *Modern Age* 37.1 (Fall 1994): 54-62.

Habermann, Ina. "Death by Water: The Theory and Practice of

Shipwrecking." Klein. 104-20.

Haklyut, Richard. *The Principall Navigations Voyages Traffiques and Discoveries of the English Nation*. Vols. 1, 5, 7, 12. New York: Macmillan, 1903-07. 12 vols.

Hambnet, Wendy C. "Beasts, Heroes, and Monsters: Configuring the Moral Imagery." Bassham and Walls 143-54.

Hannay, Margaret. *C.S. Lewis*. NY: Frederick Ungar, 1981.

Hardie, Philip. *Ovid's Poetics of Illusion*. Cambridge UP, 2002.

Hardy, Elizabeth Baird. *Milton and Spenser and* The Chronicles of Narnia. Jefferson, NC: McFarland, 2007.

Harris, Stephen L., and Gloria Platner, eds. *Classical Mythology: Images and Insight*. 5th ed. Boston, MA: McGraw-Hill, 2008. 282-86.

Hawkins, Peter S., ed. *Civitas: Religious Interpretations of the City*. Atlanta: Scholars, 1986.

---. "Nightmare and Dream: The Earthly City in Dante's *Commedia*." Hawkins 71-83.

Hefferman, James A. W. *Museum of Words: the Poetics of Ekphrasis from Homer to Ashbery*. Chicago: U of Chicago P, 1993.

Henderson, Jeffrey. "Demos, Demagogue, Tyrant in Attic Old Country." Morgan 155-79.

Hesiod. *The Works and Days, Theogony, the Shield of Herakles*. Trans. Richmond Lattimore. 1991. Ann Arbor, MI: U of Michigan P, 1994.

Hinten, Martin D. *The Keys to the Chronicles: Unlocking the Symbols of C.S. Lewis's Narnia*. Nashville, TN.: Broadman & Holman, 2005.

Homer. *Odyssey*. Trans. Robert Fitzgerald. New York: Doubleday, 1961. NY: Vintage Classics, 1990.

Hooke, S. H., ed. *Myth, Ritual, and Kingship: Essays on the Theory and Practice of Kingship in the Ancient Near East and in Israel*. Oxford: Clarendon P, 1958.

Hooper, Walter. *C. S. Lewis: A Companion & Guide*. London: Fount, 1996.

---. *Past Watchful Dragons: The Narnian Chronicles of C.S. Lewis*. NY: Collier, 1979.

Hopkins, Gerard M. "God's Grandeur." *The Norton Anthology of English Literature*. Ed. Stephen Greenblatt. 8th ed. Vol. 2. NY: Norton 2006. 1516.

Huard, Roger L. *Plato's Political Philosophy: The Cave*. NY: Algora, 2007.

Hulse, Clark. *Metamorphic Verse: The Elizabethan Minor Epic*. Princeton, NJ: Princeton UP, 1981.

Huttar, Charles A. "C. S. Lewis's Narnia and the 'Grand Design.'" Schakel 119-35.

Huxley, Aldous. *The Doors of Perception and Heaven and Hell*. New York: Harper, 1954.

Isocrates. "Panagyrics" and "To Philip." *Opera. Greek and English*. Vol 1. Trans. George Norlin and La rue Van Hook. London: Heinemann, 1928.

Jacobson, Diane. "The City in the Bible: Implications for Urban Ministry." *Word and World* 14.4 (Fall 1994): 395-401.

Janson, H. W. *Apes and Ape Lore in the Middle Ages and the Renaissance*. London: U. of London, 1962. Studies of the Warburg Institute 20.

Jensen, Chris. "Shine As The Sun: C. S. Lewis and the Doctrine of Deification." Oxbridge. The C. S. Lewis Foundation Institute. Oxford, UK. 28 July 2005 Address.

Kallet, Lisa. "Demos Tyrannos: Wealth, Power and Economic Patronage." Morgan 117-53.

Khoddam, Salwa. "Balder the Beautiful: Aslan's Norse Ancestor." *Mythlore: A Journal of J. R. R. Tolkien, C.S. Lewis, Charles Williams, and Mythopoeic Literature* 22.3 (Winter 1999): 66-75.

---. "Where Sky and Water Meet: Christian Iconography in C.S. Lewis's *The Voyage of the Dawn Treader*." *Mythlore: A Journal of J. R. R. Tolkien, C.S. Lewis, Charles Williams, and Mythopoeic Literature* 23.2 (Spring 2001): 36-52.

---. "The Enclosed Garden in C.S. Lewis's *The Chronicles of Narnia*." *CSL: The Bulletin of The New York C.S. Lewis Society* 37.1 (Jan./Feb. 2006): 1-10.

---. "From Ruined City to Edenic Garden in *The Magician's Nephew*." *Truths Breathed Through Silver: The Inklings' Moral and Mythopoeic Legacy*. Eds. Jonathan B. Himes, Joe. R. Christopher, and Salwa Khoddam. Newcastle, UK: Cambridge Scholars Publishing, 2008. 27-50.

Kilby, Clyde. "What is Myth?" *Christian Mythmakers: C.S. Lewis, Madeleine L'Engle, J. R. R. Tolkien, George MacDonald, G. K. Chesterton & Others*. Ed. Rolland Hein. 2nd ed. Chicago: Cornerstone Press, 2002. x-xiv.

Klein, Bernhard, ed. *Fictions of the Sea: Critical Perspectives on the Ocean in British Literature and Culture*. Burlington, VT: Ashgate, 2002.

Knowles, James. "'Can you tell a man from a marmoset?' Apes and Others on the Early Modern Stage." Fudge 138-63.

Ladner, Gerhart. *The Idea of Reform: Its Impact on Christian Thought and Action in the Age of the Church Fathers*. Cambridge, MA.: Harvard UP, 1959.

La Croix, Robert de. *Mysteries of the Islands*. Trans. Anne Carter. London: Frederick Muller Ltd., 1960.

Lehan, Richard. *The City in Literature: An Intellectual and Cultural History*. Berkeley: U of California P, 1998.

L'Engle, Madeleine. *Walking on Water*. Wheaton, IL: Shaw, 1980.

Lewis, C. S. *All My Road Before Me: The Diary of C.S. Lewis, 1922-1927*. Ed. Walter Hooper. San Diego: Harcourt Brace Jovanovich, 1991.

---. *Abolition of Man*. 1943. London: Fount, 1978.

---. *Allegory of Love*. Oxford: Oxford UP, 1936.

---. *Arthurian Torso*. Oxford UP, 1948. Rpt. in *Taliessin Through Logres, The Region of the Summer Stars*. Grand Rapids, MI: Eerdmans, 1974.

---. *Christian Reflections*. Ed. Walter Hooper. 1967. Grand Rapids, MI.: Eerdmans. Rpt. 1978.

---. "Christianity and Literature." *Christian Reflections*. 1-11.

---. *Collected Letters of C.S. Lewis*. Ed. Walter Hooper. 3 vols. London: HarperCollins, 2002, 2004, 2006.

---. "De Audiendis Poetis." *Studies in Medieval and Renaissance Literature*. 1-17.

---. *The Discarded Image: An Introduction to Medieval and Renaissance Literature*. 1964. Cambridge UP, 1981.

---. *English Literature in the Sixteenth Century Excluding Drama*. Oxford: Clarendon, 1954.

---. *An Experiment in Criticism*. Cambridge UP, 1961. rpt. 1979.

---. *The Four Loves*. NY: Harcourt Brace, 1960.

---. *God in the Dock: Essays on Theology and Ethics*. Ed. Walter Hooper. Grand Rapids, MI: Eerdmans, 1970.

---. *The Great Divorce*. NY: HarperSanFrancisco, 2001.

---. *A Grief Observed*. 1961. NY: Bantam. 1976.

---. "Historicism." *Christian Reflections*. 100-113.

---. *The Horse and His Boy*. NY: HarperTrophy, 1994.

---. Introduction. *The Incarnation of the Word of God. The Treatise De Incarnatione Verbi Dei*. By St. Athanasius. Trans. A Religious C.S.M.V. 1944. Crestwood, NY: St. Vladimir Seminary P, 1993. 3-10.

---. "Is Theology Poetry?" *Screwtape Proposes a Toast and Other Pieces*. 1965 London: Collins, 1974. 41-58.

---. *The Last Battle*. NY: HarperTrophy, 1994.

---. *Letters to Malcolm: Chiefly on Prayer*. NY: Harcourt Brace, 1964.

---. *The Lion, the Witch, and the Wardrobe*. NY: HarperTrophy, 1994.

---. *The Magician's Nephew*. NY: HarperTrophy, 1994.

---. *Mere Christianity*. NY: Collier, 1952.

---. "Miracles." *God in the Dock*. 25-47.

---. *Miracles: A Preliminary Study*. 1947. London: Fount, 1974.

---. "Myth Became Fact." *God in the Dock*. 63-71.

---. "The Mythopoeic Gift of Rider Haggard." *On Stories and Other Essays on Literature*. 97-100.

---. *Narrative Poems*. Ed. Walter Hooper. 1969. San Diego: Harvest, 1979.

---. *On Stories and Other Essays on Literature*. Ed. Walter Hooper. NY: Harcourt, 1982.

---. *The Pilgrim's Regress: An Allegorical Apology for Christianity,*

    Reason, and Romanticism. Grand Rapids, MI: Eerdman, 1994.

---. *Poems*. Ed. Walter Hooper. 1964. San Diego: Harcourt Brace, 1992.

---. *A Preface to Paradise Lost*. 1942. Oxford UP, 1979

---. *Prince Caspian*. NY: Harper Trophy, 1994.

---. *The Problem of Pain*. NY: Macmillan, 1962. Rpt. 1986.

---. "The Quest of Bleheris." Bodleian MS English lett. c220/5. Published with Permision of The Lewis Company Pte. Ltd.

---. *Reflections on the Psalms*. San Diego, CA: Harcourt, 1958.

---. *The Silver Chair*. NY: Harper Trophy, 1994.

---. *Spenser's Images of Life*. Ed. Alastair Fowler. Cambridge: Cambridge UP, 1967.

---. *Spirits in Bondage: A Cycle of Lyrics*. Ed. Walter Hooper. San Diego, CA: Harcourt Brace, 1984.

---. *Studies in Medieval and Renaissance Literature*. Ed. Walter Hooper. Cambridge UP, 1968.

---. *Surprised by Joy: The Shape of My Early Life*. NY: Harvest, 1956.

---. *That Hideous Strength. The Cosmic Trilogy*. 1938. London: Pan Books, 1989.

---. *Till We Have Faces: A Myth Retold*. 1956. San Diego: Harcourt Brace, 1985.

---. *The Voyage of the* Dawn Treader. NY: Harper Trophy, 1993.

---. *The Weight of Glory and Other Addresses*. 1949. Rpt. Grand Rapids, MI: Eerdmans, 1979.

Lindow, John. *Handbook of Norse Mythology*. NY: Oxford UP, 2001.

Lönnroth, Lars. "The Founding of Miygardyr ("Völuspá" 1-8)." Trans. Paul Acker and Larrington 1-25.

The Lyfe of Saynt Branden (London: Wynkyn de Worde, [1520]) (STC 3600)

Macmullen, Ramsay. *Enemies of the Roman Order*. Cambridge: Harvard UP, 1966.

McGovern, Eugene. "C.S. Lewis & Islam." *CSL: The Bulletin of The New York C.S. Lewis Society* 41.5 (Sept./Oct. 2010): 1-8.

McGrath, Alister. *The Journey: A Pilgrim in the Lands of the Spirit*. London: Hodder & Stoughton, 1999.

McLaughlin, Sarah. "The City of God Revisited: C.S. Lewis's Debt to Saint Augustine." *CSL: the Bulletin of the New York C.S. Lewis Society* 23.6 (April 1992): 1-9.

Majeske, Andrew. *Equity in English Renaissance Literature: Thomas More and Edmund Spenser*. NY: Routledge, 2006.

Mallet, M. *Northern Antiquities*. Trans. Bishop Percy. 1770. London: Bell and Daldy, 1873.

Marlowe, Christopher. "Tamburlane the Great, I & II," "The Jew of Malta," and "Dr. Faustus." *Drama of the English Renaissance*. Eds. Russell Fraser and Norman Rabkin. Vol. 1. The Tudor Period. Upper Saddle River, NJ: Prentice Hall, 1976. 205-61; 263-265; 295-322.

Markos, Louis. "The Good Guys and the Bad Guys: Teachable Moments in *The Chronicles of Narnia*" http://edu/~markos/narniaessay. November 20, 2005.

Masereel, Frans. *The City: A Vision in Woodcuts*. NY: Dover, 2006.

Maundeville, Sir John, *The Voiage and Travayle of Sir John Maundeville, Knight*. Ed. John Ashton. London: Pickering & Chatto, 1887.

Metzner, Ralph. *The Well of Remembrance: Rediscovering the Earth Wisdom. Myth of Northern Europe*. Boston, MA: Shambala, 1944.

Milton, John. *Complete Poems and Major Prose*. Ed. Merritt Y. Hughes. Indianapolis, IND: Odyssey Press, 1957.

Moorman, Charles A. *The Precincts of Felicity: The Augustinian City to the Oxford Christians*. Gainesville, FL: U of Florida P, 1966.

Moorman, Frederic W. *The Interpretation of Nature in English Poetry from Beowulf to Shakespeare*. Strassburg: Karl J. Trübner, 1905.

Morgan, Kathryn A., ed. *Popular Tyranny: Sovereignty and its Discontents in Ancient Greece*. Austin: U of Texas P, 2003.

Munch, Peter A. *Norse Mythology: Legends of Gods and Heroes*. Trans. Sigurd Bernard Hustvedt. NY: The American-Scandinavian Foundation, 1926; Detroit, MI: Singing Trees Press, 1968.

Munn, Mark. *The Mother of the Gods, Athens, and the Tyranny of Asia*.

Berkeley: U of California P, 2006.

Muscoguiri, Patrizia. "Cinematographic Seas: Metaphors Crossing and Shipwreck on the Big Screen (1990-2001)." Klein 203-20.

Myers, Doris. *C.S. Lewis in Context*. Kent, OH: Kent State UP, 1994.

Nathan, Peter. "Jerusalem: Center of the Earth?" *Vision: Insights and New Horizons*. www.vision.org. March 20, 2007.

Nicholson, Mervyn. "C. S. Lewis and the Scholarship of Imagination in E. Nesbit and R. Haggard." *Renascence* 51.1 (Fall 1998): 41-60.

Nicolson, Marjorie Hope. *Mountain Gloom and Mountain Glory: The Development of the Aesthetics of the Infinite*. 1959. Seattle: U of Washington P, 1997.

Ober, Josiah. "Tyrant Killing as Therapeutic Stasis: A Political Debate in Images and Texts." Morgan 215-250.

Oppenheim, Leo. "On Royal Gardens in Mesopotamia." *Journal of Near Eastern Studies* 24 (1965): 328-33.

Orwell, George, "Politics and the English Language." *Language Awareness: Reading for College Writers*. Ed. Paul Eschholz et al. 9th ed. Boston: Bedford/St. Martin's, 2005. 138-49.

Ouspensky, Léonide, and Vladimir Lossky. *The Meaning of Icons*. Trans. G. E. H. Palmer and E. Kadloubovsky. Rev. ed. Crestwood, NY: St. Vladimir's Seminary Press, 1982. Trans. from *Der Sinn der Ikonen*.

Ovid, *Metamorphoses*. Trans. A. D. Melville, Oxford UP, 1986.

Palmer, Barbara. "The Inhabitants of Hell: Devils." *The Iconography of Hell*. Ed. Clifton Davidson and Thomas H. Seiler. Kalamazoo, MI: Western Michigan U, 1992. 20-40. Early Drama, Art, and Music. Medieval Institute Publications.Monograph Series 17.

Panofsky, Erwin. *Imagination: Meaning in the Visual Arts*. Garden City, NY: Doubleday-Anchor, 1955.

Patterson, Nancy-Lou. "Narnia and the North: The Symbolism of Northerness in the Fantasies of C.S. Lewis." *Mythlore* 4.2 (1972): 9-16.

---. "The Bolt of Tash." *Mythlore* 16.4 (62) (Summer 1990): 23-26.

Pearl. The New Pelican Guide to English Literature. Vol. 1. *Medieval Literature: Chaucer and the Alliterative Tradition*. 1982. Ed. Boris Ford. Trans. Thorlac Turville-Petre. London: Penguin, 1997.

Pearsall, Derek, and Elizabeth Salter. *Landscapes and Seasons of the Medieval World*. London: Paul Eleck, 1973.

Peck, John. *Maritime Fiction: Sailors and the Sea in British and American Novels. 1719-1917*. NY: Palgrave, 2001.

Perry, Kathryn. "Unpicking the Seam: Talking Animals and Reader Pleasure in Early Modern Satire." Fudge 19-49.

Perutelli, Alessandro. "Remembrance of Forms Lost." Dente 23-32.

Pitts, Mary Ellen. "The Motif of the Garden in the Novels of J. R. R. Tolkien, Charles Williams, and C. S. Lewis." *Mythlore: A Journal of J. R. R. Tolkien, C.S. Lewis, Charles Williams, and Mythopoeic Literature* 30 (Winter 1982): 3-6, 42.

Plass, Paul. "Augustine and Proust on Time and Memory." *Soundings* 73.2-3 (Summer/Fall 1990): 343-360.

Plato. "Gorgias." *Complete Works*. Ed. John M. Cooper. Trans. W. D. Woodhead. Indianapolis, IN: Hackett, 1997. 791-68.

---. "Laws." Trans. Trevor J. Saunders. Cooper 1318-1616.

---. "Meno." Trans. G. M. A. Grube. Cooper 870-97.

---. "Phaedrus." *Complete Works*. Trans. Alexander Nehamas and Paul Woodruff. Cooper 506-56.

---. *The Republic*. Trans. Francis M. Cornford. New York: Oxford UP, 1967.

---. "Timaeus." Trans. Donald J. Zeyl. Cooper 1224-291.

Poems of the Elder Edda. Trans. Patricia Terry. Rev. ed. Philadelphia: U of Pennsylvania Press, 1990.

Pontoppidan, Erich. *The Natural History of Norway*. London: A. Linde, 1775.

Porteous, Alexander. *The Forest in Folklore and Mythology*. 1928. Rpt. NY: Dover, 2002.

Proud, Linda. *Icons: A Sacred Art*. UK: Pitkin Uruchrome Ltd, 2000.

Puchniak, Robert. "Augustine's Conception of Deification." Finlan and Kharlamov. 122-33.

Puckett, Thomas. "Communicology and Memoria in St. Augustine." *Semiotics Around the World: Synthesis in Diversity*. Ed. Immengard Rauch and Gerald F. Carr. I-II. Berlin: Mouton de Gruyter, 1997. 863-66.

Quinn, Patrick. "The Erosion of Sexual Power in the *Femme Fatale*: D'Annunzio Transforms Swinburne." Dente 200-11.

Quinn, Mary Bernetta. *Metamorphic Tradions in Modern Poetry*. NY: Gordian Press, 1966.

Quint, David. *Epic and Empire: Politics and Generic Form from Virgil to Milton*. Princeton UP, 1993.

Raaflaub, Kent A. "Stick and Glue: The Function of Tyranny in the Fifth-Century Athenian Democracy." Morgan 59-93.

Rakestraw, Robert V. "Becoming Like God: An Evangelical Doctrine of Thèōsis." *JETS* 40.2 (June 1997): 257-69.

Rackham, Arthur. *Rackham's Color Illustrations for Wagner's "Ring."* NY: Dover, 1979.

Ramos, Manual João. *Essays in Christian Mythology: The Metamorphosis of Prester John*. Lanham, MD: UP of America, 2006.

Rees, Christine. "The Metamorphosis of Daphne in Sixteenth-and Seventeenth-Century English Poetry." *MLR* 66.2 (April 1971): 251-63.

Rhodes J .T., and Clifford Davidson. "The Garden of Paradise." *Iconography of Heaven*. Ed. Clifford Davidson. Kalamazoo, MI: Western Michigan University, 1994. 69-103. Early Drama, Art, and Music. Monograph Ser. 21.

Root, Jerry. Personal conversation, 2001.

Russell, Fraser A., and Norman Rabkin. *Drama of the English Renaissance*. Vol. 1. The Tudor Period. Upper Saddle River, NJ: Prentice Hall, 1976.

Ryken, Leland. *The Literature of the Bible*. Grand Rapids, MI: Zondervan, 1974.

Ryken, Leland, and Marjorie L. Meade. *A Reader's Guide Through the Wardrobe*. Downers Grove, IL: InterVarsity Press, 2005.

---. *Triumphs of the Imagination: Literature in Christian Perspective*. Downers Grove, IL: InterVarsity Press, 1979.

Sandburg, Carl. "Chicago." *The Norton Anthology of American Literature*. 3rd ed. NY: Norton, 1989. 1751.

Sayer, George. *Jack: A Life of C. S. Lewis*. Wheaton, IL: Crossway Books, 1994.

Schakel, Peter, ed. *The Longing for Form: Essays on the Fiction of C. S. Lewis*. Grand Rapids, MI: Baker, 1977.

---. *The Way Into Narnia: A Reader's Guide*. Grand Rapids, MI: Eerdmans, 2005.

Schmidt, Arnold. "Walter Scott's *The Pirate*: Imperialism, Bourgeois Values, Nationalism, and Fictions of the Sea." Klein 89-103.

Scully, Stephen. *Homer and the Sacred City*. Ithaca: Cornell UP, 1990.

Seaford, Richard. "Tragic Tyranny." Morgan 95-115.

Seidel, Michael. Robinson Crusoe, *Island Myths and the Novel*. Boston, MA: Twayne, 1991.

Sennett, James F. "Worthy of a Better God: Religious Diversity and Salvation in *The Chronicles of Narnia*." Bassham and Walls 245-46.

Shakespeare, William. *The Complete Works of Shakespeare*. 5th ed. Ed. David Bevington. NY: Pearson/ Longman, 2004.

Shaw, Luci. *Breath for the Bones. Art, Imagination, and Spirit: Reflections on Creativity and Faith*. Nashville, TN: Thomas Nelson, 2007.

Shelley, Percy B. "The Cloud." *The Norton Anthology of English Literature*. Ed. Stephen Greenblatt. 8th ed. Vol. 2. NY: Norton, 2006. 815-16.

Silva, Francisco Vaz da. *Metamorphosis: The Dynamics of Symbolism in European Fairy Tales*. NY: Peter Lang, 2002.

"Sir Gawain and the Green Knight." Trans. Marie Borroff. *The Norton Anthology of British Literature*. Ed. M. H. Abrams. 7th ed. Vol.1. NY: Norton, 2000. 156-210.

Slochower, Harry. *Mythopoesis: Mythic Patterns in the Literary Classics*. Detroit: MI: Wayne State UP, 1970.

Smilansky, Saul. *Free Will and Illusion*. Oxford: Clarendon Press, 2000.

Smith, Jonathan. "Jerusalem: The City as Place." Hawkins 25-38

Smith, Mark Eddy. *Aslan's Call: Finding Our Way to Narnia*. Downers Grove, IL: InterVarsity P, 2005.

Smith, Robert Houston. *Patches of Godlight: The Patterns of Thought in C.S. Lewis*. Athens, GA: U of Georgia P, 1981.

Sørensen, Preben Mevlengrack. "Religions Old and New." *The Oxford Illustrated History of the Vikings*. Ed. P. H. Sawyer. Oxford UP,

1997. 202-24.

---. "Thorr's Fishing Expedition" [Hymiskvida]. Trans. Kirsten Williams. Acker 119-38.

Spenser, Edmund. *The Works of Edmund Spenser*. Ed. Henry John Todd. London: Edward Moxon, 1856.

Stanton, Leonard J. *The Optina Pustyn Monastery in the Russian Literary Imagination: Iconic Vision in Works by Dostoevsky, Gogol, Tolstoy, and Others*. NY: Lang, 1995.

Starkey, John. Personal correspondence, 2008.

Stewart, Stanley. *The Enclosed Garden*. Madison, WI: Wisconsin UP, 1966.

Stewart, T. C. *The City as an Image of Man*. London: Latimer Press, n.d.

Sturluson, Snorre. *The Younger Edda*. Trans. Rasmus B. Anderson. Chicago: S.C. Griggs, 1880.

Terry, Patricia. "Notes." *Poems of the Elder Edda* 1-10.

Teske, Roland. "Augustine's Philosophy of Memory." *The Cambridge Companion to Augustine*. Ed. Eleonore Stump and Norman Kretzmann. Cambridge UP, 2001. 148-58. Cambridge Companions to Philosophy.

Thomas, Keith. *Man and the Natural World*. NY: Pantheon Books, 1983.

Tinkler-Villani, Valeria, ed. *Babylon or New Jerusalem? Perceptions of the City in Literature*. Amsterdam: Rodopi, 1990.

Tolkien, J. R. R. "On Fairy-Stories." *Tree and Leaf Including Mythopoeia and the Homecoming of Bearhtnoth Bearhthelm's Son*. London: Harper Collins, 2001. 1-81.

Treneer, Anne. *The Sea in English Literature from Beowulf to Donne*. UK: Liverpool UP, 1926.

Turville-Petre, Gabriel. *Myth and Religion of the North: The Religion of Ancient Scandinavia*. NY: Holt, Rinehart and Winston, 1964.

Virgil. *The Aeneid*. Trans. Robert Fitzgerald. NY: Vintage, 1990.

Von der Thusen, Joachim. "The City as Metaphor, Metonym and Symbol." Tinker-Villani 1-11.

Walker, Andrew. "Under the Russian Cross: A Research Note on C.S. Lewis and the Eastern Orthodox Church." Walker and Patrick 63-67.

Walker, Andrew, and James Patrick, eds. *Rumours of Heaven: Essays in Celebration of C.S. Lewis.* Guildford, Surrey, UK: Eagle, 1998.

Walker, Peter W. L. *Holy City, Holy Places: Christian Attitudes to Jerusalem and the Holy Land in the Fourth Century.* Oxford: Clarendon P, 1990.

Walsh, Chad. *The Literary Legacy of C. S. Lewis.* NY: Harcourt Brace and Jovanovich, 1979.

Ward, Michael. *Planet Narnia: The Seven Heavens in the Imagination of C. S. Lewis.* Oxford: OUP, 2008

Ware, Kallistos. "God of the Fathers: C. S. Lewis and Eastern Christianity." *The Pilgrim's Guide: C. S. Lewis and the Art of Witness.* Ed. David Mills. Grand Rapids, MI: Eerdmans, 1998. 53-69.

Warner, Marina. *Fantastic Metamorphoses, Other Worlds: Ways of Telling the Self.* Oxford UP, 2002.

Watson, Thomas Ramey. "Enlarging Augustinian Systems: C. S. Lewis's *The Great Divorce* and *Till We Have Faces*." *Renascence* 46.3 (Spring 1994): 1-13. EBSCOhost. Delaney-Browne Library, Oklahoma City University. 20 Oct. 2010.

Wilken, Robert Louis. "Augustine: Enduring Legacy." American Enterprise Institute for Public Policy. January 9, 2006. Bradley Lecture.

Williams, Charles. *Descent into Hell.* 1937. Grand Rapids, MI: Eerdmans, 1949.

Williams, Kathleen. "Spenser: Some Uses of the Sea and the Storm-Tossed Ship." *Research Opportunities in Renaissance Drama* 13-14 (1970-71): 135-42.

Wilson, John A. "Egypt: The Nature of the Universe." *Before Philosophy: The Intellectual Adventure of Ancient Man.* Ed. Henri Frankfort and John Albert Wilson, 1946. Baltimore, MD: Penguin, 1960. Chapter 2.

Wilson, Robert R. "The City in the Old Testament." Hawkins 3-13.

Wiseman, D. J. "Mesopotamian Goddess." *Anatolian Studies* 33 (1983): 137-44.

Wood, Ralph C. *The Gospel According to Tolkien: Visions of the Kingdom in Middle-earth*. Louisville, KY: Westminster John Knox P, 2003.

Yates, Frances A. *The Art of Memory*. Chicago: Chicago UP, 1966.

INDEX

Main titles of C. S. Lewis's individual works are in boldface.

A

Abolition of Man, The, 33, 64, 122n1
Aeschylus, *Persians,The*, 104, 106, 111
   Prometheus Bound, 107
acedia, 10, 139, 144
Acker, Paul, 197
Alberegino, Jacobello, 194
Albertus Magnus, 18, 36, 55
allegory, 13, 44
   in Plato, 95, 99, 100, 103n9
Allegory of Love, The, 24, 30, 47, 75
Allen, Richard, 184
All My Road Before Me, 201n1
Ambrosini, Richard, 61
Anderson, Rasmus B, 195, 198, 201n2
Annas, Julia, 103n9, 114
ape, 12, 73, 136, 180-81, 183-85, 187-89, 192, 199
Apocryphal New Testament, The, 129,
apocalypse, 4, 43, 81, 93, 121, 149, 180-82, 185, 187, 194, 199, 200, 204-05
Aptekar, Jane, 45, 46
Apuleius, 89, 120, 146, 158n7, 205
Arendt, Hannah, 16, 60
Aristophanes, *Wasps, The*, 104, 111
Aristotle, 17, 55, 72
   De anima, 18
   De memoria, 18, 54, 60
   Historia animalium, 155
   Politics, 106, 107, 114
Arnold, Matthew, 134n5, 201n1
Arthurian Torso, 47
Asker, D. B. D., 30, 89

Athanasius, Saint, 35, 39, 137
Augustine, Saint, 3, 21, 38, 107, 145, 184
   Acts, 61
   Civitas Dei, 61, 70-72, 78, 100-101, 124, 125, 132, 220
   Confessions, 18, 21, 50-53, 81-82, 134n2, 145
   De beata, 161, 179n1
   De trinitate, 60
   "Enchiridion," 197
   free will, and, 70-71
   language, 35, 53, 60
   memory, 17, 18n1, 38n1, 50-53, 54, 59-61
   time, 82
Auden, W. H., 27, 72, 164

B

Bacon, Francis, 27, 159
Barasch, Moshe, 41
Barkan, Leonard, 7, 20, 26, 29, 30, 37, 39n10, 56, 99, 211, 212
Bassham, Gregory, 122n3
Beowulf, 28, 190, 199
behemoth, 166, 167
Bergvall, Åke, 61, 66
Berkeley, David S., 103n8, 128, 134n4, 176
Besson, Françoise, 4, 56
Blake, William, 22, 70, 102n1
Bloch, David, 18
Briant, Pierre, 108, 111, 114
Brown, Devin, 105
butterfly, 155, 158n7

Bynum, Caroline Walker, 32, 170

C

Cair Paravel, 21, 43, 51, 55-60, 62, 63, 67, 73, 74, 82, 84, 85, 87, 99, 100, 104, 106, 120, 123, 125-27, 130-33, 162, 181, 191, 194, 207, 219-21
Camôes, 27
Carruthers, Mary, 38n1, 55
Charbit, Yves, 25, 105, 106
Chaucer, 24, 90, 158n7
Chesterton, G. K., 81
Chew, Samuel, 41
Christian Reflections, 1, 53, 103n7
"Christianity and Literature," 17
Christopher, Joe R., 38n3, 39n11, 103n5, 134n4, 158n1
Chronicles of Narnia, The, 1, 15n1, 38n5, 122n3, 223
Cicero, 61
Circe, 83, 85, 210
Cirillo, A.R., 103n8
Cirlot, J. E., 45, 85, 126, 127
city, 55, 57, 58, 70, 71, 81, 220, 222, 223
  biblical, 126, 127, 152, 194
  classical, 102n1, 136
  God, of, 61, 70-74, 100, 105-06, 123-26, 127, 128, 129, 133, 149, 152, 162, 181, 194, 220, 221
  Dante, 70, 72, 75, 83, 93, 99
  Eliot, 70, 78, 99, 102
  Ellul, 127
  Haggard, Rider, 78, 103n5
  Man, of, 70, 71, 72, 74, 105, 108, 120, 124, 135, 186
  Satan, of, 71-75, 77, 78, 100, 101, 135, 139

motifs, of, 72, 82
Plato, 106, 109, 119-21, 131
Williams, Charles, 131-32. See also Lewis, C. S.
Clark, Stuart, 33, 66, 184, 188
Colbert, David, 122
Coleridge, Samuel, 1, 172
Collected Letters of C.S. Lewis, 1, 33, 44, 49n2, 63, 69n2, 85, 86, 113, 137, 157, 162, 196, 200, 217, 222
Comes, Natalis, 29
Corbin, Alain, 25-27, 136, 158n2, 166, 174-76, 179n1
correspondence, doctrine of, 31, 56
Crago, Hugh, 77, 78, 102n5
Cranz, F. Edward, 124
Crawford, Robert, 22, 220
Cyril, Saint, 124, 125, 132, 134n2
Curtius, Ernest Robert, 26, 27

D

dance, 9, 19, 44, 64, 65, 98, 124, 153, 212
  as *theōsis*, 19, 214
Daniélou, Jean, 161, 175, 176, 179n2
Dante, 1, 45, 75, 82, 145, 219
  Inferno, 1, 27, 62, 70, 72, 73, 75, 78, 83, 84, 91-94, 97, 99, 108, 119, 145, 158n4, 189, 206, 208, 210
  Paradiso, 177, 214
  Purgatorio, 122n2, 155, 158n1
Davidson, Clifford, 23, 151, 152
Davidson, H. R. Ellis, 181, 197, 198, 201n2, 204
Dewald, Carolyn, 107, 114
Discarded Image, The, 19, 134n2, 151

Doebler, John, 41
donkey, 73, 120, 185, 187, 205, 209, 210
Donne, John, 28, 134n5
Dougherty, James, 21, 71, 102n1, 108,
Downing, David C., 25, 40n14, 79, 102n3
Drake, Francis, 163, 164, 165
Dundes, Alan, 20, 228
Dunn, Charles W., 198-99
Duriez, Colin, 1
Dürer, Albrecht, 47, 49n2, 128

E
Easterbrook, Gregg, 122n1
Edwards, Philip, 159, 161
Eliade, Mircea, 6, 7, 15n4, 22, 123-25, 127, 129, 132, 171, 181, 196
Eliot, T. S., 22, 70, 78, 99, 102n1, 134n5
Ellul, Jaques, 22, 127, 220
Engetsu, Katsuhito, 168, 179n4
English Literature in the Sixteenth Century Excluding Drama, 33, 44, 162, 175
Eschholz, Paul, 69
esemplastic, 1, 2, 218
eucatastrophe, 9
   and *evangelium* 34, 223
   Tolkien, 4, 8, 9, 34
Euripides, *Orestes*, 114
Eusebius, Saint, 124, 125, 127, 129, 132, 134n2
Experiment in Criticism, An, 2, 3, 8, 16, 19, 34, 44, 69n1
Ezekiel, 127, 148, 191, 208, 215

F
fairy tales, 13-19
   evangelium, and, 4, 9, 10, 223
   eucatastrophe, 4, 8-9, 13, 34, 42-
Farrer, Austin, 182, 186, 191, 201n3
Father Christmas, 55, 58, 87
Faustus, 30, 33, 39n11
femme fatale, 90
Ferguson, A.S., 106
Ferzoco, George, 12, 32
Fiddes, Paul, 4, 36, 222
Filmer, Kath, 64, 85, 179n5
Finch, Jeffrey, 35
Finlan, Stephen, 34, 35
Ford, Paul, 61, 75, 77, 81, 122n1, 126, 184
Four Loves, The, 44, 45, 179n7, 185
Fowler, Alastair, 44, 45, 46
Friedrich, Andreas, 46
Frost, Robert, 30

G
garden, general, 4, 12, 23, 24, 26, 28, 78, 140-143, 152, 158n2, 174, 219, 221- 23
   art, and, 23
   biblical, 23- 26, 38n6, 113, 135, 136, 138, 140, 143, 144, 154
   classical, 23, 136, 140, 151, 156
   Dante, in, 158n1
   earthly, 88, 113, 122n2, 149, 153, 154, 172
   enclosed, 23-24, 25, 38, 82, 135, 139, 140, 143, 152, 156
   imagination, and, 2 136
   medieval, 23-25, 139, 140, 152
   Milton, in, 112, 138-140, 143, 144, 151

memory, 37
metamorphoses, 16, 22, 31, 135, 175
   motifs, of, 23, 24, 25, 88, 135, 136, 138, 139, 140, 146, 147, 149-53, 156, 172, 194-96, 198-200, 212, 221-23
   mythopoeia, 18
Pearl, 140
Spenser, 139, 149. See also Lewis, C. S.
Georgi, Dieter, 21
Giamatti, A. Bartlett, 24-25, 87, 136
God in the Dock: Essays on Theology and Ethics, 2, 3, 179n10, 204, 211, 218
goeteia (or black magic), 8, 33, 34, 84, 96, 134n5, 178, 215
Goffar, Jeanine, 69n3
Gombrich, Ernst Hans, 188
GoodKnight, Glen, 83, 85-87, 134n4
Gopnik, Adam, 13-14
Grant, John, 181
Great Divorce, The, 8, 45, 52, 73, 93
Greeks, ancient, 106-09, 111, 121, 160
Green, Roger L., 201n1
Greeves, Arthur, 49n2, 102n4
Grief Observed, A, 157
Griffiths, Dom Bede, 33, 52, 134n2, 200
Guerber, H.A., 201n2
Guroian, Vigen, 20

H

Habermann, Ina, 28
Haggard, Rider, 56, 77, 103n5, 162, 179 n6n3
Haklyut, Richard, 161-62, 163, 164, 165, 167, 172, 175, 179n9n3

Hambnet, Wendy C., 73, 220
Hannay, Margaret, 45
Hardie, Philip, 211
Harris, Stephen L., 211, 217n3
Hawkins, Peter, 21, 71, 220
Henderson, Jeffrey, 107
Hefferman, James A. W., 31
Hein, Rolland, 1
hell, general, 10, 72, 93, 123, 183, 189
   Christian, 85
   Dante, 72, 73, 91-94, 99, 108
   Homer, 92, 93, 99
   medieval, 22, 36, 93, 195, 208
   Milton, 138
   Nordic, 197
   Virgil, 83, 99. See also Lewis, C.S.
Hesiod, 23
Himes, Jonathan, 38n3, 103n5
Hinten, Martin D., 32, 95, 105, 126
"Historicism," 1, 53
Homer, 136, 211
   Iliad, 123, 168, 241
   Odyssey, 17, 27, 73, 83, 93, 99
Honorius of Autun, 46
Hooke, S. H., 106, 108
Hooper, Walter, 2, 13, 49n2, 52, 103n7, 131, 138-39, 179n6, 201n1
Hopkins, Gerard M., 5
Horse and His Boy, The, 48, 50, 62, 73, 104, 105, 109, 110, 112, 114, 117, 118, 120, 121, 131, 147, 153-54, 163, 177, 179n8, 180, 185, 205, 206
Huard, Roger L., 21, 99-100, 103n9
Hugo, Herman, 142, 166
Hulse, Clark, 158n7
Huttar, Charles A., 182

Huxley, Aldous, 149

I
Isocrates, 111
images, general, 3, 150, 118, 212, 217n3, 219
   classical, 3, 218
   fairy tales, and, 18
   iconic, 43, 44, 45, 149, 178, 214, 218, 219
   literary, 2, 18, 97, 82, 150, 198, 214
   memory, 18, 50, 53, 55, 59, 60, 102, 218
   metamorphoses, 218
   mythic, 19, 150, 181, 223
   scriptural, 2, 46, 82, 150, 182, 186, 191, 194, 218
   Spenser, 20, 44, 126, 145, 153, 189, 218, 219, 233
   symbolic, 4
   théōsis, 37, 43-44
   traditional, 44
   verbal, 44
The Incarnation of the Word of God: Th Treatise De Incarnatione Verbi Dei.
   Introduction, 35, 137
"Is Theology Poetry?", 58
George MacDonald: **An** *Anthology.*
   Introduction, 2, 52, 53, 85

J
Jacobson, Diane, 20, 22, 105
Janson, H. W., 76, 184, 185
Jensen, Chris, 35-36, 43-44

K
kairos, 50, 52, 60, 82
Kallet, Lisa, 106-07

Keats, John, 1, 91
Kilby, Clyde, 2
Khoddam, Salwa, 38n5, 103n5, 158n3n5
Klein, Bernhard, 26
Knowles, James, 184
kronos, 17, 50, 52, 54, 60

L
Ladner, Gerhart, 23
La Croix, Robert de, 160
language, general, 7, 66, 69n3, 187
   Augustine, 35
   evil, and, 64, 66, 187
   images, 44
   memory, 50, 61, 138
   metamorphoses,138
   Ovid, and, 204
   poetic, 36
   technical, 42
   théōsis, and, 35, 36, 40. See also Lewis, C. S.
Last Battle, The, 9, 21, 43, 48, 73, 74, 81, 93, 117, 121, 129, 131, 136, 138, 147, 148-50, 152, 153, 163, 170, 178, 180, 182, 183, 185-89, 191, 192, 195, 196, 198, 199, 205, 206, 210, 213, 221
Lehan, Richard, 72, 74, 78, 100
L'Engle, Madeleine, 48
Letters to Malcolm: Chiefly on Prayer, 5, 10, 11, 19, 39, 61
leviathan, 166-68, 176, 197
Lewis, C. S.
   eucatastrophe, and, 10, 12, 42
   Chronicles, in, 145, 203, 210
   HHB, 120

    LB, 153, 200
    LWW, 51
    MN, 145
    PC, 63, 212
    VDT, 149
fairy tales, 9-10, 12, 14, 20, 34, 38n1, 90
    evangelium, and, 4, 10, 13, 223
hell, 11, 73, 80, 83, 91-94, 99, 123, 138, 193, 196, 221
images, 3, 13, 15n4n6, 16, 18, 19-20, 21, 37, 42, 44, 78, 82, 85
    HHB, 104
    LB, 182, 186, 191, 194, 213
    LWW, 85
    MN, 75, 76, 78, 79, 85, 102
    SC, 94, 97
    PC, 212
    VDT, 150
language, 63, 64, 66, 69n3, 11
    Abolition, in, 64
    divine, 36, 40n14
    HHB, in, 110, 118
    Hideous Strength, 64
    LB, 187
    LWW, 187
    SC, 65
    théōsis, 36
magic, *Chronicles*
    Deep, 33, 82
    Deeper, 34, 80, 82, 222
    goetia (black magic), 84, 126, 215
    LWW, 84, 85, 130, 205
    magia (white magic), 33, 34, 36, 154, 199, 204, 209
    metamorphoses, and, 76
    MN, 34, 43, 75, 76, 82, 143

    PC, 212
    SC, 94
    VDT, 169, 173
Memory, 3, 16
    Chronicles, in, 17, 53, 56, 50
    Divorce, and, 52
    God, 17, 53. 65. 207, 223
    images, 18, 19, 37, 51, 59, 218
    imagination, 69n1, 74, 156
    language, 50, 61
    metamorphoses, 37, 51, 94, 138, 218
    mythopoeia, 16, 17, 68, 105, 109, 218, 219, 221
    PC, 50, 51, 56-60, 95, 96, 206, 212
    SC, 62, 63, 66, 68, 156
    théōsis, 36, 65, 68, 218
    time, 51, 52, 60
    VDT, 207
Metamorphoses, *Chronicles*, in, 2, 13, 14, 20, 60, 81, 162, 170, 181, 202, 204, 215, 219, 223
    fairy tales, and, 12-13
    LB, 181, 200, 205
    LWW, 87, 129, 208
    magic, 32, 215
    memory, 16, 37, 51, 59, 138
    metaphor, 16, 37
    MN, 74, 81, 82, 145
    PC, 59, 209-10
    SC, 67, 88, 96-97, 99, 100, 206
    thèōsis, and, 6, 29, 34, 36, 37, 39n14, 87, 138, 175, 205, 214, 218, 222
    types of, 29-32
        destructive, 34, 62-63, 83, 135, 184, 206, 221

individual, 205
pageants, 205, 210
positive, 12, 30, 31, 34, 64, 66
VDT, 146, 151, 160, 162, 165, 169-171, 175, 178, 206, 207, 213

Metaphor, *Chronicles*, in:
HHB, 17
LWW, 130
MN, 141, 145
PC, 59
VDT, 53, 160
City metaphor in *Chronicles*, 72, 74, 100, 124
motifs, of, 78, 92, 94
City, types of,
God, City of, 123, 132, 149
Cair Paravel (*LWW*), 74, 99, 124-26, 130-33, 162, 181, 220
Man, City of,
Tashbaan and Anvard (*HHB*), 74, 91, 104, 105, 108-10, 112, 113, 116-17, 119-21, 154, 163
VDT, 161, 165
Satan, City of,
Charn (*MN*), 73-78, 80, 82, 83, 94, 104, 112, 143, 146, 184, 220
Ruined City and Underland (*SC*), 62, 63, 67, 87, 91-93, 94, 98-131, 156, 220
Garden metaphor in *Chronicles*, 20, 25, 35, 38n5, 42, 43, 78, 112, 135, 136, 141, 142, 145, 156, 157, 219, 221-222
motifs, of, 23-25, 88, 135, 138-39, 147, 149, 150, 151, 155-56, 172, 179n1, 221
Garden, types, of
Celestial Garden in *LB*, 9, 21, 136, 147, 148, 149, 150, 151, 152, 153, 181, 186, 195-200, 213, 221
Created Garden in *MN*, 21, 38n3, 73, 74-76, 81, 82-83, 84, 88, 104, 135, 136, 139, 140, 141-42, 143, 148, 150, 151, 187
Garden of Restoration in *VDT*, 21, 88, 136, 146, 147, 150, 151, 213, 221
minor gardens in Narnia, 153-56
underwater, 162, 173-75
Light metaphor, *Chronicles*, in, 6, 13, 20, 21, 38n2, 223
Aslan, and, 19, 48, 43, 93, 137, 146, 148, 169, 170, 172, 175, 178, 188, 207
HHB, 117, 207
LB, 148, 150, 151, 188, 189, 193, 197-99
LWW, 56, 86, 125, 129, 145
MN, 77, 137, 142, 145
PC, 57, 212
SC, 92-99, 155
VDT, 146, 148, 149, 156, 169, 171, 173, 174, 175, 21
Perelandra, in, 214
thèōsis, and, 175, 17
Sea metaphor in *Chronicles*, 20, 21, 25, 42, 177, 219, 22, 223

    baptismal, 173, 175, 178
    bifurcated, 160-61, 174
    HHB, 154, 177,
    LB, 186, 191
    LWW, 125, 126, 127, 130
    motifs, of, 28, 29, 160, 162, 178, 179n1
    PC, 129
    SC, 130
    sea serpent, 62, 98, 161, 167, 176, 178
    tempests, 219, 221, 222
    VDT, 126, 149, 159, 160-64, 171-78, 213
myth, 2, 3, 35, 36
    Chronicles, in, 4, 12, 13
    evolution, and, 103n7
    God, and, 15, 218
    LWW, 132
    PC, 210
    SC, 95, 98
    théōsis, 36
Mythopoeia, 16, 37, 175, 218
    Chronicles, in, 20, 223
    metamorphoses, and, 175
    metaphor, 175
    mythopoeic aesthetics, 2, 16, 20, 31, 36, 37, 99, 218, 223
nature, 4, 22, 30, 57
    Chronicles, in, 5, 30, 81, 148, 209, 210
    art, and, 84
    Aslan, and, 43
    beauty, of, 178
    evil, and, 81, 83, 87, 88, 89, 165, 183, 185, 189, 209
    God, and, 45, 126, 148, 152, 173, 196, 204

    Hideous Strength, in, 33
    inner, 62, 210
    théōsis, 44, 65, 68
Orthodox Church, Eastern, 35, 39, 40, 134, 205
Plato, *Chronicles*, in, 96, 99, 100
théōsis Chronicles, in, 36, 37, 68, 138, 150, 205, 218, 221, 222,
    VDT, 175,
    PC, 211-12
    Perelandra, in, 214
Serpents, Chronicles, in, 62, 87, 88, 89, 91, 95, 96, 98, 136, 197, 198
light, 41, 95
    biblical, 38n4, 45, 126, 127, 137, 149, 194
    iconic, 19, 41, 42, 48
    divine, 5, 18, 19, 34, 41-43, 45, 126, 175, 182, 189
    Nordic, 195, 197
    Pearl, 140
    Platonic, 45, 47, 137
    Dante, and, 45, 214
    Saynt Branden, 148, 172
    Tolkien, 154
    Williams, Charles, 47. See also Lewis, C. S.
Lilith, 85-86
Lindow, John, 197
Lion, the Witch, and the Wardrobe, The, 5, 9, 18, 21, 33, 40n14, 43, 48, 50-58, 62, 68, 73, 80, 82-87, 89, 94, 96, 100, 101, 104, 109, 110, 117, 125, 127-31, 143, 145, 147, 154, 163, 165, 170, 173, 187, 205, 06, 208, 210, 213, 215, 219, 221

Livre des merveilles, 170
Lönnroth, Lars, 197
Lossky, Vladimir, 35, 193
The Lyfe of Saynt Branden, 138, 149, 167, 172

M

MacDonald, George, 2, 52, 53, 85
Macmullen, Ramsay, 134n3
McGovern, Eugene, 122n1
McGrath, Alister, 22, 52, 147, 221
magic, 29-33
    classical, 85
    medieval, 8, 72
    metamorphoses, 32
    mythopoeia, 29
    Renaissance, 33
    thèōsis, 36
    Norse, 204
    Tolkien, 39n12 . See also Lewis, C. S.
Magician's Nephew, The, 11, 19, 21, 31, 34, 38, 43, 48, 56, 62, 73-78, 80-82, 86-88, 91, 94, 96, 100, 104, 109, 112, 125, 129, 131, 135-40, 142, 143, 145, 147, 148, 150, 151, 158, 162, 177, 184, 187, 190, 196, 208, 215, 221
Majeske, Andrew, 108
Mallet, M., 198, 201n2
Marlowe, Christopher, *Dr. Faustus*, 39n11, 108
    Tamburlaine, 1, 108
Markos, Louis, 10
Maundeville, Sir John. *The Voiage and Travayle of Sir John Maundeville, Knight*, 210
Mere Christianity, 12, 22, 34, 35, 45, 65, 103n7, 131, 170, 177, 179n10, 180, 205, 214
memory, 2, 16, 38n1, 50, 54- 55, 58
    Augustine, and, 18, 50, 53, 60, 61
    classical, 16, 17, 18, 60
    God, 51, 60, 61, 65, 96
    meaning, 1, 3, 16, 51
    medieval, 19, 36
    metamorphoses, and, 51, 55, 224, 226
    Milton, *PL*, 144
    mythopoeia, 3, 16, 51
    and Plato, 61, 65
    recollection, 16, 18, 51-57, 59, 61
    self discovery, 53, 60, 65. See also Lewis, C. S.
metamorphoses, 6, 7, 29, 34, 36, 91, 136
    Augustine, in, 51
    biblical, 32, 209
    classical, 12
    Dante, 206, 208
    fairy tales, and, 12
    memory, 37, 53, 54
    metaphor, 31, 37
    mythopoeia, 12, 16, 31
    negative, 7, 22, 208
    Norse, 12, 204
    Ovid, 16, 29, 31, 32, 39n10, 97, 202-04
    positive, 7, 12, 208
    Spenser, 30. See also Lewis, C. S.
metaphor, 17, 20, 26, 37
    archetypal, 37
    iconic, 219. See also Lewis, C. S.
Metzner, Ralph, 198
Milton, John, 17, 45,163, 179n4
    "Lycidas," 134, 225

"On the Morning of Christ's Nativity," 193
Paradise Lost, 11, 25, 27- 28, 68, 86, 88, 97-99, 112, 127, 136, 138, 139, 140, 143-44,151, 158n1, 163, 164, 168, 210
Miracles, 2, 34, 45, 64, 81, 82, 148, 209
monomyth, 4, 203
monopods, 169, 179n5
Moorman, Charles A., 15n6, 22, 71, 72, 131, 132, 220
Moorman, Frederic W. , 166
Morgan, Kathryn A., 108
motifemes, 62, 74, 105, 191, 197, 198
motifs, general, 20, 37, 62, 74, 104
   apocalyptic, 126
   classical, 82, 136, 156, 161, 176, 178, 219
   Dantean, 75, 82, 92, 219
   Miltonic, 136
   Ophidian, 90
   scriptural, 77, 82, 126, 151, 155, 156, 161, 178, 196, 197, 219
Munch, Peter A., 181
Munn, Mark, 106, 107
Myers, Doris, 45
myth, 1, 2-4, 103, 218
   Christian, 2, 199, 211
   classical, 27, 210, 217
      Apollo and Daphne, 210, 211
      Bacchus, (Dionysus) 203, 209, 210, 211-12, 217n3
      Cadmus and Harmonia, 53, 97, 187
      Circe, 83, 85, 210
      Charybdis, 166
      Gorgon, the, 83
      Hercules, 27, 159, 187
      Icarus, 30, 39n11
      Io, 53, 54
      Jason, 26-27
      Minotaur, 31, 32, 91, 203
      Mnemosynē, 16, 51
      Neptune, 29, 174
      Pegasus, 138
      Persephone, 98
      Psyche, 148, 155
      Scylla, 165-66
      Typhon, 89
      Ulysses, 27
   Eliade, Mircea, and, 22
   floating islands, of, 166
   Nordic, 103n6, 181, 182, 185, 194, 196, 197, 198, 201, 202
   thèōsis, and, 35. See also Lewis, C. S.
   mythic, 2, 6, 62, 125, 127, 200
mythology, 3, 30, 31
   Greek, 39n11, 47, 174, 187, 189, 212, 215
   new, 4, 7, 205
   Norse, 11, 12, 13, 79, 88, 98, 181, 182, 198, 201n1, 204-05
   Semitic, 86
   world, 127
Mythopoeia, 1, 2, 15
   memory, and, 16, 18,
   metamorphoses, 29
   metaphor, 18
   thèōsis, 29
   Tolkien, 1. See also Lewis, C. S.

N
Nathan, Peter, 124, 132
nature, 4, 5, 22, 29, 30, 31, 34, 57, 70
   classical, 29, 98

Christian, 54, 130, 152
divine, 45, 152
Eliade, and, 124
evil, 90, 91
Paradise Lost, in, 25
Plato, 53
Spenser, 30, 126, 158n4
théōsis, 34
Nebuchadnezzar, 113
Nicholson, Mervyn, 103
Nicolson, Marjorie Hope, 138
Nordeau, Max, 90

O

Ober, Josiah, 106
On Stories and Other Essays on Literature, 8, 9, 12, 14, 18
Oppenheim, Leo, 113
Origen, 132, 134n2
Orthodox church, 39-40n14, 205
Orwell, George, 64, 69n3
Ouspensky, Léonide, 42, 193
Ovid, 27, 56, 158n7, 203, 204
    metamorphoses, and, 16, 29, 31, 32, 39n10, 97, 202

P

Palmer, Barbara, 22
Panofsky, Erwin, 48
Patterson, Nancy-Lou, 117, 150
Pearl, 140, 196
    poet, 28, 148, 152
Pearsall, Derek, 151
Peck, John, 28-29
Perry, Kathryn, 184
Perelandra, 11, 214
Persians, ancient, 33, 105-106, 108, 111, 121, 185, 198
Perutelli, Alessandro, 53, 55
Pitts, Mary Ellen, 25
Platner, Gloria, 217n3
Plass, Paul, 36, 61
Plato, 3, 17, 25, 45, 53, 61, 78, 81, 105, 108, 117, 119, 175, 178, 185

    Allegory of the Cave, 95-95, 99-100, 103n9
    Gorgias, 108
    Laws, 25
    Meno, 61
    Phaedrus, 65, 185
    Republic, The, 46, 53, 103n9, 103, 106, 107, 114, 117, 119, 120-21, 131
    Timaeus, 175
Platonic, 41, 44, 47, 100, 105, 109, 119, 137, 152, 158n2, 178, 188, 199, 219
Platonists, 61
Platonists (Neo-), 17, 44, 45
Poems, 87
Poems of the Elder Edda, 199, 201n2
polis, 123
Pontoppidan, Erich, 166, 168
Porteous, Alexander, 135
Preface to Paradise Lost, A, 108
Prince Caspian, 20, 43, 48, 50- 51, 55- 56, 58- 59, 60, 62, 63, 66, 68, 69n1, 74, 96, 109, 129- 32, 156, 160, 163, 173, 180, 190, 192, 195, 203, 205, 209- 12, 217n2
Problem of Pain, The, 47, 73, 96, 106, 108-09, 121, 196, 214, 221
Prose Edda, 181, 198

Puchniak, Robert, 35
Puckett, Thomas, 54
Pullman, Philip, 122n1

Q
"Quest of Bleheris," 78, 81, 102n3
Quarles, Francis, 141
Quiller-Couch, Sir Arthur, 134n5
Quinn, Patrick, 90
Quinn, Sister Mary Bernetta, 29, 37, 155
Quint, David, 13, 27, 222

R
Reflections on the Psalms, 132, 141
Raaflaub, Kent A., 106
Rackham, Arthur, 49n2, 79, 103n6, 181, 201n1
Rágnarök, 180-83, 186, 191, 194-99, 201n2, 205
Rakestraw, Robert V., 35
Ramos, Manual João, 24, 32, 90, 172
Rees, Christine, 31
Rhodes J. T. 23, 151, 152
Nibelung, Ring of the, 1, 79, 181, 204
Ryken, Leland, 5, 10, 38n6, 183

S
Sandburg, Carl, 102n1
Salter, Elizabeth, 151
Sayer, George, 150
Schakel, Peter, 65
Schmidt, Arnold, 27
"scholarship of imagination," 17, 19, 59, 74, 82, 109, 136, 178, 218, 223
Scully, Stephen, 123
sea, 26, 28, 29, 42, 159-161, 166, 174, 202, 222, 223
Augustine, 161, 178
baptismal, 28, 29, 159-62, 165, 222
biblical, 25, 28
bifurcated, 28, 115, 159-161, 178
classic, 25, 26, 27, 29, 160-61, 174
demonic, 28, 176
Donne, John, 28
Haklyut, 162, 164, 167, 168
Milton, 25, 164
monsters, 26, 166-67
motifs, 28, 29, 160, 162, 179n1
Nordic, 186, 192, 197
Plato, 25
Romantics, 26
serpents, 167, 168, 172, 178
Shakespeare, 26, 39n8, 202
Spenser, 25, 29, 38n7, 159
and time, 26
voyages, 21, 159, 160, 162, 163, 175
   evil, as, 25-28
      tempests, 28, 164, 176
      shipwrecks, 159
      clouds, black, 172
      Virgil, 27. See also Lewis, C. S.
"Seafarer, The," 28
Seaford, Richard, 106
Seidel, Michael, 160
Sehnsucht, 11, 36, 44, 154, 199
Sennett, James F., 122n3
Serpents, general, 31, 90, 91, 98, 198
   biblical, 98, 99, 123, 166, 176, 182, 186, 197
   Dante, 62, 97, 206, 208,
   Greek, 53, 187, 189
   Ovid, 97

Milton, 88, 97
Spenser, 99
Shakespeare, William,
   Henry IV (1), 26
   King Lear, 11
   Macbeth, 33
   Othello, 10, 11
   Pericles, 29
   Tempest, The, 16, 33, 201
Shaw, Luci, 4, 5, 7, 18, 48, 219
Shelley, Percy B., 202
Silva, Francisco Vaz da, 12, 90, 92, 98
Silver Chair, The, 21, 50, 61-64, 66, 73, 77, 78, 87-91, 96-100, 129-131, 147, 154, 155, 156, 180, 187, 205, 206, 215
"Sir Gawain and the Green Knight," 90
Slochower, Harry, 1, 4
Smilansky, Saul, 188
Smith, Jonathan, 4, 131
Smith, Mark Eddy, 223
Smith, Robert Houston, 42, 48, 178, 222
Sørensen, Preben Mevlengrack, 196-97
Song of Solomon, 23, 136, 140-43, 151
Spenser, Edmund, 11, 45-47, 163, 223
   Muiopotmos, 158n7
   Two Cantos of Mutabilitie, 30
   "Prosopopoia," 188,
   Fairie Queene, The, 6, 9, 25, 29, 38-39n7, 45, 46, 85, 98, 99, 102n2, 127, 135, 139, 149, 159, 162, 164, 174, 218
Spenser's Images of Life, 10, 11, 20, 44, 126, 145, 153, 189, 218, 219, 223

Stanton, Leonard J., 42, 43
Starkey, John, 134
Stewart, Stanley, 4, 23-24, 135, 139, 141, 142, 149
Stewart, T. C., 21
Studies in Medieval and Renaissance Literature, 45,
Sturluson, Snorri(e), 181, 201n2, 204
Surprised by Joy 5, 11-12, 103n6, 132, 145, 132, 145, 181

T

Tash, 112, 113, 117, 119, 180, 181, 189, 191, 193, 198
Terry, Patricia, 195, 201n2
Teske, Roland, 60
That Hideous Strength, 30, 64, 113
thèōsis, 6, 12, 29, 34-36, 145, 149,156, 212, 214, 221
   memory, and, 65, 218
   metamorphoses, 30, 36, 37, 87, 138, 175, 202, 205, 218, 222
   metaphor, 36, 175, 218
   mythopoeia, 29, 37, 68. See also Lewis, C. S.
Till We Have Faces, 89, 148
Thomas, Keith, 23
Tolkien, J. R. R., 1, 4, 7-9, 10, 11, 13-14, 15n3, 17, 33, 34, 39n12, 49n1, 154-55, 158n5, 191
Treneer, Anne, 28, 166
Typology, Christian, 3, 46
Turville-Petre, Gabriel, 197
tyrants, 2, 81, 101, 105, 106-108, 114, 116, 119, 120-21, 182, 185, 190, 220
tyrannical cities, 108-09

V

Vendôme, Matthew of, 135
Virgil, 23, 73, 83, 93, 99
   Aeneid, 27, 92
The Voiage and Travayle of Sir John Maundeville, Knight, 210
"Völuspá," 181-82, 186, 187, 191, 192, 195, 197, 200
Von der Thusen, Joachim, 102n1
Voyage of the Dawn Treader, The, 10, 21, 29, 43, 48, 49n1, 53, 62, 66, 67, 73, 87-89, 98, 113, 129, 134n4, 136, 138, 146, 147, 149, 151, 154, 156, 158n5, 159-166, 168-72, 174-78, 197, 205- 07, 210, 213, 219

W

Wagner, Richard, 103n6, 201n1
   The Ring of the Nibelung , 1, 181
Walker, Andrew, 39, 40n14
Walker, Peter W. L., 132, 133, 134n2
Walls, Jerry L., 122n3
Walsh, Chad, 102n4
"Wanderer, The," 28
Ward, Michael, 10, 153, 200
Ware, Kallistos, 5, 40n14
Warner, Marina, 17, 32, 54, 120, 146, 155, 223
Watson, Thomas Ramey, 52, 72
Weight of Glory and Other Addresses, The, 3, 10, 35, 47, 113, 178, 179n10
Wilken, Robert Louis, 53
Williams, Charles, *Descent into Hell*, 73, 83, 131
   Arthurian Torso, 47

The Descent of the Dove, 40n14
"The Figure of Arthur," 40n14
Williams, Kathleen, 28, 29
Wilson, John A., 128
Wilson, Robert R., 38n4
Wiseman, D. J., 113
Wood, Ralph C., 15n3, 34

Y

Yates, Frances A., 18, 36, 38n1, 54, 55, 61

ABOUT THE AUTHOR

photo by Dr. Marsha Keller

SALWA KHODDAM, BORN IN LEBANON, WAS EDUCATED AT THE UNIVERSITY OF KANSAS AND OKLAHOMA STATE UNIVERSITY, GETTING HER DOCTORATE IN EARLY BRITISH LITERATURE FROM OSU. SHE HAS BEEN PROFESSOR OF ENGLISH FOR APPROXIMATELY 25 YEARS AT OKLAHOMA CITY UNIVERSITY, WHERE SHE TAUGHT COURSES IN EARLY BRITISH LITERATURE, EARLY WESTERN LITERATURE, AND C.S. LEWIS, WHOSE WORKS HAVE BECOME HER MOST IMPORTANT AREA OF RESEARCH. SHE PUBLISHED SEVERAL ARTICLES AND BOOK REVIEWS ON C.S. LEWIS AND CO-EDITED AN ANTHOLOGY ON THE INKLINGS, TITLED TRUTHS BREATHED THROUGH SILVER: THE INKLINGS' MORAL AND MYTHOPOEIC LEGACY, PUBLISHED IN 2008, TO WHICH SHE CONTRIBUTED AN ESSAY. SHE DIRECTED OCU'S FIRST ANNUAL CONFERENCE ON LEWIS IN 1998. DR KHODDAM ALSO CO-FOUNDED THE C.S. LEWIS INKLINGS SOCIETY (CSLIS) IN 2004, WAS ITS PRESIDENT AND PRESENTLY IS CHAIR OF ITS EXECUTIVE BOARD. SHE DIRECTED A CONFERENCE ON LEWIS AND THE INKLINGS IN 2003 AND IN 2010. SHE ALSO CO-FOUNDED AN INKLINGS READING GROUP FOR THE OKLAHOMA CITY COMMUNITY IN 2009. DR. KHODDAM IS NOW PROFESSOR *EMERITA* OF ENGLISH AND CONTINUES WITH HER RESEARCH, WRITING, AND TEACHING AT OCU ON A LIMITED BASIS.

OTHER BOOKS OF INTEREST

C. S. Lewis

C. S. Lewis: Views From Wake Forest - Essays on C. S. Lewis
Michael Travers, editor

Contains sixteen scholarly presentations from the international C. S. Lewis convention in Wake Forest, NC. Walter Hooper shares his important essay "Editing C. S. Lewis," a chronicle of publishing decisions after Lewis's death in 1963.

"*Scholars from a variety of disciplines address a wide range of issues. The happy result is a fresh and expansive view of an author who well deserves this kind of thoughtful attention.*"
Diana Pavlac Glyer, author of *The Company They Keep*

The Hidden Story of Narnia:
A Book-By-Book Guide to Lewis's Spiritual Themes
Will Vaus

A book of insightful commentary equally suited for teens or adults – Will Vaus points out connections between the *Narnia* books and spiritual/biblical themes, as well as between ideas in the *Narnia* books and C. S. Lewis's other books. Learn what Lewis himself said about the overarching and unifying thematic structure of the Narnia books. That is what this book explores; what C. S. Lewis called "the hidden story" of Narnia. Each chapter includes questions for individual use or small group discussion.

Why I Believe in Narnia:
33 Reviews and Essays on the Life and Work of C.S. Lewis
James Como

Chapters range from reviews of critical books , documentaries and movies to evaluations of Lewis's books to biographical analysis.
"*A valuable, wide-ranging collection of essays by one of the best informed and most accute commentators on Lewis's work and ideas.*"
Peter Schakel, author of *Imagination & the Arts in C. S. Lewis*

C. S. Lewis Goes to Heaven: A Reader's Guide to The Great Divorce
David G. Clark

This is the first book devoted solely to this often neglected book and the first to reveal several important secrets Lewis concealed within the story. Lewis felt his imaginary trip to Hell and Heaven was far better than his book *The Screwtape Letters*, which has become a classic. Clark is an ordained minister who has taught courses on Lewis for more than 30 years and is a New Testament and Greek scholar with a Doctor of Philosophy degree in Biblical Studies from the University of Notre Dame. Readers will discover the many literary and biblical influences Lewis utilized in writing his brilliant novel.

C. S. Lewis & Philosophy as a Way of Life: His Philosophical Thoughts
Adam Barkman

C. S. Lewis is rarely thought of as a "philosopher" per se despite having both studied and taught philosophy for several years at Oxford. Lewis's long journey to Christianity was essentially philosophical – passing through seven different stages. This 624 page book includes an extensive index and is an invaluable reference for C. S. Lewis scholars and fans alike

C. S. Lewis: His Literary Achievement
Colin Manlove

"This is a positively brilliant book, written with splendor, elegance, profundity and evidencing an enormous amount of learning. This is probably not a book to give a first-time reader of Lewis. But for those who are more broadly read in the Lewis corpus this book is an absolute gold mine of information. The author gives us a magnificent overview of Lewis's many writings, tracing for us thoughts and ideas which recur throughout, and at the same time telling us how each book differs from the others. I think it is not extravagant to call C. S. Lewis: His Literary Achievement a tour de force."

Robert Merchant, *St. Austin Review*, Book Review Editor

Speaking of Jack: A C. S. Lewis Discussion Guide
Will Vaus

C. S. Lewis Societies have been forming around the world since the first one started in New York City in 1969. Will Vaus has started and led three groups himself. *Speaking of Jack* is the result of Vaus' experience in leading those Lewis Societies. Included here are introductions to most of Lewis's books as well as questions designed to stimulate discussion about Lewis's life and work. These materials have been "road-tested" with real groups made up of young and old, some very familiar with Lewis and some newcomers. *Speaking of Jack* may be used in an existing book discussion group, Sunday school class or small group, to start a C. S. Lewis Society, or as a guide to your own exploration of Lewis's books.

CHRISTIAN LIVING

The Living Word of the Living God:
A Beginner's Guide to Reading and Understanding the Bible
Rev. Tom Furrer

"In a clear and straightforward style, Rev. Furrer lays out the major biblical themes, inserting commentary and scripture quotations so as never to stray far from the actual text. Each chapter ends with useful questions for reflection. This is a book you can give to someone looking for guidance with confidence that they will find the guidance they need."

Rev. Christopher Webber
Author of *A Year With American Saints*

George MacDonald

Diary of an Old Soul & The White Page Poems
George MacDonald and Betty Aberlin

The first edition of George MacDonald's book of daily poems included a blank page opposite each page of poems. Readers were invited to write their own reflections on the "white page." MacDonald wrote: "Let your white page be ground, my print be seed, growing to golden ears, that faith and hope may feed." Betty Aberlin responded to MacDonald's invitation with daily poems of her own.

Betty Aberlin's close readings of George MacDonald's verses and her thoughtful responses to them speak clearly of her poetic gifts and spiritual intelligence. Luci Shaw, poet

George MacDonald: Literary Heritage and Heirs
Roderick McGillis, editor

This latest collection of 14 essays sets a new standard that will influence MacDonald studies for many more years. George MacDonald experts are increasingly evaluating his entire corpus within the nineteenth century context.

This comprehensive collection represents the best of contemporary scholarship on George MacDonald. Rolland Hein, author of *George MacDonald: Victorian Mythmaker*.

In the Near Loss of Everything: George MacDonald's Son in America
Dale Wayne Slusser

In the summer of 1887, George MacDonald's son Ronald, newly engaged to artist Louise Blandy, sailed from England to America to teach school. The next summer he returned to England to marry Louise and bring her back to America. On August 27, 1890, Louise died leaving him with an infant daughter. Ronald once described losing a beloved spouse as "the near loss of everything". Dale Wayne Slusser unfolds this poignant story with unpublished letters and photos that give readers a glimpse into the close-knit MacDonald family. Also included is Ronald's essay about his father, *George MacDonald: A Personal Note*, plus a selection from Ronald's 1922 fable, *The Laughing Elf*, about the necessity of both sorrow and joy in life.

Behind the Back of the North Wind:
Critical Essays on George MacDonald's Classic Children's Book
Editors, John Pennington and Roderick McGillis

This collection of 16 essays by various scholars is the first compendium on a particular MacDonald book – *At the Back of the North Wind*. This novel makes a good representative study because it bridges the world of the "realistic" and the fanciful, including a fairy tale and some nonsense poetry. Plus it deals with a central MacDonald theme - death. Essays run the gamut from exploring MacDonald's Christian worldview, to examining the tension between fantasy and reality, to grappling with *North Wind* as children's literature. In every case, the essays illuminate a complex book. This book is also an excellent companion to the critical and scholarly edition of *At The Back of the North Wind* by Pennington and McGillis published by Broadview Press.

A Novel Pulpit: Sermons From George MacDonald's Fiction
David L. Neuhouser

"In MacDonald's novels, the Christian teaching emerges out of the characters and story line, the narrator's comments, and inclusion of sermons given by the fictional preachers. The sermons in the novels are shorter than the ones in collections of MacDonald's sermons and so are perhaps more accessible for some. In any case, they are both stimulating and thought-provoking. This collection of sermons from ten novels serve to bring out the 'freshness and brilliance' of MacDonald's message."

from the author's introduction

HARRY POTTER

The Order of Harry Potter: The Literary Skill of the Hogwarts Epic
Colin Manlove

Colin Manlove, a popular conference speaker and author of over a dozen books, has earned an international reputation as an expert on fantasy and children's literature. His book, *From Alice to Harry Potter*, is a survey of 400 English fantasy books. In *The Order of Harry Potter*, he compares and contrasts *Harry Potter* with works by "Inklings" writers J.R.R. Tolkien, C.S. Lewis and Charles Williams; he also examines Rowling's treatment of the topic of imagination; her skill in organization and the use of language; and the book's underlying motifs and themes.

Harry Potter & Imagination: The Way Between Two Worlds
Travis Prinzi

Imaginative literature places a reader between two worlds: the story world and the world of daily life, and challenges the reader to imagine and to act for a better world. Starting with discussion of Harry Potter's more important themes, *Harry Potter & Imagination* takes readers on a journey through the transformative power of those themes for both the individual and for culture by placing Rowling's series in its literary, historical, and cultural contexts.

Repotting Harry Potter: A Professor's Guide for the Serious Re-Reader
Rowling Revisited: Return Trips to Harry, Fantastic Beasts, Quidditch, & Beedle the Bard
Dr. James W. Thomas

In *Repotting Harry Potter* and his sequel book *Rowling Revisited*, Dr. James W. Thomas points out the humor, puns, foreshadowing and literary parallels in the Potter books. In *Rowling Revisted*, readers will especially find useful three extensive appendixes – "Fantastic Beasts and the Pages Where You'll Find Them," "Quidditch Through the Pages," and "The Books in the Potter Books." Dr. Thomas makes re-reading the Potter books even more rewarding and enjoyable.

Hog's Head Conversations: Essays on Harry Potter
Travis Prinzi, Editor

Ten fascinating essays on Harry Potter by popular Potter writers and speakers including John Granger, James W. Thomas, Colin Manlove, and Travis Prinzi.

Pop Culture

To Love Another Person: A Spiritual Journey Through Les Miserables
John Morrison

The powerful story of Jean Valjean's redemption is beloved by readers and theater goers everywhere. In this companion and guide to Victor Hugo's masterpiece, author John Morrison unfolds the spiritual depth and breadth of this classic novel and broadway musical.

Through Common Things: Philosophical Reflections on Popular Culture
Adam Barkman

"Barkman presents us with an amazingly wide-ranging collection of philosophical reflections grounded in the everyday things of popular culture – past and present, eastern and western, factual and fictional. Throughout his encounters with often surprising subject-matter (the value of darkness?), he writes clearly and concisely, moving seamlessly between Aristotle and anime, Lord Buddha and Lord Voldemort. . . . This is an informative and entertaining book to read!"
  Doug Blomberg, Professor of Philosophy, Institute for Christian Studies

Spotlight:
A Close-up Look at the Artistry and Meaning of Stephenie Meyer's Twilight Novels
John Granger

Stephenie Meyer's *Twilight* saga has taken the world by storm. But is there more to *Twilight* than a love story for teen girls crossed with a cheesy vampire-werewolf drama? *Spotlight* reveals the literary backdrop, themes, artistry, and meaning of the four Bella Swan adventures. *Spotlight* is is the perfect gift for serious *Twilight* readers.

Virtuous Worlds: The Video Gamer's Guide to Spiritual Truth
John Stanifer

Popular titles like *Halo 3* and *The Legend of Zelda: Twilight Princess* fly off shelves at a mind-blowing rate. John Stanifer, an avid gamer, shows readers specific parallels between Christian faith and the content of their favorite games. Written with wry humor (including a heckler who frequently pokes fun at the author) this book will appeal to gamers and non-gamers alike. Those unfamiliar with video games may be pleasantly surprised to find that many elements in those "virtual worlds" also qualify them as "virtuous worlds."

Memoir

Called to Serve: Life as a Firefighter-Deacon
Deacon Anthony R. Surozenski

Called to Serve is the story of one man's dream to be a firefighter. But dreams have a way of taking detours - so Tony Soruzenski became a teacher and eventually a volunteer firefighter. And when God enters the picture, Tony is faced with a choice. Will he give up firefighting to follow another call? Afer many years, Tony's two callings are finally united – in service as a fire chaplain at Ground Zero after the 9-11 attacks and in other ways he could not have imagined. Tony is Chief Chaplain's aid for the Massachusettes Corp of Fire Chaplains and Director for the Office of the Diaconate of the Diocese of Worchester, Massachusettes.

Poets and Poetry

Remembering Roy Campbell: The Memoirs of his Daughters, Anna and Tess
Introduction by Judith Lütge Coullie, Editor
Preface by Joseph Pearce

Anna and Teresa Campbell were the daughters of the handsome young South African poet and writer, Roy Campbell (1901-1957), and his beautiful English wife, Mary Garman. In their frank and moving memoirs, Anna and Tess recall the extraordinary, and often very difficult, lives they shared with their exceptional parents. Over 50 photos, 344 footnotes, timeline of Campbell's life, and complete index.

In the Eye of the Beholder: How to See the World Like a Romantic Poet
Louis Markos

Born out of the French Revolution and its radical faith that a nation could be shaped and altered by the dreams and visions of its people, British Romantic Poetry was founded on a belief that the objects and realities of our world, whether natural or human, are not fixed in stone but can be molded and transformed by the visionary eye of the poet. Unlike many of the books written on Romanticism, which devote many pages to the poets and few pages to their poetry, the focus here is firmly on the poems themselves. The author thereby draws the reader intimately into the life of these poems. A separate bibliographical essay is provided for readers listing accessible biographies of each poet and critical studies of their work.

The Cat on the Catamaran: A Christmas Tale
John Martin

Here is a modern-day parable of a modern-day cat with modern-day attitudes. Riverboat Dan is a "cool" cat on a perpetual vacation from responsibility. He's *The Cat on the Catamaran* – sailing down the river of life. Dan keeps his guilty conscience from interfrering with his fun until he runs into trouble. But will he have the courage to believe that it's never too late to change course? (For ages 10 to adult)

"Cat lovers and poetry lovers alike will enjoy this whimsical story about Riverboat Dan, a philosophical cat in search of meaning."
Regina Doman, author of *Angrl in the Water*

Fiction

The Iona Conspiracy (from The Remnant Chronicles book series)
Gary Gregg

Readers find themselves on a modern adventure through ancient Celtic myth and legend as thirteen year old Jacob uncovers his destiny within "the remnant" of the Sporrai Order. As the Iona Academy comes under the control of educational reformers and ideological scientists, Jacob finds himself on a dangerous mission to the sacred Scottish island of Iona and discovers how his life is wrapped up with the fate of the long lost cover of *The Book of Kells*. From its connections to Arthurian legend to references to real-life people, places, and historical mysteries, *Iona* is an adventure that speaks to eternal truths as well as the challenges of the modern world. A young adult novel, *Iona* can be enjoyed by the entire family.

www.ingramcontent.com/pod-product-compliance
Lightning Source LLC
Chambersburg PA
CBHW020359080526
44584CB00014B/1093